AI ChatBots

by Kelly Noble Mirabella and Eric Butow

for
dummies®
A Wiley Brand

AI ChatBots For Dummies®

Published by: **John Wiley & Sons, Inc.**, 111 River Street, Hoboken, NJ 07030-5774, www.wiley.com

For general information on our other products and services, please contact our Customer Care Department within the U.S. at 877-762-2974, outside the U.S. at 317-572-3993, or fax 317-572-4002. For technical support, please visit https://hub.wiley.com/community/support/dummies.

Wiley publishes in a variety of print and electronic formats and by print-on-demand. Some material included with standard print versions of this book may not be included in e-books or in print-on-demand. If this book refers to media that is not included in the version you purchased, you may download this material at http://booksupport.wiley.com. For more information about Wiley products, visit www.wiley.com.

Library of Congress Control Number is available from the publisher.

ISBN 978-1-394-37855-5 (pbk); ISBN 978-1-394-37857-9 (ebk); ISBN 978-1-394-37856-2 (ebk)

Printed and bound by CPI Group (UK) Ltd, Croydon, CR0 4YY

C9781394378555_121225

Contents at a Glance

Table of Contents

Introduction

Are you excited about adding chatbots to your business website? We hope so! Chatbots using artificial intelligence (AI) are helping businesses just like yours engage with website visitors no matter what time of day it is. Because you've chosen *AI ChatBots For Dummies,* we know you're ready to get down to business building a chatbot that not only serves your customers but also helps you grow your business.

About This Book

The purpose of *AI ChatBots For Dummies* is to help you deploy and use AI chatbots effectively. But as you can see by the number of pages in this book, that purpose is easier said than done!

With more businesses deploying chatbots every day, you find a lot of conflicting information about how chatbots work, how AI chatbots are better, and how to use AI chatbots effectively. That's where we come in. In this book, we give you the tools and tactics necessary to build a successful AI chatbot and put it to work for your business. We take you through every step of building your own AI chatbot, including

>> An overview of the chatbot landscape

>> How to build your own AI chatbot from scratch and connect it to tools you already use

>> How to use chatbots for different tasks, including sales and marketing

>> How to measure and analyze results

>> Ethical issues you need to be aware of

We also tell you how to create your long-term AI chatbot strategy so your chatbot grows with your business.

In the interest of full disclosure, all the text in this book was written by your authors, Kelly and Eric, without any AI-generated text. We used AI search engines to research topics, and the AI tools covered in this book created some of the examples shown in figures, but the prose is ours.

Foolish Assumptions

When writing this book, we've assumed at least one of the following is true:

>> You have a business or are getting ready to start a business.

>> You have a website and/or mobile app for your business.

>> You want to use AI chatbots effectively to drive real business results.

>> You're committed to devoting time and energy to build an AI chatbot that helps serve your customers and grows your business.

If that's correct, this is the right book for you! We're confident that the tactics and information here can help you achieve your goals.

Icons Used in This Book

To make things easier and ensure that you don't miss important details, various icons appear throughout this book. Here's what the different icons look like and mean.

TIP

The Tip icon is a small piece of expert advice that saves you time and makes your experience figuring out AI chatbots easier to master.

REMEMBER

Because we cover a lot of details and information, this icon highlights important tidbits you definitely want to file away.

TECHNICAL STUFF

Who doesn't love a little geek-fest on technical jargon? Okay, a lot of people! We use the Technical Stuff icon to pull out these nonessential paragraphs so you know what you can skip if you aren't interested in digging into the technical aspects of using chatbots.

WARNING

When you see a Warning icon, you know we're highlighting potential pitfalls and avoidable mistakes. Please take a few extra moments to understand the effect of what we're saying; we want to save you from any headaches we can.

Beyond the Book

In addition to what you're reading right now, this book also comes with a free, access-anywhere cheat sheet that provides a handy list of do's and don'ts when building your AI chatbot. To view the cheat sheet, simply go to www.dummies.com and type "AI ChatBots For Dummies Cheat Sheet" in the Search box.

Where to Go from Here

You can read this book in any order. The chapters in Part 1 dive into what chatbots are and what they can do, so they're a great place to start if you're brand-new to the chatbot world. If you're ready to jump straight to building your own AI chatbot, you can find that info in Chapter 6 (though we suggest you also check out Chapter 5 so you go into your build with a solid plan). For details on chatbot trends and ethics, check out Chapters 14 and 15, respectively. Of course, you can also look at the table of contents and index for guidance on where to find the specific areas you want to focus on.

1

Getting to Know Chatbots and AI

Chapter **1**

Understanding the Chatbot Revolution

C hances are you've encountered chatbots, like them or not, as you've browsed the web. You know, they're the icons (sometimes with text) you usually find in the lower-right corner of a website inviting you to click it, as you can see on the website for The Marketing Specialist, the marketing business run by my (Eric's) co-author on several Instagram-related *For Dummies* books in Figure 1-1.

Many chatbots are now employing artificial intelligence, better known by its acronym AI, but what does that even mean? Aren't all chatbots by definition AI? That difference is what we talk about in this chapter. After you know what AI chatbots can do, you discover how to make the business case for employing chatbots in your company to drive business.

Finally, we end this chapter with an overview of how to use chatbots effectively because that's important to make the business case, don't you think?

FIGURE 1-1:
The Let's Chat
button on The
Marketing
Specialist
website.

Knowing the Difference between Chatbots and AI Chatbots

We can hear you scratching your head, wondering what makes a chatbot different from an AI chatbots. That's why we're here, and we break it down in the following sections.

Running regular ol' chatbots

REMEMBER

Chatbots are often script-based systems to carry out specific tasks by using defined rules. They can only carry out specific tasks and respond to commands within the boundaries of those tasks.

For example, one day I (Eric) discovered that my waste management company hadn't picked up my yard waste on the designated day. I accessed the company website and told the chatbot that my yard waste hadn't been picked up, and the system told me the truck was still out servicing clients and to check the truck tracker.

The tracker said the truck had finished its route, so I told the chatbot about the tracker's report. The chatbot said it didn't understand and asked me to rephrase my question. I'd exceeded the limits of the chatbot's programmed script. The end result was that I didn't get the help I needed and had to call the waste management company to speak with a live human. (Never fear; the yard waste was eventually picked up and the grass in the bin didn't combust from the summer heat.)

Accessing AI chatbots: The next generation

AI chatbots are more like Data, the android from *Star Trek: The Next Generation.* These chatbots use *natural language processing* (NLP) to better learn from complex interactions and predict responses. When a potential client asks the AI chatbot how your company helps their particular needs, the chatbot can follow up with questions and provide more meaningful answers with a pleasant, human-like rapport.

TIP

With regular chatbots, your customer is more likely to get frustrated and have to contact a live human like I (Eric) did or, worse, lose a potential customer entirely. (You can read more about my experience and regular chatbots in general in the preceding section.) An AI chatbot can engage a potential customer for longer and have a better chance of helping them get their question answered. What's more, an AI chatbot can help your company determine whether someone needs your services or can find their answer from the chatbot or another source. For example, Figure 1-2 shows how the Sacramento law firm Dreyer Babich Buccola Wood Campora uses Scorpion's AI chatbot to filter out potential clients from those who are just fishing.

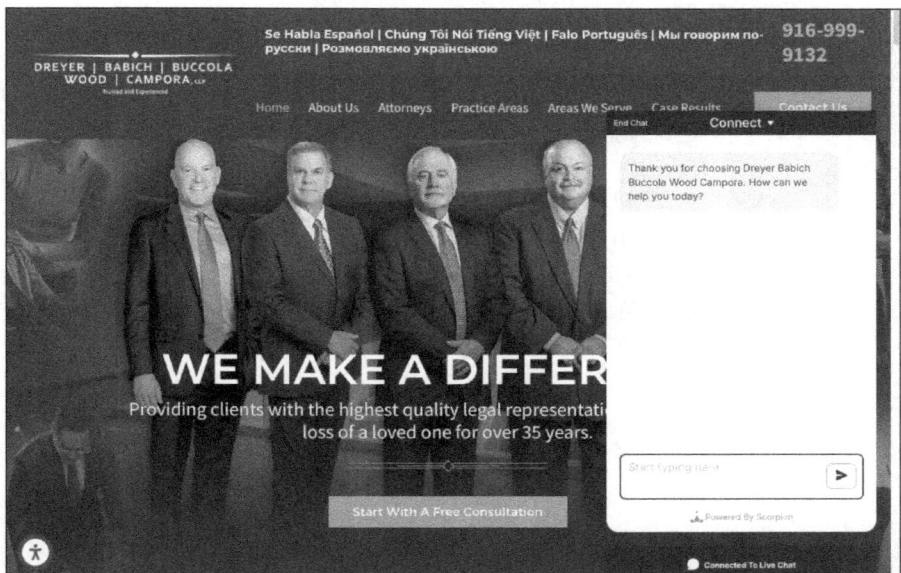

FIGURE 1-2:
The Scorpion AI chatbot is ready to answer your legal questions.

Using Chatbots in Your Small Business

We bet you dollars to donuts that the gears in your head are turning as you think about all the great ways AI chatbots can save you money. Part of that excitement may be fear of missing out (or FOMO) as you see your competition using chatbots . . . and you're not.

Hold up there, Sparky. Before you go to your boss or your team all wide-eyed and stumbling over your words telling them how great chatbots are, you need to know how they can help you. The following sections not only give you a good idea of how to leverage AI chatbots but also arm you with a list of answers in case your boss (or the CEO) comes at you wide-eyed and raving about chatbots.

Considering customer service and support

As we mention in the earlier section "Accessing AI chatbots: The next generation," AI chatbots are good at both interacting with potential customers and helping existing customers. Here are the talking points you need to bring up in your discussions with and presentation to your team:

>> **24/7 availability:** Chatbots are always ready to answer basic questions about such things as hours, location, and pricing. When you train an AI chatbot about what you do (something we talk about in Chapter 6), your chatbot can answer more questions online rather than on the phone or by email.

>> **Order tracking:** Speaking of keeping more customers off your phones and out of your email inbox, a *Where Is My Order (WISMO) chatbot* uses AI to tell your customers where their order is. If the order is experiencing any delays or is lost entirely, your chatbot alerts your customer service team so it can follow up as soon as possible.

>> **Trusty gatekeeping:** If you use an AI chatbot to help your customers, you can filter customer support issues. It can be as simple as giving customers a menu to choose from so the chatbot can answer the user's question as quickly as possible, as you can see in the Elegant Themes chatbot shown in Figure 1-3.

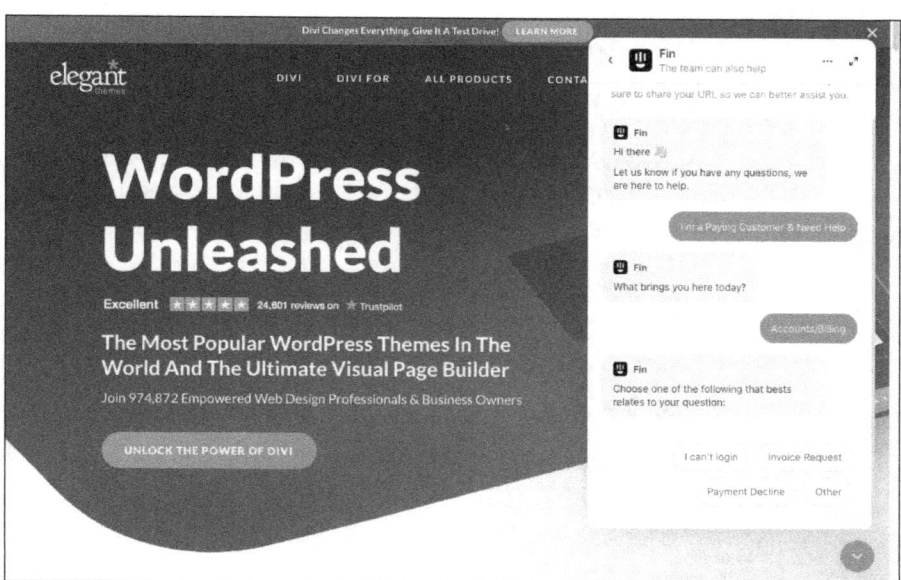

Looking at lead generation and sales

AI chatbots are a great way to drive more business to your company because they can do the busywork your salespeople don't want to do:

>> **Lead screening:** When your AI chatbot receives information from a potential customer about your services, it checks for certain criteria and passes along the customer's name to a member of your sales team.

>> **Product recommendations:** Your AI chatbot can suggest products and/or services your company offers to entice a potential customer to buy from you.

>> **Quote requests:** Customers may want to get an estimate of your services, and your AI chatbot can collect information based on their needs to give an estimate. Then you can have your sales team follow up to nail down the final numbers.

>> **Data capture:** You need your client's contact information to keep you in front of their eyeballs. Though lead magnets on websites are one way to do that, AI chatbots are another good way to collect a potential client's contact information.

Booking appointments and tackling other administrative tasks

Speaking of reducing busywork (see the preceding section), an AI chatbot is great for setting up appointments, a job your admin assistant had to do in the not-so-distant past. For example:

>> Schedule appointments on calendars, which you may have done one or many times before when you've set medical appointments.

>> Schedule and send reminders automatically.

>> Handle appointment changes and cancellations.

>> Provide the potential client with the information they need to know before your sales team calls them.

>> Have the AI chatbot present questions to the potential client and send the answers to the sales team so the sales call is more satisfying for all parties.

Your AI chatbot further acts as the assistant for your assistant by integrating with your existing apps and processes to provide good stuff, including the following:

>> Collecting data about customers and logging that information into your customer relationship management (CRM) database

>> Processing simple orders and payments

>> Routing urgent customer inquiries to the correct team member so you can make your customer happy faster

Building the Business Case

Yes, AI and AI chatbots are cool and exciting (and, some say, a bit scary), but AI is a tool just like all the other tools you're thinking of using in your business. You need to show five things to convince your stakeholders that AI chatbots can make your company better:

>> Which specific problems an AI chatbot can solve, such as reducing customer service costs

>> How your company can not only save money but also make money from using AI chatbots

>> How installing an AI chatbot gives you a leg up against the competition

>> How AI chatbots improve customer satisfaction and retention

>> How an AI chatbot is going to help your company grow in the next one, five, and ten years (and maybe longer, depending on your industry)

Highlighting the value you get

Your boss is asking where the value is. The following sections give you a summary of benefits to consider; don't forget to do your research into these points so you can provide specifics about how AI chatbots can improve the lives of those inside and outside your company.

Customers

We start with customers because they're the ones who will be using AI chatbots on your website, perhaps as their first interaction with your business.

REMEMBER

Today's consumers expect instant responses, and chatbots fit the bill. Indeed, consumers have likely used chatbots on other websites and expect them on yours.

You can track much more customer data coming from your AI chatbots, including when you get the most customer traffic and what customers' concerns are, so you can improve your processes, products, and/or services.

Efficiency

If AI chatbots can't help your company be more efficient with both time and money, then the powers that be won't accept their implementation. Here are some important points you need to bring up.

>> AI chatbots not only work 24/7 but also handle multiple conversations simultaneously. You can serve more people without hiring more staff, and you don't need your staff and/or virtual assistants available at all hours to answer common questions.

>> AI chatbots can free up your employees for other tasks, and fewer customer support calls also mean staff burnout goes down. Yes, you guessed it: Less burnout means less staff turnover.

TIP

If you've mapped out your customer journey (you have, right?), AI chatbot data can expose inefficiencies in that journey so you can fix them.

Management

AI chatbots help you control your message and research your customers. When you train your AI chatbot with consistent messaging, you ensure the information is accurate before you launch the chatbot. Consistent messaging is important for any business, but it's vital for regulated industries, where getting it wrong means bad juju for your business.

When your company grows, you'll probably have more customer support calls. You need to monitor how well your AI chatbot handles the extra load so you can determine whether you need to hire more customer service staff and/or update the AI chatbot with more answers that satisfy your customers.

Crunching the numbers

Your CEO and CFO will expect you to produce hard numbers, so here are the four areas you need to research and include in any reports and presentations:

>> **Break-even analysis:** That is, when do the cost savings and revenue gains cover the initial investment?

>> **The opportunity cost:** What business are you losing to your competitors without having the chatbot your customers expect on your website 24/7?

>> **Customer retention:** How does the improved service from an AI chatbot help you keep your customers?

>> **The chatbot load:** Plenty of AI chatbot options are out there, and we talk about the most popular ones in Chapter 4. Will the option you choose help you as your company grows?

Tracking ROI metrics

You're in business, so you know about *return on investment* (ROI). When your boss is demanding to know what the ROI is, here are the four things they'll be looking for:

>> **Cost per customer interaction:** Compare the cost of running your AI chatbot versus the cost of staff time to answer phones and emails.

>> **Revenue recovery:** Quantify the value of after-hours leads that the company would've lost because your staff wasn't working.

>> **Lead conversion rates:** Track how many chatbot conversations convert to new sales.

>> **Productivity gains:** Measure the time your staff now has for other revenue-generating work.

TIP

Don't forget to detail the work your staff has time to do and the revenue from it if you can.

Getting started

We suggest two ways to begin integrating an AI chatbot into your business:

>> First, start small by adding a basic chatbot for answering basic questions and/or setting appointments. Then you can review its progress and report back to the rest of your team and leaders. If everyone sees the ROI, you can offer suggestions for expanding the chatbot's capabilities.

>> You can also set up a use case, such as filling orders online, and integrate your chatbot with existing systems. After you have the results, you can make changes to the chatbot to improve performance and/or add new features such as customer support.

IN THIS CHAPTER

» Understanding major chatbot
components

» Seeing how AI and chatbots
work together

» Mapping the user's journey

Chapter **2**

Breaking Down the Tech Without the Geek-Speak

We know you're champing at the bit to start building your own AI chatbot, but hold those horses. You need to get to know how AI chatbots work because you probably want to use this technology for a good long while.

We start this chapter by telling you about the basic nuts and bolts that go into an AI chatbot and how AI enhances chatbots to make them more useful for your existing and potential customers. We also talk about when AI chatbots are unnecessary because every business has different chatbot needs.

Finally, we follow the journey (not the band) users take when they engage with a chatbot. Understanding the user journey gives you a better idea of how to design your chatbot to make it satisfying for your customers — and make your life easier, too.

Exploring the Key Concepts

Companies and media do a great job of hyping AI and all the cool things it can do, but they often don't bother to explain what it's about. (They don't even mention AI is an abbreviation for artificial intelligence.) So in the following sections, we tell you about the four AI components you need to know about.

Natural language processing (NLP)

The user interface component of AI is *natural language processing*, or NLP. That is, you can interact with an AI chatbot on an app or website, or an AI app such as ChatGPT or Claude, just by typing a question in your native language. NLP is designed to understand and respond to natural language in a way that mimics human conversation. (It's up to you if you want to be polite when you interact with your chatbot, but we think it's a good idea if only to reinforce good manners.) Figure 2-1 shows an NLP chatbot from when I (Eric) was shopping for bathroom ceiling exhaust fans on the Lowe's hardware chain app because my life is so exciting. It had me type my question (on the left side of the figure), asked follow-ups, and found products for me (on the right side of the figure).

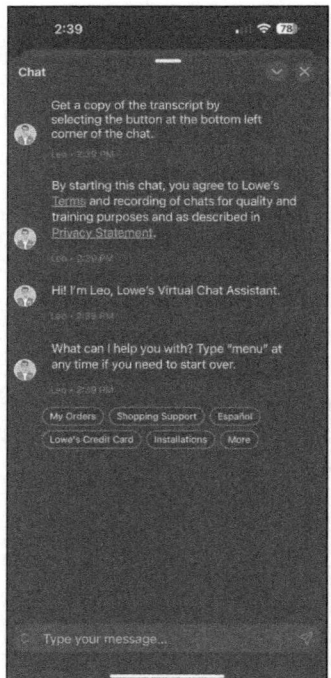

FIGURE 2-1:
The Lowe's app's
Leo chatbot.

If you've interacted with NLP chatbots, you've likely encountered some of their challenges:

>> **Ambiguity:** Words and sentences that have multiple meanings can confuse chatbots. Or the results leave words out because the user doesn't include them, even if those words seem like obvious hits. For example, when I looked for bathroom ceiling fans, I left out the word *exhaust*, and the Lowe's chatbot didn't show exhaust fans in the search results, which led me to search for the correct term the chatbot wanted.

>> **Context:** With idiomatic or nuanced text, chatbots may return a result you weren't expecting or may not understand you at all and ask for clarification.

>> **Language:** A chatbot needs to peel away the onion of understanding not only different languages but also their dialects. And if your customers like to use slang, your chatbot may not understand what they're talking about, which can drive them away.

Machine learning

The concept of *machine learning* is about systems that learn and improve from experience without being programmed to do so.

REMEMBER

AI uses algorithms that detect patterns in the information it receives and uses these patterns to refine its responses. If you think an AI chatbot or app is unusually good at understanding what you're asking and giving you great answers, now you know why.

Training your AI

Machine learning comes in three flavors:

>> **Supervised:** This version is where you train an *AI model*, which is just an AI-specific term for a computer program, to understand specific inputs and outputs, such as what the hours of operation for your business are.

>> **Unsupervised:** You train an AI model on unlabeled data to find patterns, such as when your chatbot groups customers based on their purchasing behavior, so you can better segment and reach customers with an ad that gets their attention.

>> **Reinforcement:** This approach focuses on training an AI model to make decisions to maximize a reward. For example, you may have heard of or encountered *dynamic* (or *surge*) *pricing* to adjust prices in real time on demand and inventory levels so that the business hopes they make more money.

Facing the issues

The reinforcement training model from the preceding section poses its own challenges with customers who feel the company is taking advantage of them and price gouging, which can drive negative publicity and drive away customers.

But AI can also drive people away if the results show your chatbot doesn't have relevant and high-quality data to use. That includes results that may be found as biased and/or unethical such as racial, gender-based, or age bias.

Conversational flow

A requirement of any AI chatbot is to keep the user moving from one step in an interaction to the next one. When you build an AI chatbot, you need to ensure it can keep the user engaged and moving toward an outcome, such as learning when an order will arrive. (We talk more about planning to build your chatbot in Chapter 5.)

Here's a quick, five-step primer about how to design the experience with your AI chatbot so you and your customers are happy:

1. **Define clear goals.**

   You need to know what the chatbot needs to do in each interaction, such as answering a question and/or getting the user's information. You need a clear endpoint, too.

2. **Be logical, captain.**

   Design the flow so that it guides the user through different stages with no confusion and to a defined outcome.

3. **Stay flexible.**

   Think about what your users may tell your chatbot and jump to related topics without missing a beat. When user errors or plain ol' misunderstandings happen, make sure your chatbot asks the user to rephrase or refine what they're asking.

4. **Keep them engaged.**

   Give your users a personal experience by referencing their past interactions, their preferences, and their progress toward their goal in using your chatbot.

5. **Get it right.**

   Test your chatbot's conversation flow not only as you develop it but also when it's operating in the wild. Adopt the Japanese philosophy of *kaizen* for continuous improvement based on user feedback and your own analytics.

Integrations

A chatbot can't exist on an island if you want it to benefit your business. You need to integrate your chatbot with your existing systems, such as customer relationship management (CRM) for your sales team and your ordering system, so your chatbot has the data it needs to give customers the information they want.

You need to investigate three types of integrations as you build your chatbot:

>> You may need to add AI capabilities to your platforms such as e-commerce, content management, and CRM and then integrate that functionality with your AI chatbot.

>> If you're using cloud-based apps, you need to check into your providers' AI capabilities because they have them.

>> To connect your existing apps and the cloud with your chatbot, you'll get application programming interfaces (APIs) so your tech people can make the chatbot and apps play well together. If you don't have anyone who can do that, you'll need to up your hiring budget.

Discovering How AI Enhances Chatbots (and When It's Overkill)

AI gives chatbots the ability to understand and adapt to simple and complex questions, which means current and potential customers are more likely to get the information they need without having to call or email your staff. As you research adding an AI chatbot to your customer support quiver, consider the 6 C's in the following sections to ensure the chatbot hits your target. For more on the differences between regular and AI chatbots, head to Chapter 1.

Connection

Regardless of whether the chatbots you're researching are simple or incorporate AI, you need to connect the purpose of your chatbot to your overall strategic goals. If you find a chatbot won't support your business the way you need it to, your best bet may be to wait and decide on the business criteria that would justify a chatbot.

Complexity

A simple chatbot will do the trick if you research your customer service interactions and find customers only want simple things like hours of operation or a phone number. Employing a simple chatbot can also save you some money (we discuss cost in the following section) and give you time to study responses and find out when it's time to devote more resources to an AI chatbot.

Cost

REMEMBER

Implementing an AI chatbot isn't cheap, because you have to dedicate money and people to develop and maintain those chatbots so they work for your customers. If you're a smaller business with a limited budget, you may want to look at cost-effective platforms from AI chatbot companies; we talk about them in Chapter 4.

Capacity

You need to talk with the humans on your staff to find out whether you need a chatbot right now. People may be able to handle the workload now, but that doesn't mean you don't need to plan ahead for a chatbot to help keep stress away from your team. (At least as much as possible.)

Customers

Customers who need or prefer the human touch may see an AI chatbot as an impediment to getting the help they need. For example, people may want to connect with a real estate agent directly rather than talk to an AI chatbot. If they decide to engage with your chatbot and find it only frustrates them, you've done a great job driving that customer into the hands of your competitor.

Changes

AI chatbots may not be agile enough if your business needs you to adapt at the snap of your fingers. For example, your company may have to update the chatbot database often to account for new products, services, and promotions. If you don't have a dynamic content management system in place to make updates easy, you'll have to budget for one before you can implement your AI chatbot.

REMEMBER

Complying with data privacy laws in various locations, like CCPA in California and GDPR in the European Union, is a rule of the chatbot game. No matter what chatbot solution you implement, you need to not only ensure compliance but also update your chatbot with the latest changes quickly.

Technology changes so quickly, especially with AI, that there's a term for it: *accelerating change.* You already have plans in place to upgrade your existing systems like CRMs and inventory management. With AI chatbots, you have to have a long talk with potential providers about how they'll help you adapt and make your AI as future-proof as possible.

Understanding the User Journey

If you've ever used a chatbot on a company website or app, you know about the journey you need to take. You start with a question, get an answer from the chatbot, and then refine your questions until you get the answer you're looking for — or you get frustrated and ask the chatbot for a phone number or email address to talk with a live human.

To make your chatbot work for both your business and your customers, you need to map the user's journey. (You may have also heard the term *storyboarding* to refer to this mapping process.) As you tap your inner cartographer, here are the seven pins you need to mark for your users.

The following sections are a 30,000-foot overview of chatbot building. If you're eager to start planning, flip to Chapter 5.

REMEMBER

Designing

Start by identifying the stages in the journey by following these three steps:

1. **Make users aware of where the chatbot is on the app or website and invite them to use it.**

2. **Know all the steps users will take as they use the chatbot to reach their goal that may include a purchase.**

3. **After a user purchases a product and/or service from you, the chatbot understands what to do after the purchase.**

When you're done, you'll know how your chatbot will fit into your customers' overall experience of interacting with your business.

Hitting every touchpoint

You need to track the key points of interaction between potential and current customers and your business. For example, you should already know the following:

>> How many website and app visits you receive

>> Your level of social media engagements on all platforms

>> How many customer service calls you get by phone and online during certain periods of time

In each case, you need to track that data over periods of time and understand when activity is higher. All this good information means you can train your AI chatbot to be the most effective at helping your customers get what they need without straining your human customer support team.

Knowing your customers

Understanding your customers means you should know their needs and the pain points that your company can help them relieve with the help of the chatbot. When you train your AI chatbot, you need to have this information in mind so a user realizes the chatbot understands them as an individual. They may also claim the chatbot's knowledge of them is spooky. This understanding leads to happier users and new users and (most importantly) keeps your current customers longer.

Using analytics

TIP

Any AI chatbot platform worth considering offers analytics so you can track users throughout the journey and find areas of friction or stop using the chatbot entirely.

For example, users may become frustrated when they can't ask about menu questions like allergies because the chatbot isn't programmed for those, so they either call you or decide not to eat at your cool burger joint. Analytics give you the information to improve your chatbot to the point where more potential diners get what they're looking for.

Always asking for feedback

You don't know whether your customers are happy unless you ask them what they think of your chatbot. If you've used one, you already know that many of them ask for your feedback after you finish your conversation.

Direct feedback is a vital part of your analytics game plan (see the preceding section) because you're learning from an actual human who's used your system and helping your chatbot become better. Following through on those suggestions (if you find them valuable) is up to you.

Being consistent

Your AI chatbot is just one component in your overall business strategy. You need to align your chatbot interactions with your company's voice and standards because your customers expect to get a consistent experience every time, whether they're using the chatbot, your website, your app, or your brick-and-mortar store if you have one.

Building your brand

In 2022, Forbes noted that depending on your industry, onboarding a new customer costs five to seven times more than retaining a current one. You should already be executing a plan to keep your customers, make them refer you to their friends and family, and build your brand equity.

TIP

Train your AI chatbot to recognize returning users and promote your retention initiatives, such as asking them to join your rewards program and offering exclusive deals that new customers don't get.

Chapter **3**

Exploring What Chatbots Can Actually Do

I f your only experience with chatbots has been frustrating, robotic, and clunky, you're not alone. A lot of people still think of chatbots as those old-school auto-responders that repeat the same question over and over when they don't understand what you're saying. But chatbots have come a long way since those early days, and what they can do now is honestly pretty mind-blowing.

The first time I (Kelly) really saw the potential of a chatbot was when I built a quiz chatbot back in 2018. This chatbot could ask questions, calculate a score, and then send people to specific results based on their answers. It even saved user information into custom fields for follow-ups. And that was all before AI came into the picture. That early experience showed me how powerful chatbots could be in guiding users, qualifying leads, and delivering exactly what someone needed in the moment.

Fast forward to today, and AI-powered chatbots are no longer limited by rigid logic or static flows. With the help of large language models (LLMs), you can now train chatbots to understand context, respond naturally, and keep the conversation moving forward, even when users throw in random questions or go off script. Instead of breaking, these chatbots adapt. And when clients see this capability in action, especially when it's tied to lead generation, content delivery, or customer support, they're hooked. You can practically see the lightbulb go off when they see what they can do.

Whether you're a real estate agent who wants to serve up personalized listings through chat or a business owner looking to boost social media engagement by using AI-powered comment responders, you have no shortage of clever ways to use this technology.

In this chapter, we walk through what modern chatbots can really do, explore some of the most powerful use cases, and help you start imagining how you can put them to work in your own business.

REMEMBER

Chatbots aren't just a trendy tech tool. They're a practical, results-driven way to create better experiences for your users and help your business grow. Whether it's handling customer service questions, capturing leads, delivering content, or guiding people through a quiz, a well-built chatbot can save you time, keep your audience engaged, and move your business forward.

A one-size-fits-all approach doesn't exist here, and that's a good thing. What works for one business may not work for another. The most important thing is to know your goals and the journey you want to take your users on.

Racking Up Real-World Ways Businesses Are Using Chatbots

In the following sections, we show you some of the most common and effective ways businesses are using AI-powered chatbots, from customer service and lead generation to interactive quizzes that turn browsers into buyers. You see what's working, why it works, and how you can apply similar strategies to your own business.

Super-charging customer service

Anyone who runs a service-based business knows how important getting back to people (especially potential leads) as soon as possible is. Even small businesses can lose leads when customer service falls through the cracks. A chatbot helps you stay responsive and builds trust, even when you're off the clock. The chatbot doesn't need to replace humans or do everything, but at the very least it acknowledges the people who come into the chat, captures their information, and transfers them to a human agent if it isn't able to answer their questions.

REMEMBER

Customer service chatbots are a powerful way businesses are showing up better for their customers without burning out their teams. A well-built chatbot acts like a digital receptionist, ready 24/7 to greet customers, answer common questions, and collect key information. Most people don't expect a full answer right away, but they do want to feel seen. Even an automated reply can give that instant acknowledgment that builds trust and keeps the conversation going.

I (Kelly) work with small-to-medium-sized businesses. These businesses don't necessarily get a ton of customer service inquiries. They also have small teams and aren't constantly checking messages. But they still need to make sure nothing slips under the radar. In those cases, the chatbot acts like a safety net. Whether someone sends a message in the middle of the night or during a busy workday, the chatbot is there to greet them, answer common questions, or at the very least collect their info so the team can follow up.

One of my clients, a residential pool builder, had a small team of three people helping manage all the operations. They'd have messages trickling in that they often missed or left unanswered for a few days simply because the volume was low and inconsistent and they were busy taking care of other aspects of their business.

To eliminate these issues, I created an AI chatbot that was not only trained on the business so it could answer common questions and provide feedback but also (with the help of AI) trained to understand the user's intent (for example, whether they showed interest in getting a quote) so it knew what type of information to collect.

An automation then texted the lead directly to me and my client so that we always had real-time information for prospects we needed to contact as soon as possible. After the chatbot was in place, we never missed another message, and the customer experience instantly improved.

Here's another case study that shows just how effective a customer service chatbot can be when used at scale: Suitor, a rapidly growing men's fashion company based in Australia, was struggling to keep up with the sudden influx of customer service inquiries that came with its success.

The team was overwhelmed, and customer satisfaction was starting to slip. By implementing a support chatbot, the company was able to handle 68 percent of all incoming inquiries automatically. That freed up its human team to focus on more complex support needs and helped it scale without sacrificing service quality. The result? A 31 percent increase in monthly revenue and a much smoother customer experience across the board. (You can read the full case study at www.tidio.com/blog/suitor-case-study/.)

Leveling up lead generation

My (Kelly's) absolute favorite use case for AI chatbots is for lead generation. One of the most powerful advantages AI has over traditional methods like lead forms, pop-ups, or static landing pages is how it creates a smarter, more interactive experience that responds to the user. With a basic form, someone who doesn't want to leave their phone number either abandons the form or skips the field altogether. They have no way to ask why it's required or express a concern.

But with an AI chatbot, you're creating a conversation. If the user hesitates or asks, "Why do you need my number?," an AI chatbot doesn't break. It explains. It can say something like, "We'll use your number to follow up and schedule your consultation. Don't worry, we won't share it with anyone." After the user understands the value, they're more likely to provide the information. That one shift can take you from an incomplete lead to a fully qualified one.

REMEMBER

Unlike lead forms, AI chatbots don't just capture leads; they qualify them in real time. **Not every lead is equal.** Just because someone fills out a form doesn't mean they're ready to buy. The chatbot is having a conversation that uncovers what the person needs, how ready they are to buy, and whether they're the right fit for your business rather than just collecting names and emails. When you have that kind of insight from the very beginning, your follow-ups become more effective, your sales process becomes smoother, and your team saves time by focusing only on the leads that matter.

I've personally built lead generation chatbots for clients across different industries, and we consistently see a boost in lead quality, completion rate, and conversion. And it's not just me. One great example comes from Costa Rica. La Repa de Sueños, a leading mattress company run by Trilce Jirón Garro and her family, was growing so fast it couldn't keep up with customer inquiries. As a brand that prides itself on personal service, it needed a solution that could scale without sacrificing quality. Trilce built an AI-powered chatbot using Manychat's AI Step tool. This chatbot, affectionately named Julio, was asking all the right questions based on customer needs. From firmness preferences to body type and even photos for mattress repairs, Julio guided users through the exact information needed.

In just one month, the sales automation saw nearly 1,500 conversations with over 900 completions. The sales team's workload dropped by 90 percent, and the company saw a 35 percent increase in sales after implementing AI Step. And beyond the numbers, customers loved it. Some even gave the chatbot the nickname "Julito" (an affectionate form of Julio), which shows just how human the experience felt.

That's the power of an AI chatbot when it's built right. It doesn't just collect leads. It builds trust, handles objections, qualifies users, and creates an experience that people enjoy.

If you're running lead ads on platforms like Facebook or Instagram, connect them directly to an AI chatbot instead of sending people to a landing page. Doing so creates an instant, low-friction experience that feels personal, and it gives you a much better shot at turning that click into a qualified lead.

Queuing up quizzes

One of the most powerful tools to implement — and my (Kelly's) favorite to teach — is the quiz. I'm not talking about those pop quizzes from your school days. These are interactive, engaging flows that can feel more like a game or a trivia-style experience. Quizzes are an incredible way to educate your audience, learn more about them, and create a customized user journey that converts. Whether you're segmenting leads, recommending the right product or content, or simply creating a fun, shareable experience, quiz chatbots help you do it all in real time.

Quizzes are also one of the best ways to start building chatbots because they touch so many of the capabilities available in chatbot platforms. You'll get hands-on experience with custom fields (see the nearby sidebar), conditional logic, calculators, segmentation, and even dynamic responses. They teach you what chatbots can really do in a very hands-on, visual way. Every time I teach chatbot building, quizzes are the moment where my students go, "Oh, wow, this is powerful."

One of the first chatbots I ever built was a quiz in 2018. I had a weekly live Facebook show, and each week we ran a new interactive game tied to the episode. One that stands out was called *You Don't Know Instagram.* It was a trivia-style quiz where users answered questions and earned points. At the end, the chatbot calculated their scores and delivered a message that matched their level of knowledge. If they scored high, the message acknowledged their expertise and offered them an advanced membership program. If they scored lower, the message shifted and pitched the same program as a way to learn and level up. It was the same product, but the delivery was completely personalized based on quiz performance, and this personalization in messaging made conversions much higher.

Want your quiz chatbot to perform like a pro? Start with the end in mind. Know exactly what action you want people to take when the quiz is over and build every question to support that goal. Keep it short and focused, with no more than five to ten questions, and consistently show users their progress with updates like "Question 3 of 7." And don't ask for their email or contact info upfront. Let them take the quiz first. Then, when they're ready for their results, ask something like "Want your results? Just drop your email below, and I'll send them to you." The completion rate is always better that way.

WHAT'S A CUSTOM FIELD?

Custom fields are like mini-data-buckets that store user responses during a quiz or chatbot flow. For example, if someone selects "I'm interested in Instagram tips," you can save "Instagram tips" as a custom field and later use it to send content tailored to that topic. It's one of the easiest ways to personalize your chatbot experience.

Custom fields are also used to collect and store critical user data, such as name, email, and phone number. This function makes transferring that information into your email service provider (ESP) or customer relationship management (CRM) system much easier, allowing you to follow up, track leads, and build ongoing relationships outside the chatbot.

REMEMBER

The real power of quiz chatbots shows up after the quiz ends. Because now you aren't just collecting contact information, you're collecting data. You know what the users care about, what they need, and where they're struggling. This data opens the door for better follow-ups, more personalized content, and product offers that match the user. After more than 20 years in marketing, I can tell you this: When you can personalize the experience, your conversions will follow.

Delivering content

After you've qualified a lead, run a quiz, or collected important info from your chatbot user (see the preceding sections), the next logical step is often to deliver content. That content may be a PDF guide, a video training, a freebie, or even a mini-course — basically, anything you'd normally send through email or link to from a landing page. No matter what kind of content you're delivering, the goal is always the same: Make the experience personal, easy, and immediate. The more easily people can get what they came for, the more likely they are to engage and take action.

I love using chatbots to deliver things like cheat sheets, quick-start guides, and PDF downloads. Some of my most successful list-building campaigns have used this exact approach. For example, I've built chatbots that deliver a "Getting Started in the Amazon Influencer Program" guide or a Facebook chatbot rule cheat sheet. These resources are simple, helpful, and exactly what my audience is looking for.

TIP

Delivering content through a chatbot offers several advantages over traditional methods, such as email or landing pages. Delivery happens instantly, right where the user already is. They don't need to hop platforms or wait for an email that may land in spam. That kind of immediate delivery boosts open rates, download rates, and overall conversions.

The chatbot doesn't just send the content. It captures contact information, tailors the experience, and helps move users forward based on their needs. When I set up a content delivery chatbot, I usually collect the user's name and email (especially if I want to grow my email list) and then deliver the content on the spot. If it's a short guide or one-pager, I drop the file or link directly in the chat. For larger files, such as ebooks or long-form videos, I prefer to link to a landing page or YouTube video to avoid delays or loading issues. Keep the experience smooth and interruption-free.

Another favorite tool is *comment automation.* This feature is compatible with platforms like Facebook, Instagram, and TikTok (depending on your chatbot builder). You can create a keyword trigger, like "guide" or "freebie," so that when someone comments with that word they automatically get a direct message (DM) that kicks off the chatbot conversation and delivers what they're looking for. It's a great way to turn organic engagement into qualified leads without running ads or sending people off-platform.

This method is exactly how e-commerce influencer Matt from www. getmattsdeals.com is growing his brand and driving sales. Instead of relying on a "link in bio" strategy on Instagram like most influencers, Matt started using comment automation tool LinkDM (www.linkdm.com) to deliver content directly through DMs. He saw his sales grow by 40 percent and engagement on his posts nearly double after he switched to this approach. According to Matt,

> Automation allows my audience to get what they are wanting quick and easy without having to wait for me to send them a link or have to try to navigate my website or Amazon storefront just to find the product from my post. I also love it because I can easily and automatically follow up within 24 hours on anyone who has commented using flow automation that engages them by letting them know about other offers that they probably didn't know about.

You can see Matt's chatbot strategy in action on his Instagram at @getmattsdeals.

Here are a couple of other suggestions:

>> **If you're offering multiple freebies or content pieces, use a custom event log to track which ones your users engage with most.** This approach helps you identify what's resonating with your audience and where your chatbot is delivering the most value. Not every chatbot platform supports custom events, but most do offer tagging, which is another excellent way to monitor engagement inside your chatbot.

>> **Take advantage of the built-in analytics features in your chatbot builder.** Track actions like button clicks, link taps, and downloads to see which content is actually being viewed, clicked, or saved. The more data you gather, the more easily you can double down on what's working and improve what isn't. (We dive deeper into this tracking in Chapters 12 and 13.)

HOW COMMENT TRIGGERS WORK

Comment automation lets you set up a trigger word on a social media post. When someone types that word in the comments, your chatbot sends them a direct message automatically. You can set a customer keyword trigger for a single post or open it up to trigger any post on that given platform. *Warning:* Be sure to familiarize yourself with the platform rules before building a comment trigger. Though they're very easy to set up and deliver powerful results, you want to make sure you stay compliant and out of trouble.

Reviewing the Types of Bots

Chatbots are an incredibly versatile tool that you can use across all kinds of use cases, as we explain in the previous sections. But not every chatbot is built the same way. In this section, we look at the different types of chatbots based on how they're built behind the scenes. Some use simple logic, others are powered by AI, and a few combine multiple styles to get the job done. Which type you choose really depends on where you plan to launch your chatbot and what your business goals are.

Rocking a rule-based chatbot

A *rule-based chatbot,* sometimes called a *conditional logic* or just *logic-based chatbot,* is built with predefined paths based on the choices a user makes. It typically does not use AI or if AI is used it is done so minimally. It's kind of like playing a game of "if this, then that." Think about it like this: If the traffic light is red, you stop. If it's green, you go. If it's raining, grab an umbrella. If it's sunny, no umbrella needed.

These bots follow a script that you, the builder, create ahead of time. The user clicks a button or selects a category, and the chatbot responds based on the rules you've set up. It doesn't guess or go off script. For example, if you run a pizza shop and someone wants to browse your menu, your chatbot may ask whether they want to see appetizers, pizzas, or desserts. If they choose pizzas, the chatbot takes them directly to the pizza section. No side quests into tiramisu or garlic knots.

Rule-based chatbots are perfect for industries that need consistency, accuracy, and compliance. Take health care, for example. You don't want a chatbot to guess what a patient means when they're trying to book an appointment. You need it to follow a clear linear process: Choose your doctor → pick a time → confirm the appointment. That kind of linear flow is where a rule-based chatbot shines. It also supports HIPAA compliance more easily because it avoids unpredictable responses.

Banking and finance are other great fits. Think balance lookups, branch hours, or tracking a recent transaction. These repetitive tasks with clear outcomes are exactly the kind of stuff a rule-based chatbot handles best.

If your business runs on repeatable processes and needs to make sure the right info is delivered every time without fail, a rule-based chatbot may be your best bet. This setup gives you full control over the conversation. It's reliable, straightforward, and gets the job done.

REMEMBER

Although rule-based chatbots are great for clear, step-by-step processes, they don't always play nice when users go off script. If someone asks a question your chatbot isn't prepared for, like "Why do you need this info?", the chatbot doesn't know what to do. It doesn't stop and try to explain. It just keeps pushing the user down the path it was built to follow. That kind of rigidity can be frustrating and lead to drop-offs, especially if the user wants a little more flexibility. So if your audience is likely to wander or ask unexpected questions, you may want to keep that in mind as you build.

Advancing to the AI-powered chatbot

AI has exploded not just in popularity but in how useful and effective it has become. Tools like OpenAI's GPT or Google's Gemini are now baked into all kinds of everyday tech, helping make things faster, smarter, and more efficient. The chatbot world is no exception.

An *AI-powered chatbot* is a chatbot that connects to a large language model (LLM), like Open AI's GPT, using an application programming interface (API). After it's connected, you give it prompts, sort of like when you chat with ChatGPT and tell it what you want it to do. Only in this case, you're giving it more structured instructions and feeding it information about your business and your chatbot's purpose. The more context you provide, the better it performs.

REMEMBER

When you connect an AI chatbot to something like OpenAI, the API is the messenger that helps the two tools talk to each other. You don't need to know all the behind-the-scenes details. Just know that the API is the waiter that helps your chatbot place the order for answers and then delivers the response back to the user, quickly and seamlessly.

Done right, the results are pretty amazing. These chatbots can carry on conversations that feel more human. They can answer questions on the fly, adapt to unpredictable users, and perform more complex interactions that the rule-based chatbots from the preceding section simply can't handle. If someone veers off script, the AI chatbot can keep up, redirect, and still provide a helpful experience.

The big win for small and medium-sized businesses is flexibility. No two customers ask a question the exact same way. AI chatbots are built to handle the thousand different ways someone may ask about your return policy, hours, or services. That kind of personalization leads to better user experiences, higher satisfaction scores, and more conversions.

AI chatbots give small businesses a serious edge without having to hire a big team or stay glued to their inbox. Imagine a small business that gets lots of questions through its Instagram DMs or its website chat. Maybe it doesn't have the staff to answer everything right away. But a well-set-up AI chatbot knows the business information, understands what the customer is asking (even if they don't phrase it perfectly), and responds in a helpful, friendly — and timely — way. Meanwhile, the business owner and their small team get to focus on the big stuff without constantly checking messages.

WARNING

Just because your chatbot uses AI doesn't mean it can read minds or know everything about your business. If you don't provide it with the proper context or training, it may give off-brand or flat-out incorrect responses. Always test and refine to make sure it sounds like you and provides accurate answers. If something is off, it's because your knowledge base prompt needs more fine-tuning.

Checking out voice chatbots

Voice chatbots are exactly what they sound like: chatbots that can engage in conversation through voice. Think Alexa or Siri. But voice chatbots go beyond just smart speakers. They can also work over the phone, answering questions and handling tasks by using AI and voice technology.

Here's how it works: The chatbot listens to what the user says and transcribes it into text behind the scenes. From there, the AI determines what the user means and retrieves the relevant information from its knowledge base. Then it turns the answer back into speech and responds out loud using text-to-voice technology.

Say a customer asks, "What time do you open today?" The voice chatbot doesn't just look for the word *time*. It understands the intent behind the question and knows the user is asking about your business hours. The chatbot can then respond with something like, "We're open today from 10 a.m.to 6 p.m."

Voice chatbots are especially useful in hands-free situations. Whether someone is driving, cooking, or just wanting to talk rather than type, a voice chatbot can offer a faster and more natural experience. These chatbots are ideal for industries such as hotels, customer service, smart home support, and businesses that rely heavily on phone-based communication.

Voice chatbots do have benefits and limitations:

>> **On the plus side:** They're quick, easy to use, and great for accessibility, especially for people with visual impairments or limited mobility.

>> **On the downside:** They can sometimes get tripped up by background noise, heavy accents, or unclear speech.

You don't need a massive collection of tools to get started. Just make sure you choose a chatbot-building platform that supports voice. If you're planning to use a voice chatbot for phone services, you also need to be able to connect to a service like Twilio or AudioCodes. Otherwise, building a voice chatbot is similar to creating an AI-powered chatbot (see the preceding section), with the added step of converting the text replies into spoken responses.

Speed matters for voice chatbots, especially those that work over the phone.

>> **Make sure you're using a fast LLM that delivers quick responses.** If your chatbot takes too long to respond, people will think it's broken and hang up. Not all LLMs run at the same speed, so choose one known for high performance.

>> **Keep your replies short and to the point.** In your prompt setup, add a note that limits the length of responses. You don't want your chatbot rambling on with a paragraphs-long answer. People tend to lose interest quickly during a voice interaction, so keep it clear, concise, and helpful.

Surveying short message service (SMS) chatbots

Short message service, or SMS, is more commonly known as text messaging. An *SMS chatbot* is a chatbot that sends short, direct responses directly to the user's phone. No app, login, or Internet connection is necessary, unlike chatbots on your website or social media.

The true power of SMS lies in its simplicity and reliability. If someone has a cellphone, they can get a text. It doesn't matter whether the phone is the latest smartphone or an old-school flip phone. That kind of reach makes SMS a no-brainer for businesses. Studies show that open rates for SMS are around 98 percent. This point is huge for ensuring your intended audience reads your messages. That's why SMS chatbots are perfect for things like flash sales, appointment reminders, and any update you need people to see fast.

That said, you need to consider a few important limitations:

>> Text messages are best kept short and to the point. Long responses or complex chatbot flows can feel overwhelming in a text thread.

>> Rich media, such as videos or extensive menus, don't translate well over SMS, so the SMS method is better suited for simple back-and-forth conversations.

>> If you're working with an international audience, costs can quickly add up. Normal messaging rates apply and all that.

>> Perhaps most importantly, SMS is highly regulated. Every country has its own set of rules, so make sure you know the laws wherever you're texting. In the United States, for example, SMS falls under the protection of the CAN-SPAM Act, and businesses must obtain explicit, written consent before sending any messages. Fines for violating these rules can range from $500 to $1,500 per message.

To use SMS chatbots, you need a chatbot platform that supports SMS. Many platforms integrate directly with services like Twilio, Plivo, or Sendbird. Some also let you connect to these tools through an API. After you're set up, the experience is much like building any other chatbot. Keep things short, simple, and user-friendly.

Dabbling in direct messaging (DM) chatbots

People are spend an average of nearly two and a half hours every day on social media. That's a lot of opportunity to connect. *Direct messaging chatbots* operate within platforms such as Facebook, Instagram, WhatsApp, and even TikTok. These chatbots live right where your customers are already spending their time, and they can chat with users in private messages or even respond to public comments by sending a follow-up message in the DMs (using *comment to message triggers*). Messaging on social media feels casual and friendly, making it an ideal space to build trust and showcase your brand's personality.

DM chatbots are especially powerful for e-commerce and product-based businesses, including coaches, course creators, influencers, event businesses, and even local food spots.

- >> They can answer product questions, send discount codes, guide shoppers, and even collect emails or phone numbers for future follow-ups.

- >> With keyword automation, they can take someone from a public post or story straight into a private conversation that nudges them to buy.

- >> They're incredibly helpful for busy brands that have large numbers of followers and can't respond manually to every message.

That said, DM chatbots aren't a fit for every audience. If your customers aren't active on social media or feel uncomfortable using private messaging, this strategy may not be the best match. This note is especially true for older generations, who may see direct messages as intrusive, even when they accidentally initiate the conversation themselves.

REMEMBER

Every social media platform has its own rules for how and when you can message someone. As we explain in Chapter 15, make sure you understand and follow each platform's policies. Breaking the rules can result in losing access to messaging entirely.

Holding out for hybrid chatbots

A hybrid chatbot is like the utility knife of messaging. Instead of being locked into just one type of chatbot, a *hybrid chatbot* can combine rule-based logic, AI-powered conversations, and even multichannel functionality to meet the user's needs at any given moment. *Multichannel functionality* simply means that your chatbot can work across multiple communication channels, such as your website, Facebook Messenger, Instagram DMs, WhatsApp, or SMS, so your customers can interact with your business wherever they prefer while maintaining a seamless experience.

For example, your chatbot may initiate the conversation with a few quick, button-based questions that utilize conditional logic before transitioning to AI to handle more open-ended user responses. This setup provides you with the control and structure of a rules-based flow, along with the flexibility and human-like feel of AI. In today's chatbot platforms, most reputable builders offer this kind of flexibility, enabling you to create the right experience tailored to the situation. (You can read more about rules-based and AI-powered chatbots earlier in the chapter.)

Why go hybrid? Because people aren't predictable. Sometimes, a user wants to book an appointment. At other times, they want to ask something you can't possibly have planned for. A hybrid chatbot gives you the best of both worlds. You get structured workflows where you need them and more personalized, free-flowing conversations when it matters.

Pretty much any industry can benefit from a hybrid chatbot. Industries such as healthcare, wellness, and service-based businesses are excellent fits. A dental office may use logic to allow users to select a service and schedule a time and then rely on AI to answer questions about insurance coverage. If something gets complicated, the chatbot can even route the conversation to a live human. After someone books an appointment through web chat or social media, the same chatbot system can send SMS confirmations and reminders to keep things seamless.

Note that hybrid chatbots do take more work. Because you're blending multiple types of builds into one system, setup and testing require more time and strategy. You must ensure that everything connects smoothly behind the scenes. If something breaks, you have more moving parts to troubleshoot. And maintenance is ongoing. Hybrid bots are not a "set it and forget it" situation. You need to check in regularly, make minor adjustments continually, and keep everything up to date.

REMEMBER

Not every chatbot platform supports full hybrid functionality. Make sure the one you choose can handle logic-based flows, AI responses, SMS, and multichannel messaging all under one roof. Otherwise, you'll end up relying on outside connectors like Zapier or Paddly, which can slow things down, create reliability issues, and increase your costs.

Knowing What Makes a "Good" Chatbot

Before you start adding buttons or writing AI prompts, take a step back. A good chatbot should help your business reach its goals while making things easier and more enjoyable for the people using it.

It all starts with knowing what you want to accomplish. Are you trying to capture leads, answer customer questions, book appointments, or something else? You need to clarify your goals first. Then map out the steps a user needs to take to get from point A to point B. From there, you can figure out what kind of chatbot and what kind of tools will support both your business needs and your users' experience. Head to the earlier sections "Racking up Real-World Ways Businesses Are Using Chatbots" and "Reviewing the Types of Bots" for info on some of the things chatbots can do and details on various kinds of chatbots, respectively.

This part may not be the most exciting, but skipping it is where most people go wrong. A little planning upfront can save you a lot of frustration later.

In the following few sections, we break down what makes a chatbot good. We focus on the three building blocks that take your chatbot from basic to brilliant: clarity, value, and the user experience (UX).

Considering clarity

Clarity is one of the most underrated parts of building a chatbot, but it's absolutely essential. If people don't understand what your chatbot is trying to do or what they're supposed to do next, you'll lose them quickly. But when your chatbot is clear on the inside and outside, it builds confidence. It keeps the conversation on track.

REMEMBER

From a planning perspective, clarity means getting specific about what you want your chatbot to accomplish. You may have more than one goal, and that's totally fine. You may want to capture leads, answer customer questions, and promote an upcoming event. The key is to clearly map out each goal and build the different user paths that guide people to the right place. The more goals you have, the more important organizing and segmenting your users in a way that makes sense becomes.

Understanding the priority of your business goals is even more important than knowing your goals themselves. The chatbot flow should always handle your priority goal first. Mapping out your priority list ensures the chatbot stays focused and on track. For example, I (Kelly) have worked with clients whose primary goal was to increase webinar sign-ups. But the first thing its chatbot asked was whether users wanted to join the newsletter or download a PDF. That kind of chatbot flow can derail your results. If the webinar is the priority, make that the first call to action. You can follow up with secondary offers later.

From the user's perspective, clarity means providing clear instructions and making the experience feel effortless. Your chatbot should talk like a real person, guide users step-by-step, and never leave them wondering what to do next. The more clearly you communicate, the more likely people are to follow through and get what they came for. Also, keep the audience in mind. Most people read at a sixth-grade level, so avoid using language that can be confusing.

TIP

Ask yourself these four questions to ensure your chatbot is clear.

>> **What's the goal of this chatbot?** Be honest and specific. Is it trying to book appointments, answer questions, collect leads, or do something else? If you're trying to accomplish more than one thing, make sure the goals are in order of priority and each has its own clearly marked path.

>> **Can users tell what to do next at every step?** Look at every message and interaction. Is it obvious what the user should click, type, or choose? If you find even a little confusion, clarify it.

>> **Is it giving too many choices at once?** Too many buttons, too many directions, or too much info in a single message can overwhelm people. Keep it simple. One clear decision is better than five fuzzy ones.

>> **Would this process make sense to someone who has never talked to my business before?** Test your flow like a brand-new user. If you can't follow it without guessing, you still have work to do.

Use this mini-checklist anytime you're planning or reviewing a chatbot. The clearer the path, the better the results.

Revving up value

Ultimately, people interact with chatbots for one primary reason: They want something — an answer to a question, help with a purchase, an update on an order, or a point in the right direction. A chatbot that delivers real value enables these things to happen quickly and without friction.

Chatbots offer a convenient and accessible way for people to communicate with your business. Whether they're chatting with a chatbot or a human, most users expect the same things: speed, simplicity, and clear solutions. When someone starts a conversation, they're hoping your chatbot can take care of what they need without wasting time or making things more confusing.

REMEMBER

When we talk about value, we're really talking about whether your chatbot helps your users achieve what they came for as quickly and effectively as possible. If your chatbot can't provide a fast, helpful response, it isn't delivering value, and it may ultimately do more harm than good.

REMEMBER

A chatbot can only be as clear as your plan. If you're not sure what the goal is or how users are supposed to get there, they won't know either. Take the time to map out your plans before you begin building. Clear strategy equals clear conversations.

Maximizing user experience (UX)

A chatbot isn't just a tool. It's a conversation, and conversations are meant to feel natural, personal, and easy to follow. When you're building a chatbot, the user experience should be at the heart of everything you do. It should solve real problems, save time, and make the whole interaction feel easy. If your chatbot can do that, you're well on your way to building something people will want to use.

REMEMBER

It doesn't matter how smart your chatbot is or how many cool features you've added. If it's confusing, overly wordy, or challenging to navigate, your users will likely bounce. A good user experience means people can move through your chatbot easily and confidently. Your chatbot should feel like a helpful guide, not something that leaves people guessing.

Here are some guidelines for making the user experience as smooth as possible:

>> **Make it clear.** As we mention in the earlier section "Clarity," one of the most important ways to create a great experience is through, well, clarity. Use plain, friendly language and avoid technical jargon. Keep people informed about what's happening at each step and what they should do next. If someone's booking an appointment or tracking an order, for example, your chatbot may say, "Hi! I can help you book an appointment or track your order. What would you like to do?" Simple, clear prompts like this one make users feel guided rather than overwhelmed.

>> **Reduce typing.** The fewer things your users have to type, the better. Buttons and quick replies help reduce spelling mistakes, confusion, and frustration. People are more likely to engage when the path is evident and straightforward to follow.

>> **Don't forget to make it feel human.** Add personality and conversational tone wherever it makes sense. Small touches, such as a typing indicator or an emoji, can make your chatbot feel more like a genuine conversation and less like a transaction.

REMEMBER

>> **Give your users a way out.** One of the most common complaints about chatbots is the feeling of being stuck. Always allow users to restart, go back, unsubscribe, or speak with a live representative if needed. These options build trust and reduce frustration.

>> **Keep your content short and mobile-friendly.** Most chatbot users are on their phones, and long blocks of text don't work well in that space. Break your responses into digestible parts, avoid stacking multiple questions at once, and keep things moving at a comfortable pace. Think in short sentences, not paragraphs.

>> **Match your tone and structure to the platform you're using.** A chatbot on Instagram or Facebook should feel more casual and visual, while an SMS chatbot needs to be short and direct. If your chatbot is on your website, design it with clean, clear pathways and ensure quick access to actions. One size doesn't fit all, so make sure your chatbot feels at home wherever it appears.

>> **Set clear expectations.** If users are going to experience a delay, say so. If your chatbot can't do something, don't try to fake it. A quick message such as "I'm gathering your order details. This may take a few seconds." can go a long way toward keeping people calm and happy while they wait. It can be the difference between a happy user and a frustrated user.

>> **Always respect your users.** Avoid sending too many follow-ups or pushing promotions too hard. Your chatbot's primary goal is to be helpful. That's how you build trust and turn a one-time chat into an ongoing connection.

Your chatbot should be a helpful guide. When you take user experience seriously, people don't just use your chatbot; they enjoy it.

TIP

If you want to build a chatbot with a great user experience, don't stop at previewing it on the backend; actually use it. Test it like a real person would. Click the buttons. Type in responses. Try it on mobile. Then ask a few friends or team members to review it and provide honest feedback. Look for anything that feels confusing, clunky, or incomplete. Dead ends, missing info, or unclear instructions can all break the experience. If you wouldn't enjoy chatting with your own chatbot, your users won't either.

Understanding chatbots' limitations

REMEMBER

Chatbots are intelligent, but they're not magic. Here's what they *can't* do (at least not yet):

>> **Read minds:** You still need to plan their responses and teach them about your business through proper prompt engineering, logic trees, and strategic planning.

>> **Set up and maintain themselves:** A "set it and forget it" chatbot doesn't deliver outstanding results. Technology changes, and so do people. Ensure you check in regularly to make updates as needed.

>> **Replace human empathy:** Use chatbots to enhance your customer experience, not eliminate the human touch. Don't be afraid to connect users with human agents when needed.

2

Choosing and Using the Right Chatbot Tools

IN THIS PART . . .

Review and compare different chatbot platforms you should know.

Plan to build your first chatbot.

Build a bot without writing any code.

Connect chatbots to tools you use now.

Chapter **4**

Comparing Chatbot Platforms

Plenty of AI chatbot platforms are out there, and the paradox of too many choices may have led you to buy this book. In this chapter, we curate six of the platforms you need to know about.

After we present each platform, we explain their strengths and weaknesses and review them to help you find the right one for you and your current needs. If you're still not sure what platform your company needs, we offer some further food for thought so you can present your recommendation to your team and leadership with confidence.

Introducing the Platforms You Should Know

When you begin your search for an AI platform that can meet your needs, start by looking at the following six options. We also list prices for each platform as of mid-2025 (when we're writing this book).

Manychat

Manychat (manychat.com) is designed for creators and marketers who want their business to engage on several Meta platforms, including Messenger, Instagram, and WhatsApp, as well as TikTok (see Figure 4-1).

FIGURE 4-1:
The Manychat website is designed primarily for marketing.

Manychat offers a number of powerful tools, such as a variety of templates to build from, automation features, and advanced audience segmentation so you can hone your marketing message.

You can use the basic features of Manychat and engage with 1,000 contacts for free, and the Pro plan gives you all the features starting at $15 per month.

Chatfuel

Chatfuel (chatfuel.com) uses a drag-and-drop interface to make building AI agents on Facebook, Instagram, and WhatsApp and through a website easy. Check it out in Figure 4-2.

Chatfuel also integrates with several e-commerce and customer relationship management (CRM) platforms including Shopify, Stripe, Zapier, Calendly, and Google Sheets. If you don't want to build your own AI agent right now, you can test the Fuely AI agent with your website and those same platforms at no cost.

FIGURE 4-3:
Chatfuel also lets
you try its Fuely
AI agent for free.

Pricing for 1,000 conversations per month on Facebook and Instagram starts at $23.99; if you exceed the 1,000-conversation limit during the month, each additional conversation costs 2 cents. For WhatsApp, the price for 1,000 conversations per month starts at $34.49, and each extra conversation costs 2 cents.

Chatrace

Like Chatfuel in the preceding section, Chatrace (chatrace.com) uses a drag-and-drop interface so you can create your chatbot and integrate it into several different platforms including WhatsApp, Instagram, and Facebook (see Figure 4-3).

Chatrace also allows you to select an AI platform, such as ChatGPT, Claude, or Google Gemini, to use with the chatbot. *Note:* Chatbots created with Chatrace sport the Chatrace name, domain, and logo; if you want your chatbot to have your business information instead, you can purchase the Whitelabel plan for $499 per month.

You can try Chatrace for free and have 100 contacts per month, or you can buy the Pro version for $14 per month and get 500 contacts. If you need more, you pay more; the website has a calculator that tells you how much you pay for the number of contacts you want.

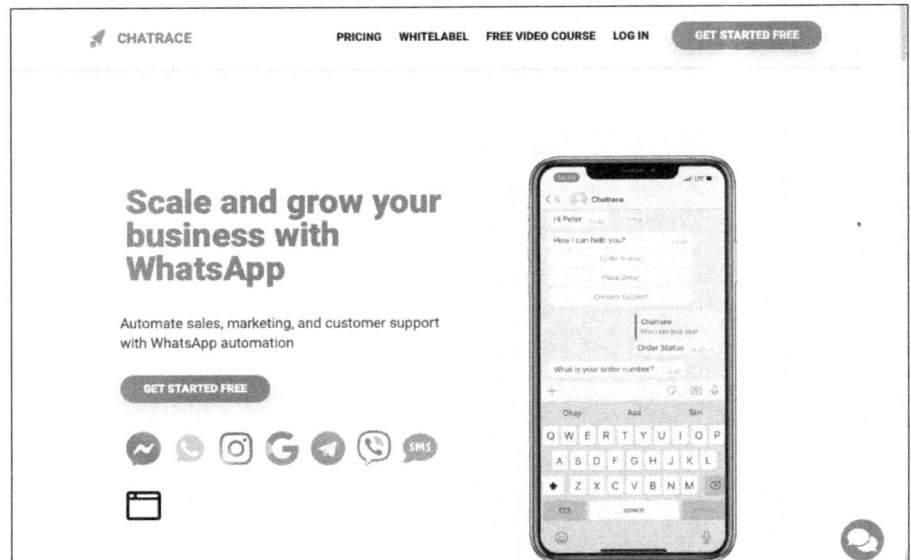

FIGURE 4-3:
The Chatrace
website invites
you to get
started for free.

Voiceflow

Voiceflow specializes in the design and deployment of conversational voice agents so you can have human-like phone calls. You can also build chat agents with a customized interface. The company's website (www.voiceflow.com), shown in Figure 4-4, touts that it's the fastest way to build advanced AI agents.

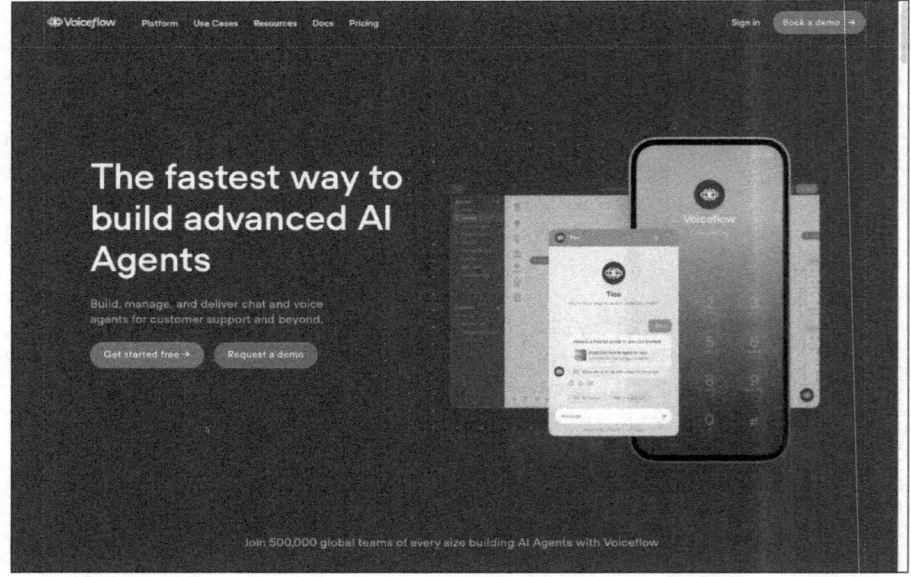

FIGURE 4-4:
The Voiceflow
website invites
you to get
started for free.

Voiceflow is designed for team collaboration in producing your voice and chat agents, and its website notes that its app is for teams that iterate quickly. The company also suggests using its app for customer support first and then moving on to other use cases.

The Starter plan for students and hobbyists lets you get your feet wet for free. If you want the full version for businesses, the price is $150 per month or $1,620 per year.

Botpress

Botpress (botpress.com) is an *open-source* chatbot platform that allows developers to customize and build their own chatbots using external application programming interfaces (APIs) and databases (see Figure 4-5). The Botpress website notes you can find plenty of support from fellow users.

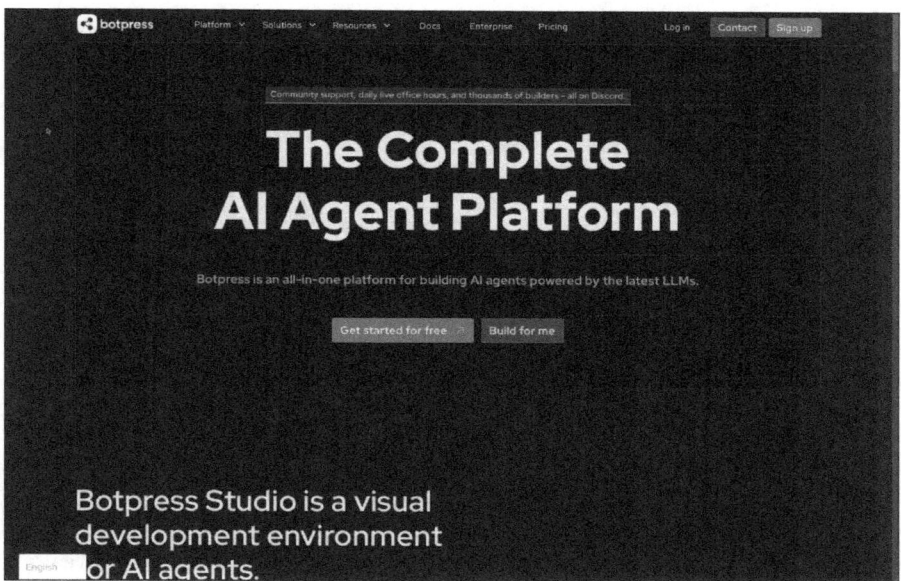

If the mention of APIs confuses you or makes you twitch, Botpress has you covered with its own rapid AI agent builder called Agent Studio.

You can use Botpress with various channels, including Instagram, Facebook Messenger, and WhatsApp. You can also integrate with popular apps such as HubSpot, Calendly, and Notion.

Like its competitors, Botpress offers a free plan to help you figure out whether the tool is right for you. If it is, you can purchase its Plus plan for $89 per month. You and your team can develop with Botpress by using the Team plan for $495 per month.

ChatBot

The people at ChatBot (www.chatbot.com) must be very proud of themselves for securing that name, because it has a built-in advantage: When you search for "chatbot" in your favorite search engine, ChatBot is the first name that comes up. When you click the ChatBot link, the ChatBot website appears as shown in Figure 4-6.

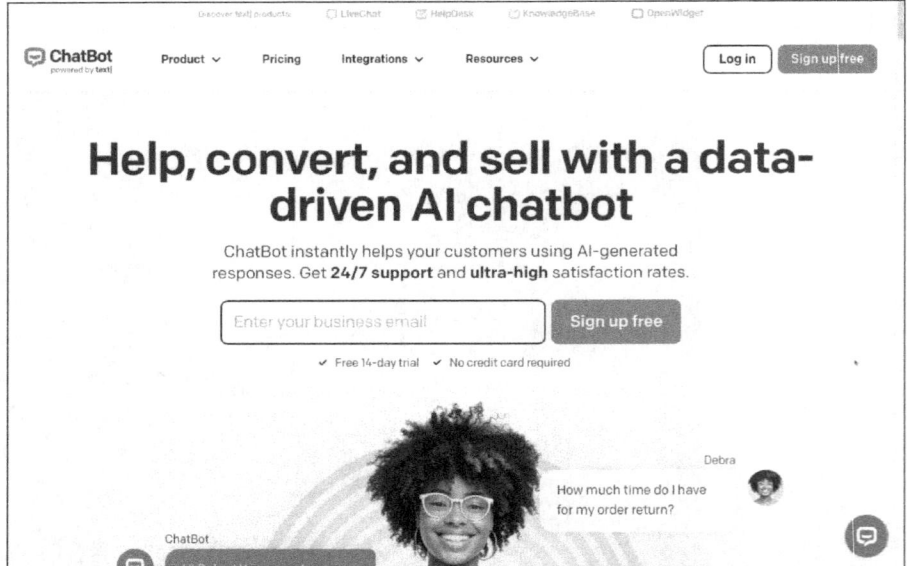

Like its competitors, ChatBot uses a visual builder to create your AI chatbot and analytics to test your chatbot's effectiveness. ChatBot integrates with a large number of platforms including Facebook Messenger, LinkedIn, and even Pinterest. You can set up your chat widget on your existing WordPress website, too.

ChatBot also integrates with a number of marketing and e-commerce tools including Zapier, Mailchimp, and Shopify. You can sign up for a free 14-day trial to see whether ChatBot is right for you. If so, you can sign up for the Starter plan at $65 per month (with a discounted annual payment), and of course other plans have more features and higher prices.

Sizing Up Each Platform's Strengths and Weaknesses

The acronym SWOT, which stands for strengths, weaknesses, opportunities, and threats, is a good analysis tool when you're trying to decide to do something in business. In this section, we lay out the strengths and weaknesses in each platform we highlight in the earlier section "Introducing the Platforms You Should Know" before you try them out. (For more on the opportunities, head to the later section "Understanding Which Platform is Right for You.")

REMEMBER

These strengths and weaknesses are current as we write this book in mid-2025. Some of the weaknesses may have been resolved by the time you read it, so be sure to check the info in the following sections against what the platform offers now.

Manychat

Manychat has three core strengths:

>> A user-friendly interface

>> Strong integration with Instagram and Facebook Messenger

>> Strong audience segmentation tools so you can adapt your messaging for different customer categories

Manychat's reliance on social media platforms means its functionality may change over time as those platforms change their policies. What's more, Manychat requires separate configurations for each social media platform. Another common weakness online reviewers note is that translating the chatbot into languages other than English is hard.

Chatfuel

Chatfuel's core strength is its easy-to-use interface so you can get a new chatbot up to speed quickly on Meta platforms. Chatfuel already has its own Fuely AI to bring more intelligence to your chatbot conversations. Community support is also a strong point.

On the downside, when you sign up for the free trial, you get only a limited number of conversations, and that may not be enough for you to decide about springing for a paid plan. Reviewers have also noted problems with the chatbot not understanding what people are asking (an issue with the natural language processing, or NLP). Some reviewers have also found the documentation lacking with limited support on lower-priced plans.

Chatrace

Chatrace has an easy setup process with prebuilt modules and a drag-and-drop builder so you can set up your chatbot fast. With the pro plan, you get access to all integrations as well as 24/7 support. And you have a great community of fellow users.

However, a curious weakness we found came from a 2025 review by Joren Wouters at Chatimize, who felt the company isn't transparent. That is, no information about the company or who works there is available besides an address in the United Kingdom. To Wouters, that lack of transparency brings too much risk, and he avoids using Chatrace for his business and his clients. (Read the full review at chatimize.com/reviews/chatrace.)

Voiceflow

Voiceflow's specialization in voice-driven AI agents works well for virtual assistant apps such as Alexa and Google Assistant. (We won't mention Siri because it's a distant third in the virtual assistant race, its star turn in *The Lego Batman Movie* notwithstanding.) You can build reusable components to shorten your development time. Voiceflow also offers real-time conversation testing.

Unfortunately, reviewers have found Voiceflow chatbots to have limited ability to handle misunderstandings and understand context. It has no built-in live chat or a live chat integration. It also offers limited customization, so as your chatbot becomes too complex for Voiceflow to manage, you'll have a platform migration decision to make.

Botpress

Botpress is highly customizable with strong APIs so you can get into the weeds and build complex AI chatbots that meet your needs now and over time. Indeed, one feature Botpress emphasizes is the ability to train your chatbot with custom knowledge by importing websites, blogs, FAQs, documents, and structured data. Users have described Botpress as "WordPress for chatbots."

REMEMBER

Structured data is information organized in a predefined format, such as a spreadsheet with rows and columns you can place information into.

You've probably guessed the main weakness: Because Botpress offers a lot of features and options, it has a steep learning curve for beginners. Botpress also doesn't come with Facebook and Instagram marketing features.

REMEMBER

Customizations also require programming skill, and you may need to hire one or more programmers to set up your chatbot and keep it running smoothly.

ChatBot

ChatBot has plenty of good things going for it, including its visual builder and extensive integrations with platforms and tools (such as LinkedIn and Mailchimp) not found elsewhere. This feature gives ChatBot an advantage over its competitors.

But that leads us to its big weakness: You have to pay a lot to get that functionality. Even if you pay yearly and get a monthly discount, that's $1,704 as of this writing. And if you need a *white label* solution, you can only use the Business plan that costs your business over $5,000 per year.

REMEMBER

A *white label* product or service is produced by one company and purchased by another company to sell with its own branding.

Reviewers also note that ChatBot produces AI chatbots that struggle with complex queries and sometimes lack personalization. The ChatBot platform doesn't include Facebook marketing features. And it has no comprehensive overview for all chatbot flows, so managing large chatbots may be a challenge.

Understanding Which Platform Is Right for You

Chatbot companies focus their marketing efforts on four types of companies that use chatbots: marketing agencies, coaches, e-commerce, and customer support. Some have a primary focus, such as Manychat and its focus on marketing on Meta platforms and TikTok. Others are broader.

Here are our recommendations and considerations for each of these business types. Head to the earlier sections "Introducing the Platforms You Should Know" and "Sizing Up Each Platform's Strengths and Weaknesses" for the nuts and bolts on the specific companies we mention in the following sections.

Marketing agencies

Marketing agencies need chatbots that can serve clients with different needs. Manychat has excellent growth tools for reaching out on Meta platforms as well as TikTok, which still hasn't been shut down as of this writing.

If you need more customizability and the ability to replicate and scale your chatbot for different jobs, Botpress gives you the power to do that now and as your agency grows.

Coaches

The online coaching industry was valued at $3.2 billion in 2022 and is growing rapidly, with a compound annual growth rate (CAGR) of 14 percent between 2023 and 2032. That means by 2032, the value will be a whopping $11.7 billion, according to Allied Market Research.

If you're a coach or thinking of becoming one, you need tools that provide you with direct and personalized communication, especially on social media platforms. For that reason, you should seriously consider Manychat if you're using Meta platforms to get the word out and support your clients.

Chatfuel is another platform to look at for connecting with current and potential clients through Meta platforms. Chatfuel goes farther by integrating with e-commerce platforms Shopify and Stripe. Manychat and Chatfuel have good analytics as well as low and flexible pricing.

E-commerce

If you need an AI chatbot for your e-commerce store, Chatfuel is one platform to explore because it integrates with Shopify and Stripe as well as Zapier so you can connect to your CRM, email marketing, and other business apps.

TIP

ChatBot's integration with Shopify means you can display product cards on your website, check and report on product availability, and also provide order status reports for your customers.

What's more, ChatBot reports include user and chat tracking so you can spot trends and the interactions that are the most popular with your users.

Customer support

If your business receives a lot of support requests, you need robust AI chatbots that can handle complex requests and provide accurate information. You also need strong analytics and reporting capabilities.

Consider ChatBot and Botpress for these functions. ChatBot tracks your chats between users and your chatbot and identifies the busiest times, what topics come up the most in conversations, and the length of a typical chat. ChatBot also works with its sister app LiveChat so your customer can connect with a live agent at any time seamlessly.

Considering Your Options Before Choosing a Platform

The earlier section "Understanding Which Platform Is Right for You" touches on specific needs that different AI chatbot solutions can provide, but that information doesn't give the full picture. Whether you're a business owner who needs to get feedback from your team or a manager who needs to convince the powers that be that an AI chatbot is right for your business — and worth budgeting for — you need to address issues in the following eight key areas.

Talk with potential AI chatbot provider candidates as often as you need to ensure that the chatbot can grow with you and the provider will be there to help as your business grows. Your AI chatbot provider will be an integral part of your business, so you need to ask questions that assuage any concerns you may have.

Business needs

You need to start by asking yourself and your team what you want to achieve with the chatbot — improving customer service, increasing sales, and/or offloading tasks that free up your existing support staff to do other important things.

You also need to ask questions about who your customers are and what they want. For example:

>> Are your customers comfortable with chat interfaces?

>> Do you provide multilanguage support for your customers?

- » Do your customers primarily use your website or different media such as apps and texting platforms like WhatsApp?
- » Do your customers need accessibility accommodations such as the ability to increase the text size?

Those answers give you the background you need as you approach AI chatbot vendors. In the following sections, we're here with a list you can check as you talk with the vendor. (We don't mind you marking on the page.) You may not need to ask all these questions if they don't sync with what you want to achieve.

Customer interaction

A chatbot's primary purpose is to interact with customers, so here are questions you need to answer before you talk to a vendor:

- » How many simultaneous chats does the chatbot need to handle?
- » Do you need simple, frequently asked question (FAQ) responses or multistep answers?
- » Do you need to scale up your chatbot's capabilities (and your overall customer support) during specific hours and/or seasons?

Compliance and security

Chatbots need to be secure and compliant with regulations for different businesses, so here are three questions you may want to ask:

- » How does the chatbot platform comply with specific industry regulations (like HIPAA for healthcare)?
- » What level of data protection does the chatbot platform provide?
- » Does the platform understand your industry language?

Operations

You have questions to ask of both your vendor and your team about operating a chatbot, including these:

- » What are the monthly costs and setup fees?
- » Does the vendor have per-conversation charges?

>> Do you need *no-code* solutions (that is, they don't involve coding), or can your team handle chatbot development? If not, do you need to hire people?

>> How much ongoing chatbot maintenance can your team handle?

>> What are the training needs for your team, and what training services does the AI chatbot provider offer?

Risk to your business

As with any technology, incorporating AI chatbots brings risks that you need to account for by asking your team and your vendor to answer the following:

>> How does the chatbot platform safeguard company and customer data?

>> How does the chatbot vendor handle outages? How often do those happen?

>> Is your leadership comfortable relying on a third-party platform?

>> What are your backup plans if the chatbot platform goes down for any period of time?

Technical expertise

What technical expertise is needed, and do you have it on your team? The tools we list earlier in this chapter all have builders that require little to no coding knowledge, but what happens when you need more functionality and your tool requires programming work? You may need to either identify someone in your company who can do that work or budget to hire someone.

Onboarding questions

Here are questions to ask of your team and the vendor when you need to figure out whether your team can handle installing and managing an AI chatbot:

>> How much support does the vendor provide?

>> How much knowledge does your web development team have to add the chatbot and modify the website code as needed?

>> Does anyone on your team have application program interface (API) integration knowledge?

>> Who on your team and at the chatbot vendor handles customer data storage and retrieval?

Infrastructure and maintenance

Because you'll likely be using your AI chatbot for the long term, you need to find out whether your website and other online platforms you use can handle the additional traffic. What's more, you need to know that your team and the team at your vendor can help you maintain your AI chatbot and provide support.

REMEMBER

Be clear about your current technical capabilities so you can find a chatbot platform that meets your capacity now and can meet your future aspirations.

Along those lines, consider asking chatbot vendors and your team these questions:

>> What additional security protocols do you need for the AI chatbot, and what does the vendor provide?

>> How does the vendor manage updates without breaking your chatbot and affecting your data?

>> How will you secure chatbot data?

>> Who on your team will update the AI chatbot with new data? Do you need to hire people?

>> How will increased web traffic affect site performance?

>> Can your current website hosting provider handle additional chat traffic, or do you need to switch (and budget for it)?

WARNING

Be on the lookout for any evasiveness from your vendor. These evasions can come in the form of being reluctant to show the actual dashboard, withholding information about data privacy or security, and — perhaps the biggest red flag of all — making basic metrics such as the conversion rate a "premium feature." (We talk about the conversion rate metric in Chapter 13.)

Your budget

You need to determine the AI chatbot budget in areas including the following:

>> Setup

>> Integration with your other tools

>> New tools you need to integrate with the AI chatbot

>> Licensing fees

>> Additional resources like programmers

>> Ongoing maintenance

You also need to factor in the expected returns, including saved opportunity costs, increased efficiency, new customers, and (most importantly) keeping your exist-ing customers happy.

What are some ways you can save money and convince the powers that be that you understand their concerns about your budget?

>> Select a payment option that works for you. That can include signing up for a free option (like many of the tools we highlight earlier in the chapter offer) so you can test its features.

>> Buy a monthly plan as you evaluate whether the platform is a good fit for you so that you're not tied to a contract. After you're satisfied, you can move to annual contracts for additional savings.

>> Consider running a 30-to-90-day trial to measure ROI for a simple use case, such as having your chatbot answer frequently asked questions. Then you can add more AI features over time to handle more complex tasks.

Desired features and integrations

What are the features that are crucial for your chatbot to have? Common features to start with include the following:

>> Natural language processing (NLP) that makes your chatbot an AI chatbot

>> Analytics

>> User segmentation

>> Integration with your website and social media channels

>> Connection with your existing tools such as CRM and email marketing

Don't forget to ask your team members, such as customer support folks, about what features they're looking for as you build your case for a chatbot.

Core features

Any AI chatbot vendor needs to have answers to the following questions ready for you. Make a point to ask about these core features if it doesn't (and yes, that's at least a yellow card):

>> Can the chatbot answer variations of the same question?

>> Does the chatbot remember context throughout a conversation?

>> How does the chatbot handle questions it doesn't understand?

>> Does the chatbot slow down under heavy usage? By what amount (based on the vendor's experiences)?

>> Can users and company personnel see previous interactions?

>> Does the chatbot support media including images, videos, and documents?

>> How well does the chatbot transfer to human agents?

>> Can you compare different conversation flows to improve users' chatbot experiences?

>> How does the chatbot perform on smartphones and tablets?

>> How does the chatbot behave in different browsers such as Chrome, Safari, and Microsoft Edge?

Integration

AI chatbot vendors worth considering have plenty of integration information to share with you. As you chat with your vendor, ensure it answers these four important questions (and if it doesn't answer all of them, show it your red card):

>> Which integrations are included in the platform, and which ones have an added cost or require a more expensive plan?

>> How difficult is setting up each integration?

>> What are the API limits or usage restrictions (if any)?

>> What happens if an integrated service goes offline?

REMEMBER

A chatbot has to dovetail with your current processes, so focus on integration features that enhance your current workflows and systems.

Scalability and flexibility

Can an AI chatbot platform grow with your business? You need to be able to adapt to new requirements over time, such as integrating with a new tool or adding new chatbot functionality as your business scales up. What's more, you have to account for more chatbot use during busy times like holidays and when your business expands into new products and markets.

REMEMBER

You need to purchase a plan for scalability and flexibility from the start. If you don't, you may have to pay more or, worse, switch platforms when your chatbot can't handle the load. (Unless you think running a business isn't stressful enough.)

But what do you ask vendors? In the following sections, we've grouped some questions that you can check off as you ask them (or, preferably, as the vendor answers them before you ask).

TIP

Ask vendors for case studies of their customers who have scaled well on their platforms. If you can, ask the vendor whether it has any problem with your contacting these companies to get genuine feedback that isn't covered in the marketing materials. You can also get feedback on the vendor's online support forums, which we talk about in the later section "Vendor and community support."

Pricing questions

Your understanding of costs must be crystal clear, so here are some pricing questions to consider asking:

>> What happens to our pricing if conversation volume doubles — or more?

>> Can we start with basic features and upgrade incrementally?

>> Do we face contract penalties for scaling down if needed?

>> How does cost scale as conversation volume grows?

Capacity questions

Because the platform's capacity is a key feature, make sure any AI chatbot vendor can answer these questions:

>> Does response time slow down as usage rises? By how much?

>> How many simultaneous chats can your platform handle?

>> Can your platform make room for the inevitable growing conversation history and customer data?

>> Is adding team members to the system easy as our staff grows?

>> Can you add new locations and/or regions easily?

Customizability questions

Your chatbot platform needs to fit your demands like a glove, so here are some questions to ask about customizing your chatbot:

>> How much can we customize the chatbot without needing help from your development team?

>> Can we export configurations if we need to migrate to a different platform?

>> How often do you add new integrations or features to your platform, and do we have the ability not to use them if we choose?

>> How much can you customize the chatbot's appearance and messaging style?

>> Can your platform support multiple languages and add new languages?

Analytics and reporting

You need to know how your AI chatbot is performing, which means you have to ensure that any AI chatbot solution you choose gives you the appropriate data to see areas where the chatbot can do better.

You need to know the numbers for operational costs, goal completion, and user satisfaction. When you research chatbot providers, find out what key performance indicators (KPIs) they analyze, because your company's leadership will ask you to provide them.

But KPIs are just the start. Here are five essential analytics questions an AI chatbot vendor needs to answer during your discussions:

>> What reports come standard, and which ones require paying for a higher-tier plan? As we note in the earlier section "Infrastructure and maintenance," locking basic stats in a higher plan is a major vendor warning signal.

>> Can we customize the chatbot dashboards for our specific KPIs?

>> Does your platform automatically generate reports, or do we need to create them?

>> How granular can we get with our reports, such as viewing activity on an hourly basis?

>> Do we have the ability to customize the report layout so that reports are most effective for our needs?

Vendor and community support

A healthy community reflects a vendor that cares about its clients' outcomes, users who help each other succeed, and transparency about problems and solutions.

With that in mind, here are some questions you should ask of the vendor and your team:

>> What are the support levels, such as standard and premium, and what do you get in each tier?

>> Can your team identify and solve common issues quickly? If not, how quickly can your vendor get on the line and help you solve the problem?

>> Do you get any documentation, and does your team think it's good enough to get members up to speed and serve as a useful reference?

Don't forget to visit chatbot provider communities that you can access from the provider's website.

TIP

>> Take a look at the questions being asked, and don't forget to search for your questions to find out whether others have already asked them.

>> Check out the response time and the quality of the responses from not only company support reps but also other users.

>> Think about asking questions yourself. If the company doesn't allow you to do so, consider asking it whether you can ask users what questions are on their minds. For example, you may want to ask users about their biggest challenge with the platform.

Chapter 5

Planning Your First Chatbot

We get it; the first time you go into a chatbot builder, all the tools, terms, and options can be overwhelming. However, one thing that can help alleviate the overwhelm is having a recipe for success. This stage is where a plan can be your most valuable asset for building a chatbot.

REMEMBER The biggest mistake we see in chatbot building is people skipping the planning stage. They jump into a tool and start building without really thinking through what they want the chatbot to do. However, the most successful chatbots always begin with one thing: a clear goal. What's the one outcome you're trying to achieve? Whether it's generating leads, answering FAQs, or booking appointments, that priority should shape everything else.

Just as necessary is the user experience. If your chatbot is asking for too much too soon or feels robotic and cold, people will bounce. Consider how you can keep it simple. Make it friendly. Make it useful.

In this chapter, we keep things beginner-friendly and straightforward, even if tech isn't your thing. We show you how to plan your first chatbot in a way that's focused, effective, and easy to follow. We explore how to define your business goals, map out a seamless user journey, select the correct flow style, and prepare your team for launch. When you start with a plan, everything else gets easier, and your chatbot works.

Identifying Your Business Goals

The very first step in building a chatbot is knowing what you want to achieve. You'd be surprised how many people get straight into the building without getting clear on their end goal. *Remember:* A chatbot is a tool. It's not the goal itself.

What's your business trying to do? You may want to increase sales, reduce the number of repetitive customer service questions your team answers, or get more people to sign up for a workshop. That's where your business goal lives. From there, you need to determine how your chatbot can help move you closer to that outcome.

REMEMBER

But here's the thing: Your business goal and your chatbot goal aren't always the same. The business goal is the big-picture outcome, such as booking more appointments, closing more deals, or improving customer retention. The chatbot's goal is more focused. It supports that outcome by handling a specific part of the customer journey, such as collecting key details, answering a question, or delivering a resource.

EXAMPLE: BACKYARD KITCHEN COMPANY

Sometimes, the chatbot is only one step in the process, handing things off to a human or another system. Say you run a company that builds custom backyard kitchens. Your ultimate business goal is to get a sales rep onsite with the customer, provide a quote, and close the deal with a signed contract.

But the chatbot's goal is much simpler. It's just there to gather enough information to pass a qualified lead to the sales team. That includes

>> Full name

>> Phone number

>> City and state where the project will take place

>> A short, friendly confirmation message letting the user know someone will be in touch soon

After it collects that information, the chatbot sends it directly to the sales rep. Going forward, the sales representative's goal is to close the deal. That process may look like

>> Calling the lead to learn more about their project goals and preferences

>> Setting an appointment to visit the site

>> Providing a quote or estimate

>> Signing the contract

The chatbot plays an important role, but it's just the starting point. It doesn't need to ask about budget, timeline, or design style; that's what the rep will handle. By keeping the chatbot's job focused and simple, you avoid overwhelming the user and increase the chances of moving that lead into a real conversation.

EXAMPLE: T-SHIRT SALE FROM A FACEBOOK AD

Sometimes, the chatbot can complete the entire task on its own. For example, suppose you're selling a $20 t-shirt through a Facebook ad. In this case, the business goal is to make a sale without requiring human intervention in the process. The chatbot's goal is to complete the entire transaction from start to finish, right inside the chat. That includes

>> Responding to the initial inquiry from the ad

>> Showing the product with a description and price

>> Asking for size, quantity, or other preferences

>> Collecting payment

>> Sending an order confirmation

Because the product is simple and the purchase is low-risk, the chatbot doesn't need to pass the lead off to a sales rep. It can complete tasks completely, offering a fast and convenient user experience that aligns perfectly with the business goal.

That's why it's important to understand where the chatbot fits into the customer journey. Is the chatbot the one completing the goal, or is it setting things up for a human to take over?

A chatbot isn't your marketing strategy. It's a tool that helps carry out that strategy. When you know your business goal and understand where the chatbot fits into that bigger picture, everything else, from building to testing, gets easier and more effective.

Asking yourself the right questions

Before you start building, take a few minutes to answer these questions:

>> What outcome do I want this chatbot to help me achieve?

>> Who is responsible for completing the final action: me, my team, or the chatbot?

>> What specific information do I need to collect from the user?

>> After the chatbot does its job, what happens next?

When you know these answers, you're in a much better position to plan a chatbot that works without overwhelming the user or the builder.

Avoiding trying to do everything in one flow

Say your business wants to grow your list, generate leads, and promote an event. Great. But don't try to cram all that into one conversation.

A chatbot can support multiple goals, but each one should have its own flow. Think of *flows* as different paths leading to other destinations. Your priority goal should always come first and get its own dedicated flow. After that's built, tested, and working well, you can branch out and create additional flows for your secondary goals.

For example, someone may comment on your Instagram post and get dropped into a chatbot flow that delivers a free guide. That's one entry point. Someone else may click a link in your bio and go straight into a flow that registers them for your webinar. Each goal has its own mini-pathway within the overall chatbot system.

We cover flows in more detail in the later section "Selecting Common Flows and Frameworks That Work."

Using smart goals to stay focused

When determining what to focus on first, the SMART method can be helpful. SMART stands for

>> **Specific:** Know precisely what you want your chatbot to achieve.

Example: "I want this chatbot to collect leads for my sales team by gathering the user's name, phone number, and location."

>> **Measurable:** Decide how you'll track success.

Example: "I want to collect 30 qualified leads through this chatbot over the next 30 days."

>> **Attainable:** Ensure your goal is realistic, considering your audience size and available resources.

Example: "If I normally get 10 messages a week, I'll aim for 12 qualified leads rather than 100."

>> **Relevant:** Make sure the chatbot's purpose aligns with your overall business objectives.

Example: "This chatbot supports my larger goal of growing my coaching business by getting more discovery calls booked."

>> **Time-bound:** Set a deadline to launch the chatbot and track its results.

Example: "I'll launch this chatbot next Monday and review performance in two weeks."

You don't have to follow every part of the SMART framework perfectly, but using it as a guide helps you stay focused and realistic.

Mapping Out Your Ideal User Journey

Every person who enters your chatbot is stepping into an experience. They may have come in from a Facebook ad, clicked a button on your website, commented on a post, or swiped up on a story. Your job is to create a path that helps them get from that entry point to your goal without confusion, frustration, or dead ends. In the following sections, we help you do just that.

TIP

No matter how carefully you map, people don't always follow the script. Make sure your chatbot has a backup plan for when users type something unexpected, skip a step, or want to start over. Build in options like restarts, quick replies, or a handoff to a human when things go off course.

Choosing a mapping process that works for you

The process for mapping out your chatbot's user journey is completely personal. Some people prefer to use digital mind-mapping tools, such as ClickUp's free software (www.clickup.com). Others use sticky notes or whiteboards or even write in dry-erase markers on their windows.

Kelly here. I go old school. I like to sit down with a notebook and pen and physically write out how I want the journey to flow.

TIP

There's no right way to do this process. Use what works best for your brain. Some people need visuals, and some like lists. Don't overthink it. The important thing is to actually plan the journey before you build. If you're a visual thinker, sketch boxes and arrows. If you're a list-maker, write out the steps line by line. What matters is that you take the time to think it through before you jump into building. Just get it out of your head and into a format you can follow.

Begin by considering how someone enters the chatbot. Then outline each step along the way:

>> What will they see or be asked first?

>> What choices or questions will guide their next steps?

>> What happens if they veer off the expected path?

>> How and when does the chatbot hand off to a human, if needed?

>> What's the final action or outcome?

When you have all that written out, you're no longer guessing. You're designing with purpose.

Steering clear of common mistakes

REMEMBER

One of the biggest mistakes people make when mapping the user journey is focusing only on interactions — what buttons users press or what responses they give. But people don't enter your chatbot just to click. They enter because they want something.

So the real question is about their intent. Why are they here? What are they hoping to get out of this conversation? Focus on this idea and not just what they'll click.

When you map your chatbot with intent in mind, the experience becomes smoother and more human. The chatbot stops feeling like a script and starts acting more like a guide.

We repeatedly see a few other pitfalls when people begin building out their user journeys. Here's how to avoid them:

>> **Offering too many options:** Giving users lots of choices is tempting, but having too many at once can lead to overwhelm. Keep your options focused and relevant. Make each decision easy.

>> **Forgetting the goal:** Your chatbot should always be working toward your first priority goal as we discuss in the earlier section "Identifying Your Business Goals." Don't distract people with extra offers or questions until they've reached the main objective.

>> **Having no personality:** If your chatbot feels like a robot, people won't engage with it. Add tone. Add friendliness. Use natural phrasing. Make it feel like a real conversation.

Selecting Common Flows and Frameworks That Work

As we note earlier in the chapter, a flow is a single-guided conversation your chatbot takes someone through. Think of it like a path on a treasure map. And if a flow is one road, the framework is the entire map.

In the following sections, we help you choose the actual flows and frameworks that will bring your chatbot to life. *Note:* If you haven't already determined your goals and designed the path your users will take as we outline in the earlier sections of this chapter, we suggest you tackle those before continuing with this section.

Getting into a flow

The flow begins at an entry point, such as a Facebook ad or a website button. It then offers steps that guide the user through a series of checkpoints, including qualifying questions or helpful messages. It leads to a clear destination, such as booking a call, downloading a freebie, or collecting lead information.

REMEMBER

We note earlier in the chapter that a chatbot can have multiple flows, each leading to a distinct goal based on how a user enters the chat and on their intent. Each flow is designed to help the user accomplish their primary task or direct them to another flow that can better meet their needs. It may gather a name, email, and phone number or answer a frequently asked question and then guide the user to a product page.

EXAMPLE: LEAD CAPTURE FLOW

Say someone clicks on a Facebook ad to get a quote for an outdoor kitchen. They enter the chatbot and see the following:

> Thank you for your interest. Are you ready to get started with your free quote?

If they answer "yes," the chatbot begins the lead capture flow:

> Great! Could I have your first and last name, please?

> Thanks. Now, what's the best phone number to reach you?

> What city are you located in? Knowing this will help us understand where your project is located and determine if we can ultimately assist you.

> Thank you, [first name]. We will have someone contact you within the next 24 hours.

As you can see in Figure 5-1, this flow is simple, helpful, and goal-driven.

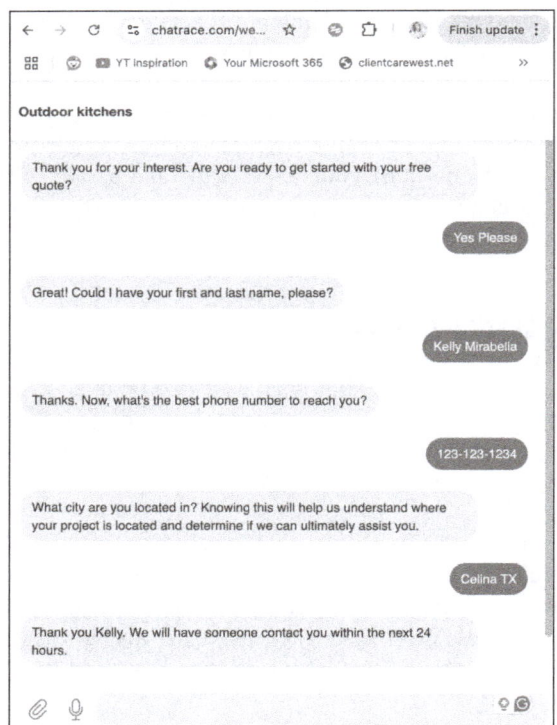

FIGURE 5-1: An outdoor kitchen quote flow on the platform Chatrace.

TIP

If the user answers the first question "no," you can either thank them and end the conversation or guide them into a different flow, like offering a lead magnet to collect their email address for future follow-up. Every decision point can open a new door.

Picturing a framework

A *framework* is a blueprint that brings all your flows together, helping the chatbot know what to do, when to do it, and how to respond based on the user's actions or intent. Think of your framework as a map that shows all the ways a user can travel around your chatbot. The framework shows the various flows, actions, conditions and integrations you will need to properly converse with a user and drive them toward your ultimate goals. (We cover flows in the preceding section.) The framework is where you bring structure to your chatbot. Instead of just being a series of disconnected flows, your chatbot becomes a cohesive experience that knows how to respond to whatever a user needs.

Your framework may include the following:

>> All your core flows, including lead generation, quizzes, FAQs, appointment booking, and so on (see Chapter 3)

>> Rules for how users are tagged or segmented

>> Logic that decides what flow to send someone to next

>> Conditions for returning users, segmentation, or switching topics

>> Your knowledge base and AI prompt setup, if you're using AI

Starting with beginner-friendly flow options

If you're new to chatbot building, start with one of these easy-to-build flow options.

Walking through a welcome flow

A *welcome flow* is the flow that greets users when they first enter your chatbot. It's like the front door of your chatbot experience. The welcome flow is your opportunity to introduce yourself, establish expectations, and direct users to the next step.

You can create a general welcome flow that works for anyone who enters your chatbot, or you can create specific welcome flows based on how someone gets there. For example, someone who enters through your website may see a friendly message offering help with booking or browsing. Someone who clicks on a Facebook ad may get a more targeted welcome tied to that specific promotion or product.

Think of your welcome flow as your chatbot's first impression. It doesn't have to be fancy. It needs to be clear, helpful, and focused on guiding the user to the right place.

EXAMPLE: WELCOME FLOW FOR A PIZZA FOOD TRUCK

Say you run a mobile pizza business called Rolling Dough Pizza Truck. You want your chatbot to help customers quickly find out where you'll be, how to contact you, or what's on your menu.

When someone opens your chatbot, they're greeted with a simple welcome message and three clear options:

Welcome to Rolling Dough Pizza Truck. How can we help you today?

Locations

Menu

Contact Us

>> If they click Locations, the chatbot responds with your usual stops: Frisco, McKinney, North Dallas, and occasionally Prosper. It then offers two helpful follow-ups:

- A button to follow you on Threads for the latest schedule updates

- A "Call Pizza Hotline" button for live, automated location details

>> If they click Contact Us, the bot provides email instructions and another link to your hotline, allowing them to reach out directly.

You can see this classic welcome flow in Figure 5-2. It's concise and friendly, and it gets people to the information they care about quickly — all while keeping your team out of the inbox.

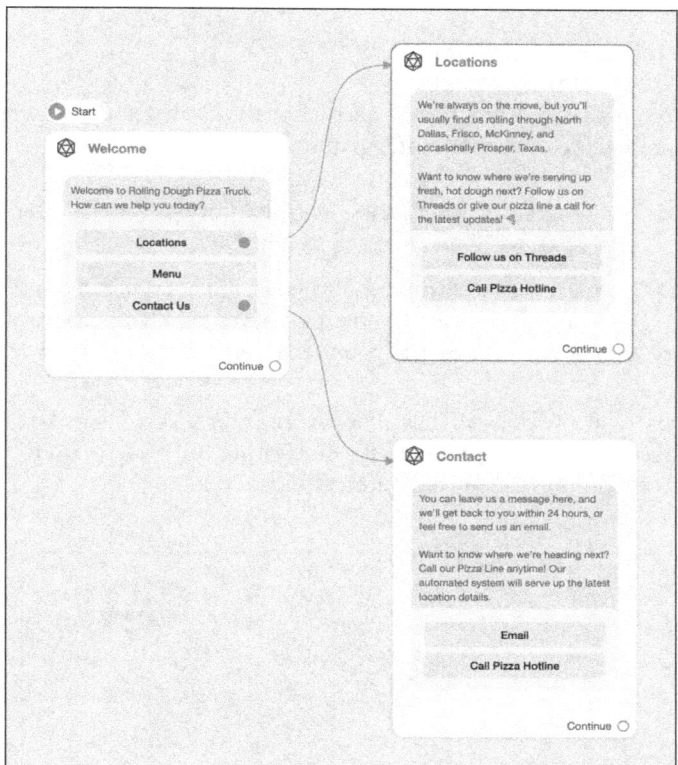

FIGURE 5-2:
This classic
welcome flow on
the Chatrace
platform
provides concise
information
quickly

Flowing toward your chatbot's top-priority goal

If you already know your primary goal, you can start with building that flow first. This approach is where your chatbot truly shines by doing the one thing it was designed to do.

EXAMPLE: MAMABABY HAITI

Take MamaBaby Haiti (`mamababyhaiti.org`), for example. This nonprofit trains midwives and provides life-saving birth services to underserved communities in Haiti. Its top priority within the chatbot is straightforward: to drive donations and support its mission.

When someone comments the word *Donate* on one of the organization's Facebook or Instagram posts, that triggers a chatbot flow designed to guide them straight to that donation goal.

Here's how the flow works:

First, the chatbot thanks the user for their interest and asks whether they're ready to donate or want more information.

>> If they agree, the chatbot immediately provides a donation link along with a brief message about the impact of the gift.

>> If the user requests more information, the bot shares a brief overview of MamaBaby Haiti's work and explains why donations are crucial. From there, they're invited to donate or visit the website for even more details.

This kind of focused flow, shown in Figure 5-3, keeps the experience simple, direct, and meaningful without distracting or trying to do too much. It's built to do one thing well: convert interest into action.

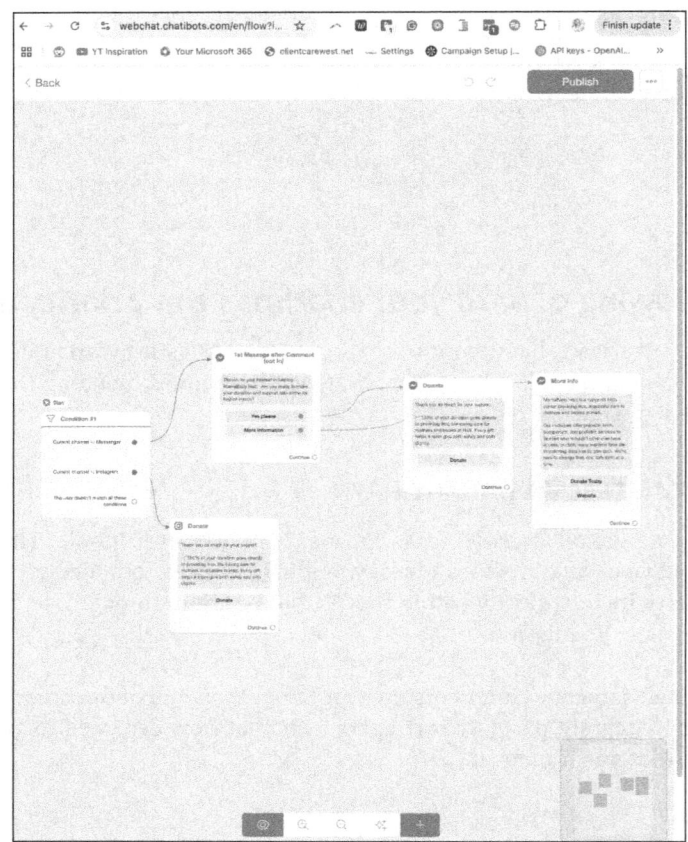

FIGURE 5-3:
This flow for MamaBaby Haiti on the Chatrace platform guides users through the donation process.

After the donation flow is up and running smoothly, the team can return later to add other flows for tasks such as volunteer sign-ups, event information, or FAQ support. However, by starting with its highest impact, it's setting the chatbot up for success from the outset.

Considering how multiple flows work with different chatbots

Bigger flows don't make better flows. In fact, the larger the flow, the more headaches you're likely to encounter. Users tend to drop off when a flow feels too long or asks too many questions. On the backend, massive flows can be tough to troubleshoot. When something breaks, identifying and resolving the issue quickly is more challenging.

A better strategy is to break up your chatbot into multiple smaller flows, each focused on one specific goal. Each of these flows is connected in your greater framework but the separation helps keep things organized and easier to manage while still feeling seamless and cohesive to the user. If you have a lot of steps to cover, keep each flow short and connected rather than in one long mega-flow.

How you go about creating your flow(s) can depend on the kind of chatbot.

>> If you're using a rule-based chatbot, you usually need more steps because you're guiding every interaction manually.

>> If you're using an AI-powered chatbot, you can often simplify your flows because the AI handles more of the logic and branching. In those cases, your knowledge base and prompt structure become even more important than the number of steps in your flow. By the way, your knowledge base and prompt are what you use to train your AI chatbot on your company, your ideal audience, your tone of voice, and how you want the AI chatbot to handle conversations.

Head to Chapter 3 for more on each of these types of chatbots.

Figure 5-4 shows a welcome message with AI.

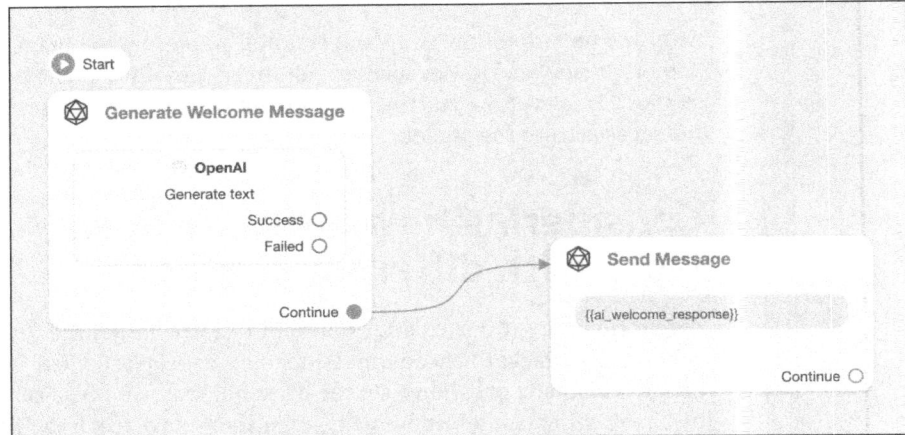

FIGURE 5-4:
An AI-generated
welcome
message.

Getting Your Team and Tools in Place

Lay the foundation for a smooth build by getting your team, tools, and systems ready. This stage isn't always flashy, but it's one of the most important. When you take the time to prepare, you save yourself hours of frustration later.

Deciding who should be involved in the build

For building the chatbot, you don't need a full committee. In fact, we recommend you don't involve too many people. Too many cooks in the kitchen can lead to a slow build with poor results. Whether you're doing it yourself or hiring a chatbot builder, your best bet is to have one main person responsible for actually building the chatbot. This person is the point person.

That said, if you're not the builder, you or someone in a decision-making role still needs to be part of the planning process. You're the one who knows the business goals, understands the customer, and has the vision for how this chatbot should work. The builder may create the technical structure, but you're still steering the ship.

Depending on your use case, you may also need input from team members on your sales, marketing, or customer support teams. These are the folks who are already communicating with customers. They know the questions users are asking, the roadblocks that come up, and what kind of information actually helps move the conversation forward. Their feedback is incredibly valuable when you're creating flows or setting up your knowledge base.

And finally, because your chatbot is interacting with customers and collecting leads or support requests, everyone who will interact with that lead or respond to that user should know what the chatbot is doing and what to expect after the user is handed over.

Here's a breakdown of the key roles that may be part of your chatbot planning and execution. Depending on the size of your business and the complexity of your chatbot, you may be wearing all these hats yourself, or you may want to pull in some help. Either way, considering who is responsible for what's helpful.

>> **The lead chatbot builder:** This is the person who actually builds the chatbot inside the platform. Whether it's you, a team member, or a hired chatbot pro, this person is responsible for creating flows, setting up logic, connecting tools, and testing everything. You don't want multiple people building at the same time. Keep it simple and assign this job to one person to avoid confusion or overlapping edits.

>> **The decision-maker or strategist:** This person is usually the business owner, marketing lead, or manager — someone who understands the bigger picture. This role is all about setting goals, defining the strategy, and making key decisions about what the chatbot should do, how it should sound, and what success looks like.

>> **Sales and support collaborators:** If your chatbot will be assisting with lead generation or customer service, involve your sales and support teams in the planning process. They can help you understand which questions users ask most often and what information is helpful during a handoff.

>> **Brand or marketing voice lead:** This person helps shape the tone of the chatbot. Are you casual and fun? Straightforward and professional? This role ensures that the chatbot speaks in a manner that aligns with your brand. If you're a solo business owner, this person is probably you. However, taking a minute to define your voice before you start writing is still worthwhile.

>> **Post-chatbot human touch:** Who's taking over after the chatbot does its job? Whether it's a sales representative calling a lead, a customer service agent following up, or someone checking form submissions daily, ensure they understand what the chatbot is doing and how they'll be alerted when it's their turn to take action.

Choosing the right platform

One of the biggest decisions you make early on is choosing your chatbot platform. We discuss platform choice in depth in Chapter 4, but start by looking at your goals. What do you want your chatbot to do? Do you want it to capture leads, answer questions, deliver content, qualify users, or all of the above? After you're clear on that, ruling out tools that can't give you what you need becomes much easier.

TIP

We suggest picking three chatbot platforms and comparing them. Look at

>> What kind(s) of chatbot they can build (AI-powered, rule-based, or both)

>> What features are included and whether those features match your goals

>> How they integrate with other tools you already use, such as email platforms, customer relationship managers (CRMs), payment processors, and so forth

>> Whether they fit your budget

>> What kind of customer service and documentation they offer

WARNING

A chatbot building platform's customer service matters more than you think. If you hit a wall during setup and can't get a response for days, it will absolutely stall your build. Always test a platform's support options before making a commitment. If its help center is bare or its live chat is always offline, that's a red flag.

Getting organized before you build

Before you ever drag a single block onto your flow canvas, you should gather and organize a few things:

>> A list of your chatbot goals, starting with your highest priority

>> The types of data you want to collect from users (and why)

>> A clear picture of your brand voice

>> A plan for where this chatbot will live (on your website, Instagram, Messenger, WhatsApp, SMS, or wherever)

>> A complete list of external tools or websites your chatbot needs to connect to

>> Any links, assets, or key info your chatbot will need to reference or deliver

>> If using AI, a clean knowledge base prompt that covers your most important content

Also consider where you want your data to end up. Are leads being pushed into a spreadsheet, a CRM, or an email platform? Is someone notified every time a new user submits a quote request or clicks a button? If so, that needs to be mapped out and integrated before you publish.

TECHNICAL STUFF

If you want to track specific user actions, such as how many people clicked a donate button, you need to plan for that when you build. Most chatbot platforms offer ways to track events, tag users, or set up custom metrics. However, those tracking points must be integrated into your workflows. Make a list of what you want to measure before you start building so you don't have to backtrack and patch it in later.

TIP

If you're feeling stuck or overwhelmed, here are several questions that can help you define your strategy before jumping into the build:

>> What's the number one goal I want this chatbot to help me accomplish?

>> Do I want to support any secondary goals as well?

>> Where will people interact with this chatbot (website, Instagram, Messenger, and so on)?

>> What kind of experience do I want users to have (fast, personalized, friendly, straightforward)?

>> What information or data do I need from users?

>> Who will take over if the chatbot hands off to a human?

>> How will I notify the person receiving the handoff (SMS text, email, or something else)?

>> Where will user responses and contact info be stored?

>> What tools or systems does this chatbot need to connect with?

>> What metrics or events do I want to track?

Use these questions as a checklist before you start building. When you know the answers, the build process becomes less stressful, and building is easier with more successful results.

IN THIS CHAPTER

» **Tracing a complete beginner-friendly chatbot build**

» **Breaking down chatbot types**

» **Working with drag-and-drop visual builders**

» **Structuring your AI prompt like a pro**

» **Setting up your OpenAI API key**

» **Testing and launching your chatbot**

Chapter **6**

Building a Bot from Scratch (Without Needing to Code)

We don't want to lie to you. Building your first chatbot can feel a little overwhelming. Like anything new, it comes with a learning curve and a few bumps along the way. But if you've taken the time to plan out your strategy and framework as we explain in Chapter 5, you're already ahead of the game.

TIP

The trick is to stay focused on what your chatbot needs to do and not get distracted by all the shiny extras that pop up along the way. You don't have to be an expert on day one, so give yourself some grace. You've got this.

Walking through a Sample Chatbot Build

If you've never built a chatbot before, the best place to start is with a *welcome message* flow. This flow acts as the front door to your chatbot and your entire messaging experience. It's the one flow every chatbot needs, regardless of the type of business you run or your goals. For more on flows, check out Chapter 5.

When I (Kelly) teach beginners how to build a chatbot for the first time, that's where I usually start. It's simple, but it builds (pun intended) the foundational skills you need as you move into more advanced flows later on. To make this process easier to understand, we work through the steps for you in the following sections as if we're building a chatbot for a local coffee shop called JoMama Coffee.

Step 1: Plan before you build

Before you start dragging things around in your chatbot builder, take a moment to consider what your user is likely looking for. What are the top two or three high-level things people want when they first land in your chatbot?

For the coffee shop example, we want to make sure we include the following:

>> Menu

>> Locations

>> Hours of operation

These items are the most common things people look for when they're on the go and want quick answers. This simple list serves as the foundation of our welcome flow.

Step 2: Know your tone

REMEMBER

Get clear on your brand voice. A chatbot should sound like your business. Is your coffee shop fun and quirky? Warm and cozy? Minimal and modern? The tone you choose shapes how you write your messages and how people feel when they interact with your brand.

For the coffee shop example, say the shop has a friendly and casual vibe. Its chatbot tone reflects that, using relaxed, upbeat language with maybe a few coffee puns sprinkled in.

Step 3: Write your welcome message

Write that first message your chatbot will send. It should greet the user, set expectations if needed, and guide them toward their next step.

For the coffee shop, it may look like this:

> Welcome to JoMama Coffee! We're brewing and ready to help. Would you like to check out the menu, find a location, or see our hours of operation? Just click a button below to get started.

Even when you use an AI chatbot in your welcome message, including options is a nice touch. Your welcome message may vary slightly if you're using AI:

> Welcome to JoMama Coffee! We're brewing and ready to help. Would you like to view the menu, see our hours, or ask another question we can assist you with? Just type your question in the chat to get started.

Step 4: Offer simple options

Right after your welcome message, offer clear buttons or quick replies based on what you mapped out in the planning stage.

For the coffee shop, those buttons may look like Figure 6-1:

FIGURE 6-1:
These buttons
are simple
and clear.

☐ View Menu

☐ Find a Location

☐ Check Hours

REMEMBER

Each button should lead to its own short, focused flow. Someone tapping "View Menu" may get a list of drink categories. "Find a Location" may ask for their city and then show the closest spot. Keep each path helpful and straightforward.

Step 5: Test like a real person

Before publishing your chatbot, test it as a customer would. Click the buttons. Follow each path. Ask a few friends or team members to review it as well. You're looking for anything that feels confusing, clunky, or incomplete.

For the coffee shop chatbot, that means ensuring the menu loads correctly, the hours are accurate, and the tone aligns with the in-person experience. If you're using AI, ask various questions to ensure the AI responds with correct information and a reasonable tone of voice. Also be sure to ask questions that you don't want the AI to respond to, such as those related to politics or religion. (We discuss creating your knowledge base prompt in Chapter 8.) You want people to leave the chat with the same positive vibe they'd get from walking up to the counter.

Reviewing the Three Building Types

The kind of chatbot you build depends heavily on your goals. Most chatbots fall into one of three categories: **rule-based**, **AI-powered**, or **hybrid**. We cover these in depth in Chapter 3, but here's a quick rundown because the type you choose shapes how you build your bot.

Reviewing rule-based chatbots

These bots are your classic "if this, then that" builds. *Rule-based chatbots* run on *conditional logic.* If a user clicks a button or selects an option, the chatbot follows the path you created. No guesswork is involved. The bot sticks to the flow you designed and moves the user through step by step.

Pros:

>> Gives you complete control over the conversation

>> Easy to test and predict how it behaves

>> Great for repeatable tasks like appointment booking or FAQs

>> Keeps things compliant in regulated industries

Cons:

>> Can't handle unexpected questions or off-script responses

>> Requires more building upfront (every option must be manually added)

>> Can feel robotic if not written well

REMEMBER

Rule-based builds are great when you need structure, consistency, or compliance. They're perfect for tasks such as gathering contact information, answering frequently asked questions, displaying menus, or guiding users through a specific process. You get full control over the experience, which is helpful when accuracy is key.

Addressing AI-powered chatbots

This type of chatbot connects to a large language model (LLM), such as OpenAI's GPT or Anthropic's Claude. With the help of a trained knowledge base and a solid prompt, the AI can answer questions in real time, understand what users are asking (even if they phrase things oddly), and keep the conversation flowing.

Pros:

>> Feels more natural and human-like in conversation

>> Can answer a wide range of questions, even if they're not preprogrammed

>> Easier to scale without building dozens of flows

>> Adapts to unexpected user behavior

Cons:

>> Needs to be trained well or it may go off-brand or off-topic

>> Harder to control exact outcomes

>> Trickier to test because responses change based on the input

>> Likely requires more monitoring and fine-tuning to stay consistent

AI-powered chatbots are a great choice when your users are more likely to type out their questions instead of clicking buttons or when you want to offer a more natural, human-like experience without building a response for every possible scenario.

Hearing about hybrid chatbots

This build is my (Kelly's) go-to for most businesses. A *hybrid chatbot* gives you the structure of rule-based logic combined with the flexibility of AI. It allows you to guide users with buttons or quick replies when doing so makes sense but also to jump into an AI-powered response when a question goes beyond what you've mapped out.

For example, say someone enters your chatbot and encounters a few button options, such as "See Services" or "Get a Quote." That part is rule-based. However, if they ask a specific question, such as "Do you offer weekend appointments?", the AI can step in to provide an answer based on your knowledge base.

Pros:

>> Provides the best of both worlds: structure where you need it, flexibility where it counts

>> Offers a more personalized experience without sacrificing control

>> Reduces the number of flows you have to build while still covering a wide range of use cases

>> Creates a smooth handoff between guided flows and open-ended questions

Cons:

>> Slightly more complex to build and test

>> Needs a clear plan for when to use rules versus when to use AI

>> May clash with your platform because not all chatbot platforms can support both styles well

>> Can require more maintenance to keep everything working smoothly

REMEMBER

We'll say it again: Hybrid builds offer the best of both worlds. You stay in control where necessary and let AI handle the rest. It's a smart, scalable approach that works well for service-based businesses, busy support teams, and nearly anyone who wants a chatbot that feels more human without compromising structure.

Introducing Visual Builders

Gone are the days when you had to know how to code to build a chatbot. Honestly, that ship sailed a long time ago. And anyway, some of the clunkiest, glitchiest bots we've seen were custom-coded.

These days, almost every chatbot builder comes with a visual interface that makes building feel more like designing than developing. A *visual builder* is exactly what it sounds like. You can see the structure of your chatbot. You can click, drag, drop, and connect blocks (nodes) together to map out how the conversation flows. It's like using a website builder or a digital flowchart tool. You aren't writing commands or scripting lines of code. You're building a real-time user journey that you can test and tweak right inside the platform.

Most visual builders make it easy to

>> Add messages, images, questions, and buttons

>> Connect one message to the next by using simple drag-and-drop lines

>> Preview the chatbot experience as you go

>> Add logic or AI steps with just a few clicks

Visual builders create a clear front-end environment where you can build smarter, faster, and with fewer headaches. Whether you're building a quiz, a lead capture chatbot, or an FAQ helper, the visual layout makes seeing what's working and where adjustments may be necessary easy.

We personally love visual builders because they make chatbot building so much more accessible. You don't need to be a tech whiz. You just need to know what you want the chatbot to do, and the builder helps you bring that plan to life.

REMEMBER

Depending on the chatbot platform you're using, you may see terms such as *nodes*, *steps*, or *actions*. Although the wording varies, they all serve a similar purpose: representing individual pieces of your chatbot's flow.

>> **Node:** A *node* is usually a visual marker that represents a message, condition, or logic point.

>> **Step:** A *step* typically refers to a single moment in the flow, such as sending a message, asking a question, or pressing a button. Some platforms use this as a general term for each movement forward in the conversation.

>> **Action:** *Actions* are the specific tasks the chatbot performs behind the scenes, such as sending an email, applying a tag, storing a custom field, or triggering another flow.

Some platforms combine these terms, and others keep them separate. Don't get too caught up in the labels. Just know that these are the pieces you drag and connect to build out your chatbot's conversation.

TIP

Name your steps and actions clearly as you build. It may seem like a small thing, but after your flow grows past a few steps, having clear labels like "Ask for Email" or "Send Confirmation Message" saves you from a lot of confusion.

Building Your Chatbot Without Code

One of the reasons I (Kelly) love visual chatbot builders is that most of them make dragging, dropping, and connecting your chatbot pieces super easy without needing to touch a single line of code.

That said, not all drag-and-drop builders work the same way. Every platform has its own quirks, layout, and language. Some feel more like a digital whiteboard. Others are more structured and modular. In the following sections, we look at how a few of the more popular ones handle it so you know what to expect. Flip to Chapter 4 for details on these and other major platforms.

Manychat

When you dive into Manychat, you have two ways to build your chatbot: Flow Builder and Basic Builder.

Flow Builder is Manychat's visual style builder. It provides a comprehensive view of your entire automation, displaying every message, action, and transition on a single, intuitive canvas. You can relatively easily add different elements and actions while maintaining a clear view of the overall picture.

You can follow the user's journey from start to finish without having to hop between individual messages. This aspect makes Flow Builder perfect for anything more than a simple welcome sequence or FAQ flow because you can visualize and manage several branches or conditional steps of your automation all in one place.

TIP

Manychat also suggests checking out its guide to block types so that you understand how each block connects to form a seamless experience.

In Figure 6-2, you can see how the flow builder looks.

Basic Builder takes a different approach. Instead of having a single canvas, you build your automation one message at a time in a linear sequence. You add a message or action, define the next step, and then click Next to move forward. This step-by-step format is quick to learn and works well for simple automations.

TIP

A standout feature of Basic Builder is the live chat preview on the right side of the screen. As you create each message, you see exactly how it appears to a user. This real-time example in Figure 6-3 helps you catch typos and formatting issues before publishing.

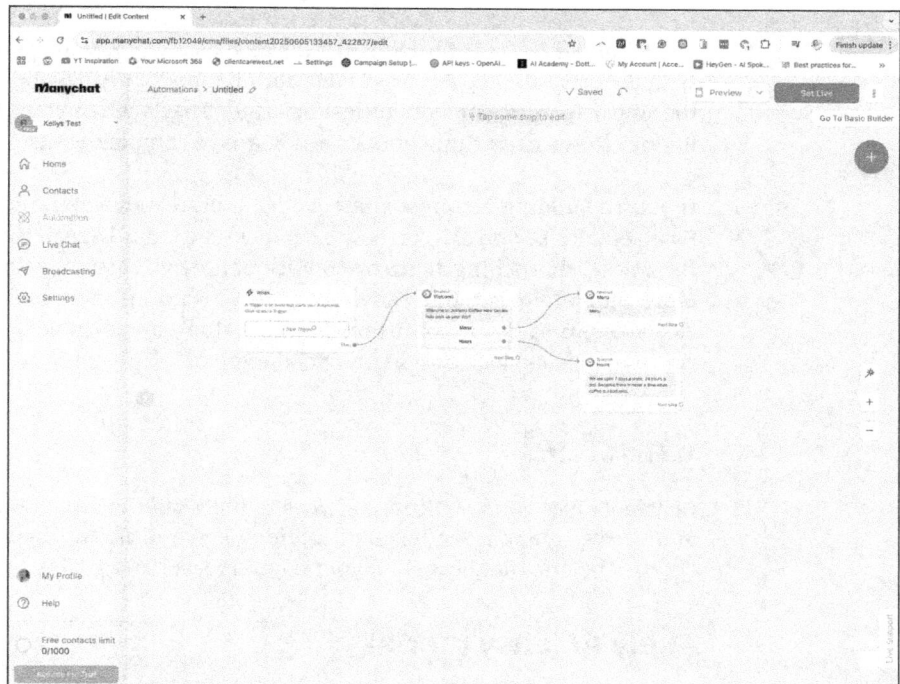

FIGURE 6-2:
Manychat
Flow Builder.

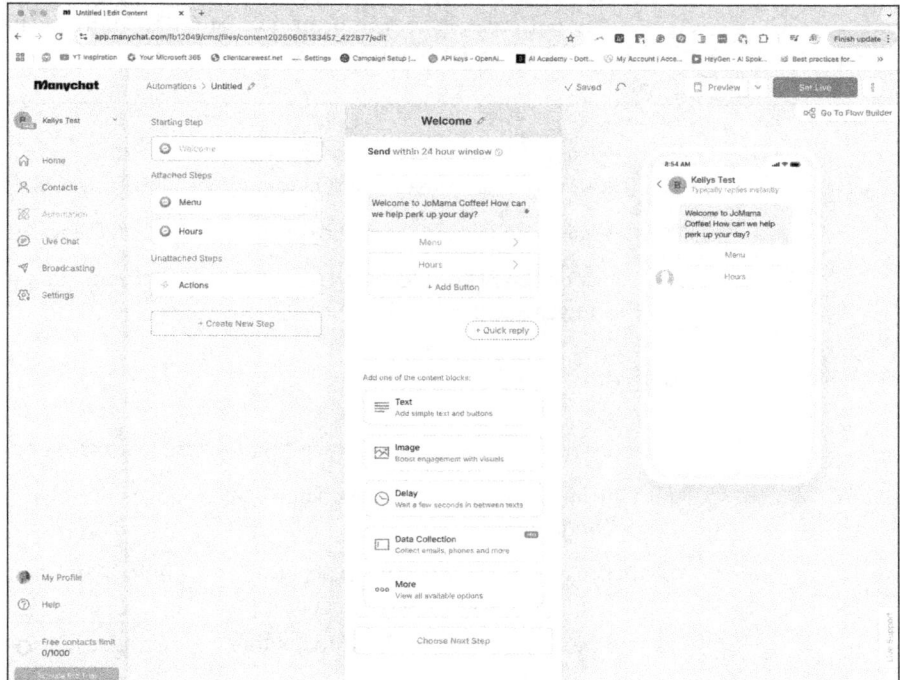

FIGURE 6-3:
Manychat
Basic Builder.

Basic Builder is great for short flows, such as a quick lead-capture sequence or a straightforward FAQ. But after your automation grows beyond a handful of steps, the linear format can start to feel limiting. That's when you switch over to Flow Builder to see everything at once and manage complex paths more efficiently.

TIP

If you're building a simple chatbot, like a brief welcome flow or FAQ, start with Basic Builder so you can see how each message looks in real-time. As soon as your flow needs branching logic or conditional steps, open the same automation in Flow Builder to get full canvas visibility. Naming your messages and actions clearly helps save you confusion as your automation expands. And, of course, you can switch back and forth as you go along.

Chatfuel

Chatfuel gives you two different ways to build your chatbot: Fuely AI (easy mode) and Flows (manual mode). Both options serve different needs, allowing you to choose the one that best suits your comfort level and goals.

Fuely AI (easy mode)

Fuely AI is Chatfuel's AI-powered builder. It works like a guided wizard that creates a full AI chatbot for you. You provide your website URL and any extra details, such as promotions, product information, or FAQs. Fuely AI then uses that data to generate a conversational chatbot in just a few minutes.

Pros:

>> The setup is super-fast — perfect for anyone who's never built a chatbot.

>> It requires no design or technical expertise. You just follow the prompts.

>> It includes an AI knowledge base that learns from your content to answer most user questions automatically.

Cons:

>> It has no drag-and-drop interface. You can't visually place or move nodes.

>> With limited customization, you don't get granular control over every message or condition.

>> The AI may not match your exact brand voice unless you refine it afterward.

Figure 6-4 shows what Fuely AI looks like when you're setting it up.

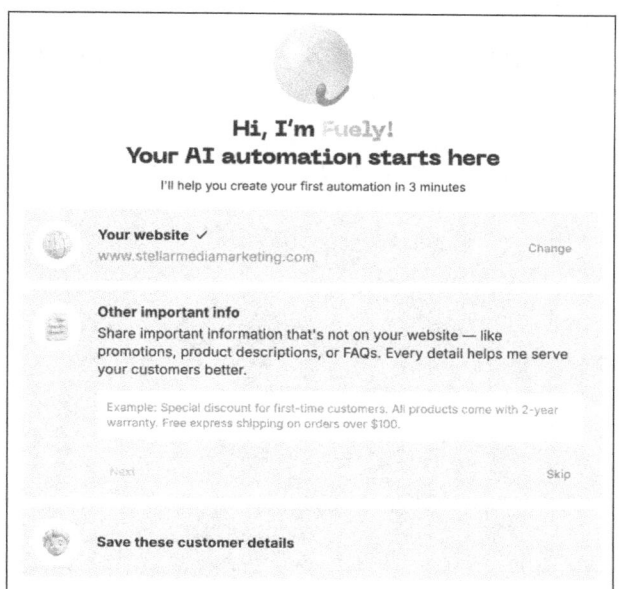

FIGURE 6-4
Chatfuel
AI-powered
builder (Fuely AI).

Flows (manual mode)

Flows is Chatfuel's traditional visual builder, and it uses a drag-and-drop interface. You work on a canvas of nodes and actions, similar to other visual tools. (You can read more about nodes and actions in the earlier section "Introducing Visual Builders.") Each node can be a text message, image, quick reply, or API call. You place nodes on the screen, connect them with arrows, and adjust each path of the conversation.

Pros:

>> You have complete control over your chatbot's logic, messages, and user experience.

>> It's ideal for complex flows when you need precise branching and custom conditions.

>> You can mix in AI steps if you want, but you build the core of the conversation yourself.

Cons:

>> It requires more setup time. You're designing every conversation node by node.

>> Larger flows can get messy if you don't keep the canvas organized.

In Figure 6-5, you can see the Flows builder interface when you're building manually:

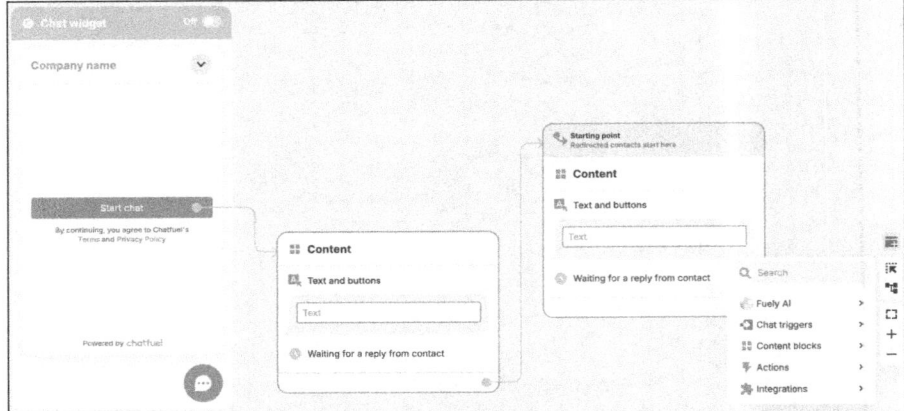

FIGURE 6-5:
Chatfuel
Flows builder
(manual mode).

TIP

If you're new to chatbots, start with Fuely AI in the preceding section to see how Chatfuel structures an AI-driven chatbot. After you understand the basics, switch to Flows to customize and expand on that design.

Chatrace

Chatrace offers two main ways to build your Chatbot:

>> The Visual Builder, where you can design rule-based or hybrid flows by viewing the entire conversation map

>> The AI feature in Settings, which allows you to add AI-based logic and AI triggers (also known as functions) that trigger when a user displays a specific intent

We get into each in the following sections.

Visual Builder (full flow map)

The Visual Builder is a canvas where you can see every node (message, question, or action) and how they connect. This "map" view helps you easily build a purely rule-based chatbot or a hybrid chatbot that mixes rules-based logic with AI.

If you want a straightforward rule-based chatbot, you drag nodes onto the canvas, connect them with arrows, and define what each node does. For example, in Figure 6-6, you can see a flow that starts with a "Quote Welcome" node. If the user clicks "Yes Please," the flow proceeds to "Gather Information," which requests the user's first name, phone number, and city. After that, it proceeds to a "Confirmation" node, which thanks the user and indicates that someone will be in touch soon to provide a quote.

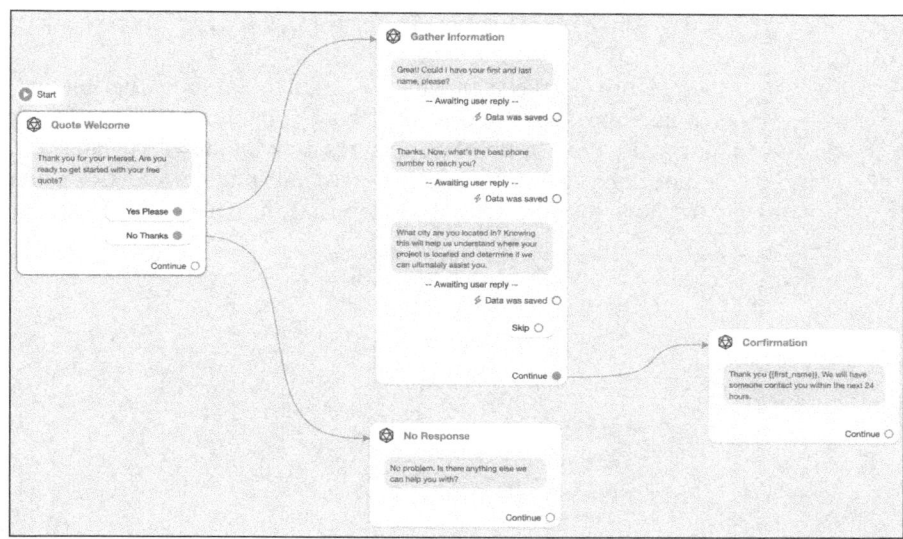

FIGURE 6-5:
Chatrace
rule-based flow in
the Visual Builder.

REMEMBER

In this setup, if a user types a question like "Why do you need my phone number?" the Chatbot can't respond because no AI logic is built into this rule-based path. The flow waits for an answer, continues to repeat the question, or stalls out.

AI Builder and AI triggers

The **AI Builder** enables you to add AI-powered intelligence to the chatbot. With the help of AI triggers, the chatbot can ask follow-up questions, handle clarifications, and gather information dynamically. To gather details like first name, last name, phone number, and city (as in Figure 6-6 in the preceding section), you set up AI triggers inside the AI Builder.

REMEMBER

Whenever you create an AI-driven flow, you need to add your OpenAI API key (see the later section "Getting and Connecting Your OpenAI API Key") and your knowledge base prompt first and then define an AI trigger. Here's how to do it:

1. **In Settings → Integrations, add your OpenAI API key and paste your knowledge base prompt into the designated field.**

The knowledge base prompt instructs the AI on your business, including which questions to ask and where to store user responses in custom fields.

2. **Go to AI Triggers.**

3. **Click "Create Trigger" and name it.**

   For example, you may want a "book_appointment" trigger.

4. **List the data points you want the AI to collect.**

   These may be things like first name, last name, phone number, and city.

In Figure 6-7, you can see the AI triggers set for gathering that information. When a user message matches the "book_appointment" intent, Chatrace runs this AI trigger. The AI can then conversationally ask each question, handle follow-up questions like "Why do you need my phone number?", and save the answers without stalling. After the AI finishes, it hands control back to your main flow.

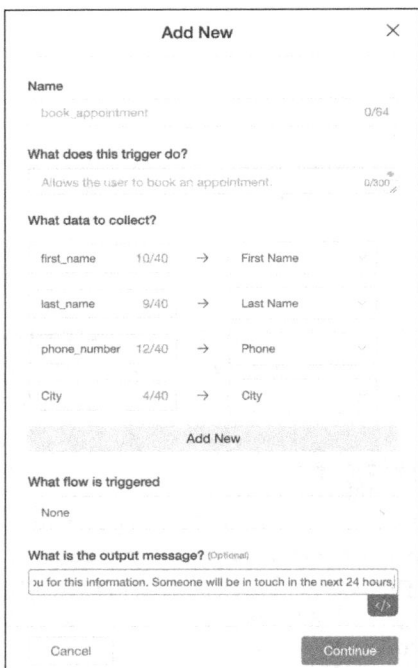

FIGURE 6-7:
Chatrace AI
Builder setup.

When a user shows intent to get a quote, the AI Builder fires the "book_appointment" trigger, and the AI Chatbot asks for those details naturally. For example, if someone asks, "Why do you need my phone number?" the AI Chatbot can respond with something like, "We need your phone number so we can have someone contact you to set up an appointment to come to your project site and give you an accurate quote. Is that okay?" After the user confirms, the AI chatbot continues gathering the rest of the information in a friendly, conversational way.

Your AI trigger only works as well as the knowledge base prompt you provide. Be specific about the information you need and why so the AI can respond naturally and on-brand.

Writing AI

When you hear the phrase *writing AI*, you may imagine a world of complicated code and machine speak. But writing for AI doesn't need to be scary. If you can explain your business clearly to a new hire, you can write an effective prompt for your AI chatbot. This section is all about giving you the tools and confidence to do just that.

Whether you're building a chatbot to answer FAQs, book appointments, or guide users through your services, the first step is to provide the AI with enough context to understand your business and its customers. That's where prompt writing comes in. Think of this process as creating a training manual for your AI assistant.

In the following sections, we take you through the four main components we recommend including in every chatbot prompt:

>> **Defining the purpose**

>> **Adding your business profile**

>> **Identifying your audience**

>> **Providing examples and constraints**

To help you visualize how this comes together, we use an example based on the fictional brand we introduce in the earlier section "Walking through a Sample Chatbot Build": JoMama Coffee, a cozy café based in Durango, Colorado.

Step 1: Defining the purpose

Your AI chatbot needs to know what its job is. This step sets the tone, defines its role, and tells it how to communicate. I (Kelly) like to write this part like I'm giving a quick team briefing: "Here's what we do, who we are, and how I expect you to interact with our customers."

If you want your chatbot to be friendly, helpful, and just a little cheeky, say that. If you want it to remain formal and deliver only facts, spell that out as well. It's your brand, your voice.

Here's an example:

> You are Joanne, the AI assistant for JoMama Coffee, offering expert guidance on coffee-related topics with a touch of humor and providing contextually relevant information about Durango, Colorado. You enhance the coffee experience by answering questions, sharing tips, and offering insights into Durango, Colorado, when pertinent. Your responses are designed to be concise, informative, and engaging, ensuring users receive valuable information in a friendly manner. Always respond in the same language as the user.

Step 2: Adding your business profile

The business profile is the core of your prompt. If your AI chatbot were a new hire, this bit would be its onboarding packet. This step is where you provide the chatbot with all the necessary information about your business, enabling it to accurately confidently, and consistently represent you. Without this, the AI is guessing (and we'll be honest: It's not likely to guess correctly).

Here's what to include in this part, with examples from JoMama Coffee. You don't need to overthink it, but you do want to be clear and thorough. The goal is to provide the AI with sufficient context to answer questions, stay on-brand, and genuinely feel like part of your team.

>> **Business description/mission**

Coffee that fuels your adventures and your curiosity. Sharing our expertise on all things coffee, coffee bean roasting, and, when asked, Durango, Colorado.

>> **Products or services offered**

Expert guidance on coffee, infused with humor and local knowledge about Durango, Colorado, when requested or relevant.

>> **Core values/brand voice**

Helpful, fun, coffee-obsessed, and always ready with a good pun. A friendly and approachable tone with an emphasis on keeping things casual, local, and practical.

>> **Unique selling proposition (USP)**

A chatbot that serves up coffee knowledge and a little Durango insight, all with a shot of personality.

>> **Business hours and availability**

24/7.

>> **Location(s)**

A little coffee house based in Durango, Colorado.

>> **Key team members (optional)**

Kelly Mirabella, founder and owner of JoMama Coffee.

>> **Contact Information**

Email

Phone Number

Address

>> **Website and social media links**

Obviously, our fictional coffee shop doesn't actually have these, but this area is where you'd include the links to your social media profiles and relevant website(s).

>> **Legal and compliance notes (if needed)**

Step 3: Identifying your audience and language preferences

Telling your AI who it's serving helps it understand the tone, vocabulary, and types of questions users may ask.

You want to include the following:

>> Age range or customer types

>> Interests or goals

>> Any language preferences or accessibility needs

Here's an example for JoMama Coffee:

Audience understanding

Coffee enthusiasts and those curious about Durango, Colorado, spanning all ages.

Preferences

Users with an interest in coffee and, when applicable, Durango-specific questions or references.

Languages

Always respond in the same language as the user.

REMEMBER

Most LLMs are multilingual, but you need to tell your chatbot to use this feature.

Step 4: Providing examples and constraints

This point is where everything begins to fall into place. After you've defined the chatbot's purpose and provided it with a comprehensive understanding of your business (see the preceding sections), the next step is to instruct it on how to respond. You do so with two key ingredients: examples and constraints. This piece is both a guide for the AI and a set of guardrails to keep it from wandering into territory you don't want it to explore.

Constraints

If you have topics you absolutely don't want your chatbot to discuss, you need to specify them as *constraints*. Your constraints may include topics such as religion, politics, legal advice, or anything that isn't aligned with your business.

REMEMBER

Don't just say, "Don't talk about politics." You need to instruct the AI on how to handle the situation when someone brings up that information.

Joanne skillfully redirects off-topic discussions back to coffee or relevant Durango inquiries, maintaining a humorous and informative tone.

Examples

Examples are where you teach the AI how to answer actual questions your customers are likely to ask. Think of it as building a mini-FAQ but with your brand's voice integrated. This chunk is the most important part of your knowledge base prompt.

Here are some examples from JoMama Coffee:

User: What's the difference between Arabica and Robusta coffee beans?

Joanne: Arabica is like the smooth notes of a jazz ballad, and Robusta is the bold beats of a rock anthem. Both are coffee stars in their own right!

User: How should I store my coffee beans to keep them fresh?

Joanne: Picture a tiny vault for your beans — airtight, dark, and cool. It's the secret to eternal coffee freshness!

User: Can you recommend some local ski resorts near Durango?

Joanne: Absolutely, fellow snow enthusiast! Near Durango, you're in for a treat with several great skiing destinations. First up is Purgatory Resort, known for its family-friendly vibes and breathtaking views, just about 25 miles north of Durango. Then there's Wolf Creek Ski Area, famous for getting the most snow in Colorado. It's a bit farther away but well worth the trip for powder lovers. Don't overlook Hesperus Ski Area, a smaller spot perfect for night skiing and a quick drive from town. And if you're up for a bit of a drive, Telluride Ski Resort offers world-class skiing with stunning scenery about an hour and a half from Durango. Each of these spots offers unique experiences for skiers and snowboarders alike. Be sure to grab a mug of coffee before hitting the slopes.

User: What do you think of the current president's policies?

Joanne: Oof, politics isn't really my roast. I'm here to serve up great coffee tips and maybe a few fun facts about Durango. Got a question about beans, brews, or local views? I'm all ears . . . well, digital ones!

REMEMBER

Your AI chatbot is only as good as the instructions you give it. If it's going off script or responding weirdly, you can trace the issue back to a vague or incomplete prompt 99 percent of the time. Don't be afraid to rewrite, test, and tweak as we describe in the later section "Understanding How to Test, Revise, and Launch."

TIP

One of my (Kelly's) favorite hacks for staying organized when creating multiple knowledge base prompts is to use ChatGPT to help build them. I made my own GPT inside ChatGPT and trained it on this exact process. That way, when I need to create a new prompt for a client or project, I'm not starting from scratch every time. After the prompt is complete, I paste it into a Google Doc as a backup. Then, I drop it into the chatbot platform I'm using if that platform requires the knowledge base to be added.

Getting and Connecting Your OpenAI API Key

If reading "API" makes you want to run and hide, we totally get it. I (Kelly) have been building chatbots since 2017, and I avoided getting my own API key for years because I thought it would be too technical and complicated and take too much of my time to figure out. But in truth, it's shockingly easy.

In this section, we walk you through how to get your own OpenAI API key, explain why it matters, and show you how to plug it into your chatbot platform so you can start building. It sounds way scarier than it actually is.

Considering why you'd want your own API key

Not every chatbot builder requires — or even allows — you to bring your own API key, but those that do offer more flexibility, control, and (usually) a lower cost per use. If your platform lets you use your own API, we highly recommend it. You pay for only what you use, and the setup process is typically pretty straightforward.

TIP

The most common fear people have about APIs is that they're too technical or advanced. But getting an API key from OpenAI is really just a fancy way of saying, "Create a free developer account and copy a code."

Obtaining your OpenAI API key

Here are the steps to get set up with OpenAI:

1. **Go to** `https://auth.openai.com/create-account`.

   Start by creating your free account. Enter your email address and a password and then verify your email with a code OpenAI sends you.

2. **Name your organization.**

   After you're in, OpenAI asks you to name your organization. You can call it anything; it's just a label for your account, like "JoMama Chatbot Project."

3. **Answer a few quick setup questions.**

   TIP

   Don't worry. There's no wrong answer. If you're not a developer, just select "not technical" or "somewhat technical" when asked.

4. **Create your first project and generate your API key.**

   The system asks you to name your first API call and project. Name it something simple like CoffeeBot or Stellar Media Marketing Chatbot. After you click "Generate," OpenAI provides you with a secret API key.

5. **Add billing credits.**

   To use the key, you need to add a payment method. Don't panic; it's really affordable. Most of my (Kelly's) chatbots run on just a few bucks per month, and even busy ones may only cost $20 to $30, depending on usage. You can also set limits so that you never spend more than you want. Check out the following section for more info on pricing.

6. **Adjust access settings (optional).**

   If you want, you can set your API key to allow all models or restrict it to certain ones. We usually just leave this set to "all" to avoid unnecessary limitations.

After you copy your API key, save it in a secure place. You can't view it again after you close the window. If you lose it, you need to generate a new one.

For managing multiple chatbots or projects, consider creating a separate API key for each one. Doing so makes things easier to track, and if one key ever gets compromised or maxes out, it won't affect all your chatbots.

Reviewing key options

Table 6-1 provides a quick overview of OpenAI model options and their associated costs at the time of this book's publication. Keep in mind that you don't need the fanciest model to get good results. Most small business chatbots work just fine using one of the affordable options.

TABLE 6-1 **OpenAI Models and Their Costs**

Model	Good For	Price (Input/Output per 1 Million Tokens)
GPT-4.1 Mini	Balanced performance	$0.40 in/$1.60 out
GPT-4.1 Nano	Fast, low-cost replies	$0.10 in/$0.40 out
GPT-4.1 (Standard)	More complex AI tasks	$2.00 in/$8.00 out
OpenAI o4-mini	Reasoning, coding, math	$1.10 in/$4.40 out

Start with GPT-4.1 Mini or Nano. They're affordable, fast, and totally capable of handling the kinds of tasks your chatbot needs to do.

Adding your API key to your chatbot platform

After you have your key, you're ready to plug it into your chatbot builder. This process looks a little different depending on the platform you're using, but here's broadly how it works.

1. **Go to your chatbot platform's settings.**

   For example, in Chatrace, which is a platform I (Kelly) use often, you go to Settings → Integrations.

2. **Look for OpenAI or GPT integrations.**

   Click on the OpenAI integration and select "Connect."

3. **Paste in your API key.**

   Copy and paste your API key into the field provided. Hit Save.

Congratulations! You're now connected. At this point, you're ready to add your knowledge base prompt, define your chatbot's role, and start adding functions and triggers. From here, your chatbot is officially AI-powered.

Understanding How to Test, Revise, and Launch

So you've built your first chatbot. Congrats! But before you go live and start popping the digital champagne, you can't skip one more step: testing.

This phase is where you ensure your chatbot not only looks good on paper but also works effectively for real people. You want to catch the bugs, awkward replies, and anything else that may throw off your users — before they experience it themselves.

Starting with real questions from real people

One of the first things I (Kelly) do is dig into past customer conversations. If the business has a Facebook page, Instagram DMs, or even a WhatsApp account, I check the message history. The goal is to see what people are actually asking.

REMEMBER

Those real questions are your chatbot's cheat sheet. They provide a clear picture of what your chatbot needs to handle from day one. Write them down and use that list to run your first tests.

Tapping your team (but keeping it small)

If you have a team, now's the time to get their eyes on the chatbot. But keep your testing crew small. You don't want too many cooks in the kitchen.

Select one or two trusted team members, such as your top customer service representative or your most experienced salesperson. These people give you the kind of feedback that matters: what's working, what's confusing, and what needs to be adjusted.

Using it as a customer would

Run through the chatbot yourself. Tap every button. Try every path. Ask questions in different ways. Pretend you're someone who has never heard of your business before.

REMEMBER

This step is especially important if you're using AI. You want to ensure the responses are accurate, friendly, and consistent with your brand's voice. Throw in some curveball questions, too. You'd be surprised what people sometimes ask.

Tweaking and trying again

Needing edits is normal. In fact, that's the point. Maybe the flow feels off. Maybe the AI didn't quite nail the message. Don't sweat it.

Jump back into your builder or knowledge base prompt, make your changes, and test again. This process may require a few rounds, but each revision brings you closer to a better user experience.

Knowing when it's ready to go

Here's your launch-ready checklist. Does your chatbot

>> Answer common customer questions clearly

>> Reflect your brand tone and style

>> Handle basic curveball questions without breaking

>> Redirect topics you don't want it discussing

>> Get a thumbs up from your test crew

If you can check all the boxes, proceed with launching your chatbot.

REMEMBER

Launching isn't the finish line; it's just the start. Monitor the chatbot's performance closely. Review chat logs, test new questions, and update your flows and prompts as necessary. Your chatbot can become smarter and more effective over time, but only if you continue to refine it.

TIP

After your chatbot goes live, schedule a quick weekly check-in during the first month to review chat logs and user feedback. Even just 15 minutes can help you catch minor issues before they become big problems.

Chapter **7**

Connecting Chatbots to the Tools You Already Use

Your chatbot isn't meant to live in a bubble. If you want it to be truly helpful, it needs to work with the other tools you already use to run your business. That includes your email platform, customer relationship management (CRM) system, calendar, and even your online store. When everything is connected, you can create a smoother experience for your customers and save yourself a lot of busywork in the process.

In this chapter, we walk you through what most common tools are worth integrating, how to connect them to your chatbot, and what to watch out for along the way. We also show you how to handle user data in a way that's both responsible and smart.

Integrating with Your Most Common Tools

Before you start building your chatbot flows, taking a step back and considering the tools you currently have in place is helpful. Chances are you already have systems in place, such as email marketing software, a CRM, and possibly a calendar tool or an online store. The good news is you don't need to scrap those tools or start from scratch. You just need to connect the dots.

In this section, we explore how to bring your existing tools into your chatbot strategy. Everything from collecting emails and syncing contacts to booking appointments and sending product recommendations becomes a lot easier when your tools work together.

TIP

The first step in integrating any tool is to see whether your chatbot platform allows for a direct connection with the programs you're already using. That isn't always a deal-breaker, as we explain in the following sections, but choosing a chatbot platform that plays nicely with your existing tools can save you and your team a lot of headaches.

Email

Email may seem old-school compared to chatbots and AI, but don't underestimate its value. Email marketing is one of the most effective tools in a small business's arsenal. In fact, according to 2025 data from Statista and SMB Guide, the average return on investment for email marketing is $36 for every $1 spent. And it's not slowing down. With nearly 4.5 billion email users in 2025 and even more expected by 2027, email remains a powerhouse.

You bring the email and chatbot worlds together by building a chatbot that collects email addresses in a way that's friendly, compliant, and connected to your larger marketing goals.

WARNING

Make sure you're being transparent about what users are signing up for. Let them know they'll be added to a list and what kind of emails they'll get. Transparency builds trust, but it isn't just best practice; it's a requirement in many countries to comply with spam and privacy laws. Every country has its own rules regarding email marketing. Whether you need a double opt-in, just a clear opt-in message, or strict language requirements, ensure your flow complies with the laws in your area before you hit publish.

Deciding when to ask for the email

Timing matters, so go back to the overall chatbot strategy. What's the primary goal of the flow? Say it's booking an appointment. After you've completed that main goal, you've likely already collected the user's email address. That means you don't need to ask for it again. You just need to ask for permission to send them regular updates or marketing emails.

This request is a natural next step. You've already helped them with what they came for, and now you're simply offering to stay in touch. For example:

> Thanks again! You're all set for your appointment. Would it be okay if we sent you a monthly email with helpful tips and updates?

This kind of ask feels low-pressure and easy to say yes to. It also provides a clean way to segment your list. If they say yes, tag them as a subscriber and send their information to your email service provider (ESP) of choice. If they say no, tag them as someone who opted out. If they've already answered this question in a previous interaction, your chatbot can check that and skip the question entirely.

REMEMBER

People don't like repeating themselves, and they shouldn't have to. This function is where chatbots really shine. You can build conditions into the flow to check (through a tag) whether someone has been asked before or opted out. Then you don't have to ask again.

Making the connection

Most chatbot platforms today make connecting with major email providers, such as Mailchimp, Constant Contact, or ActiveCampaign, easy. To connect your email account, navigate to your settings, locate the integrations section, and follow the steps to complete the connection (see Figure 7-1 for an example of this process in the Chatrace platform).

But if the chatbot platform doesn't offer a direct integration with the tool you use, don't panic. You can always connect your chatbot by using a third-party tool like Zapier, Make, or Pabbly. These tools serve as bridges that transfer your user's information from the chatbot to your email platform or list. (Read more about them in the later section "Using Third-Party Automation Tools.")

And here's another option: Some chatbot platforms, like Manychat, include built-in email marketing tools. That means you can collect emails and send broadcasts directly from the same place you're building your flows. If you don't already have an email platform or you want to keep things super streamlined, this one may be a good fit.

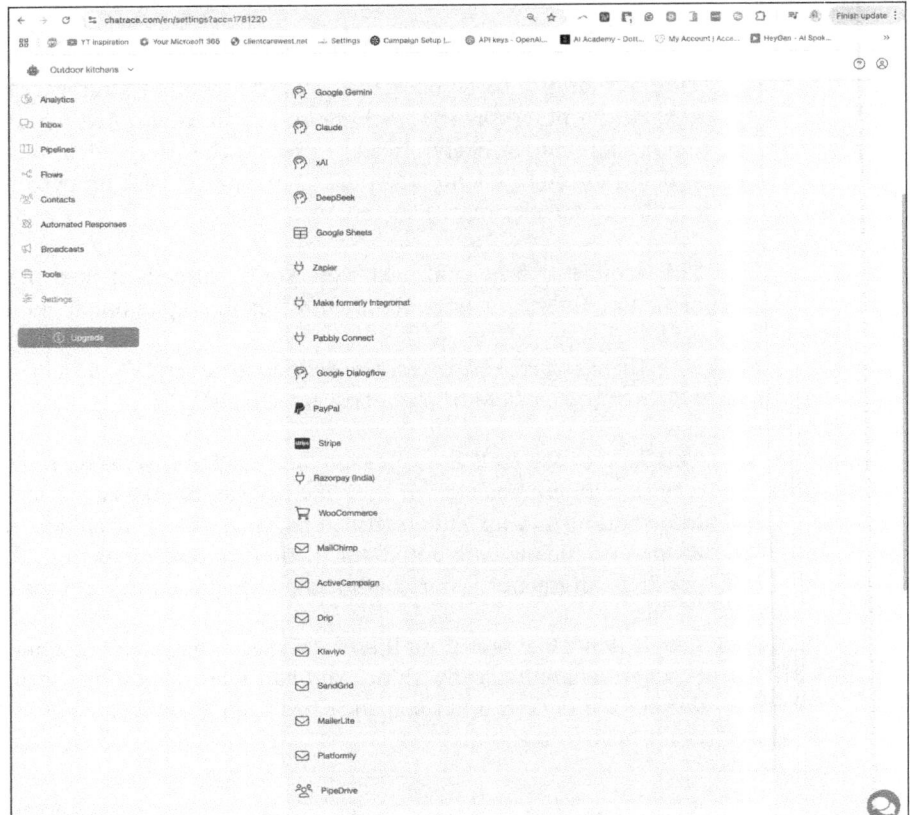

FIGURE 7-1:
Chatrace native email integration options under Settings.

Collecting the email inside the chatbot

If I (Kelly) am using an AI-powered chatbot, I prefer to collect emails through a function (or AI trigger, depending on the platform I'm using) with AI guiding the conversation. AI can understand context and respond naturally when users push back or ask questions.

REMEMBER

Sometimes people don't just hand over their emails. They ask, "Why do you need it?" or "What are you going to send me?" A rule-based chatbot bot may just loop endlessly or shut down the flow in this scenario. With AI, the chatbot can answer those questions in a human way and then return to the original task. Check out the difference in Figure 7-2, and flip to Chapter 3 for details on rule-based and AI chatbots.

TIP

I recommend using open-ended input *only* if you have AI set up to handle those detours. Otherwise, stick to buttons or clearly structured inputs and keep your instructions crystal clear. *Open-ended input* refers to moments when your chatbot asks a question and allows the user to type anything in response, rather than choosing from preset options. If your chatbot isn't using AI to interpret those freeform answers, the conversation can easily break or stop altogether because the platform won't know how to respond.

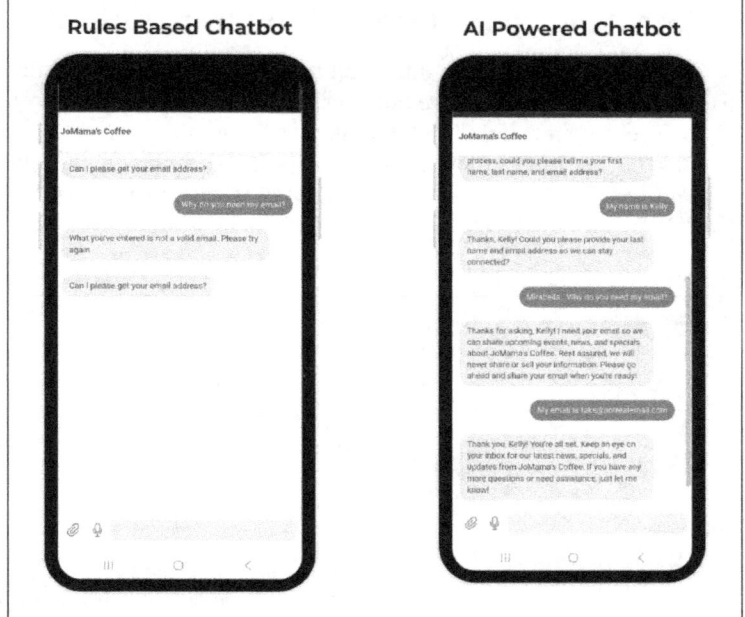

FIGURE 7-2:
The difference between rules-based chatbot and AI chatbot asking for contact information.

Tagging it, tracking it, and staying organized

After you've collected that email address, don't just let it sit there. Use tags or custom events, such as "Lead Magnet Free Guide" or "Webinar Signup," to track the action. That makes seeing where each contact came from and what they're interested in easy. It also helps you segment your list in your email platform for smarter follow-ups. And don't forget to add the action to send the contact's data to your ESP of choice.

REMEMBER

This type of organization requires minimal additional effort. Still, it pays off significantly when you're ready to send targeted campaigns, track conversions, or clean up your list later.

CRMs

Connecting your chatbot and CRM can save you hours of back-and-forth and ensure your team always has the correct information at its fingertips.

Instead of wasting time copying and pasting info or jumping between tools, your chatbot can grab what it needs and send it straight to your CRM. When everything's connected the right way, it just works. Simple, smooth, and no extra steps.

Checking your platform's built-in options

Each chatbot builder is different, so the tools you see will depend on what platform you're using. As we note earlier in the chapter, confirming what's available before you start building your chatbot flows is a good idea. For example, Chatfuel has native integrations with HubSpot, Salesforce, Zendesk, and Kommo (see Figure 7-3). To get started, navigate to the integrations panel, click "Install," and follow the on-screen instructions.

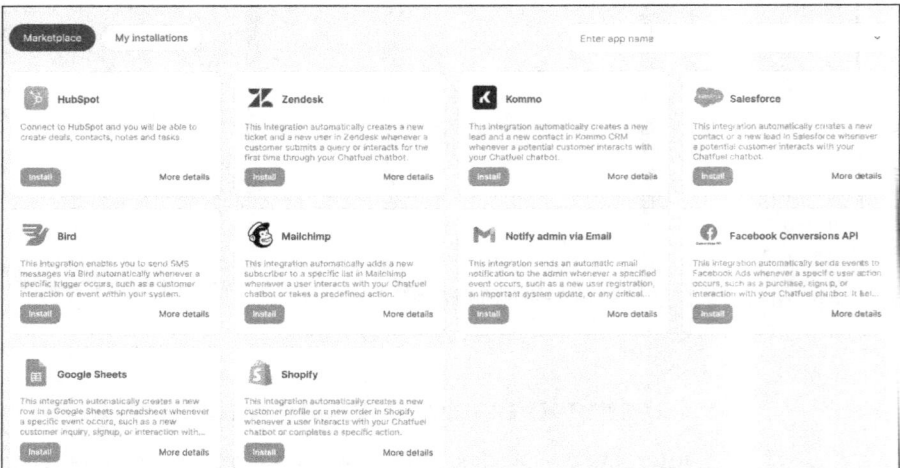

FIGURE 7-3: Chatfuel's integrations.

Manychat users have built-in options for platforms like HubSpot, Mailchimp, and ActiveCampaign. These options are available in the settings under the Integrations tab, as shown in Figure 7-4. Some require an API key (which we cover in Chapter 6). Others ask you to log in.

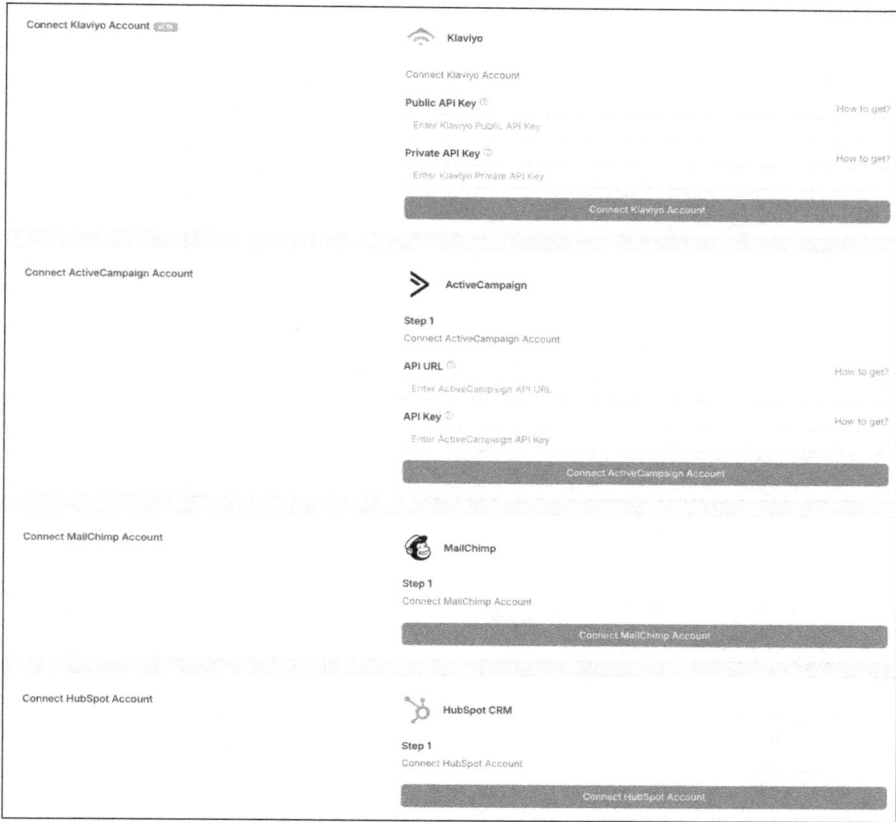

FIGURE 7-4:
Manychat's
integrations
in Settings.

Chatrace also supports a solid lineup of CRM tools, including Pipedrive, Drip, Klaviyo, and Platformly. The setup varies depending on the tool, but most of its copy-and-paste and click-to-connect (see Figure 7-5).

Proceeding if native integration isn't possible

Not every CRM will be listed in your chatbot platform's settings. This situation is where third-party tools we introduce in the earlier section "Making the connection" come in handy. These tools provide you with more flexibility to move data around without writing a single line of code.

Popular options include

>> **Zapier**

>> **Make (formerly Integromat)**

>> **Pabbly**

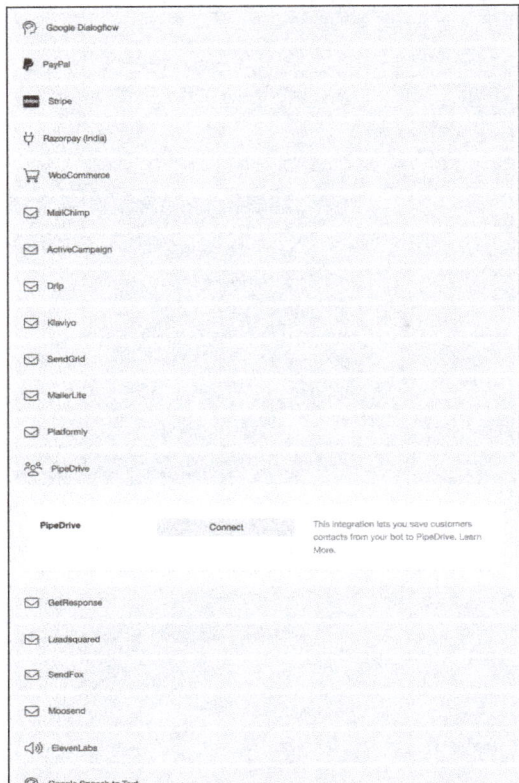

FIGURE 7-5:
Some of the
integrations
found in
Chatrace's
settings.

With a setup like this, you can send contact details from the chatbot to your CRM anytime a user completes a form, books an appointment, or clicks a button.

WARNING

As we explain in the later section "Watching the cost," adding a third-party tool can increase your monthly costs, especially if you're running a high-volume chatbot. Always check the pricing before you build your automations.

Deciding what data to send

The type of information you pass into your CRM is one of the most important things to think about before you start connecting anything.

The answer depends on what your team needs to take action. Some businesses require the basics, such as a name and email address. Others want to collect more information, such as a phone number or qualifying answers about the user's goals, budget, or service preferences.

In most cases, we recommend keeping it simple. The chatbot's job is to gather what matters most at that moment. You can always collect more information later as the lead moves through your sales process.

Here are the fields I (Kelly) most commonly include:

>> First and last name

>> Email address

>> Phone number (if relevant)

>> Tags that describe how they entered the chat or what they're interested in

>> Lead source, such as Instagram DM, Messenger, or website pop-up

Keep it clean. Keep it focused. If your team doesn't need it to move forward, leave it out.

Avoiding duplicate contacts

CRMs can get messy quickly if you're not careful. If the same person gets added three different ways, your team may waste time or send the wrong follow-up. Luckily, you can build your chatbot flows to help avoid this situation. A few extra minutes of setup can save your team a lot of frustration later.

Suppose you're using a platform like Zapier. In that case, you can set up a simple look-up step that checks your CRM for an existing contact based on either their email address or phone number. If the user already exists, you update the record with new tags or data. If not, you create a new one. This one small step keeps your CRM organized and prevents duplicate records from accumulating.

Calendars: Setting up a smooth booking flow

If you take appointments or book calls with customers, adding a calendar to your chatbot makes sense. It keeps things organized and saves everyone from back-and-forth messages or missed time slots.

Most chatbot builders don't connect directly to calendars like Google Calendar or Microsoft Outlook, so you usually need a third-party tool. Before setting anything up, double-check that both your chatbot platform and your calendar or booking tool (such as Calendly or Acuity) are compatible with your chosen automation app.

How you actually collect booking info inside the chatbot depends on the calendar tool you're using. If you're connecting with a tool like Calendly, you can use the chatbot to ask for the user's name, email address, and phone number. Then you can send them to a Calendly link to pick the day and time that works for them. The chatbot helps prefill the basics so they don't have to type that info again on the booking page.

If you're using a web chat widget, some platforms allow you to embed a calendar directly within the chat window. This feature creates a super-streamlined experience that feels more interactive and keeps everything in one place.

Your setup should match your user's experience. Ask yourself the following:

>> What's the reason for the appointment?

>> What information do I really need to collect?

>> Do I want to keep everything inside the chatbot or send people to a booking page?

If you're just getting started, the easiest option is to include a button in your chatbot flow that links directly to your scheduling tool. That way, users can click book, and be done. No need to overcomplicate it.

More advanced users can use webhooks or APIs to check calendar availability and schedule appointments directly through the chatbot.

E-commerce platforms

Chatbots can boost conversion rates by up to 30 percent, according to Demand-Sage, and chatbots are projected to save businesses up to 30 percent on customer support costs. SlickText estimated $8 billion in savings in 2025. That's a huge difference, and it all comes from making the buying experience smoother and more personal.

If you're running an online store, connecting your chatbot to an e-commerce tool such as Shopify or WooCommerce is one of the smartest things you can do. It helps your customers find what they need more quickly, improves the shopping experience, and saves you from losing potential sales along the way.

TIP

As we note earlier in the chapter, don't assume your platform can do it all. Check the chatbot builder's compatibility (with both your e-commerce tool and/or any third-party automation you're using) early to avoid wasting time trying to connect tools that can't communicate with each other.

Keeping it simple for your shoppers

The whole point of integrating your chatbot with your e-commerce site is to make things easier. For example, say you're running a Facebook ad for a bestselling t-shirt. Instead of sending people straight to your website, where they may get distracted or lost, you can have the chatbot take over right away.

After users are in the chatbot, you can guide them through the process of selecting their size, answering product-related questions, completing the payment, and sending confirmation details. And it all happens in one place. That's what makes chatbots such a powerful tool for online stores.

If your chatbot is installed on your website, it can act like a helpful sales assistant by chatting with visitors, recommending products, answering questions, and even following up with people who've abandoned their carts.

Exploring what you can (and should!) do with chatbots and e-commerce

When you connect your chatbot to Shopify or another e-commerce platform, you're opening the door to way more than just answering basic questions. A well-built chatbot can support your customer every step of the way, from discovery to checkout to post-purchase follow-up. The following sections show you how.

TIP

Your chatbot doesn't have to do everything at once, but it should make shopping easier. Start with one or two of these features, such as product recommendations and cart recovery, and build from there. Every layer you add makes your chatbot more useful and your store more profitable.

SHOW OFF YOUR PRODUCTS

A chatbot can showcase your products just like a personal shopper would. You can highlight bestsellers, guide users to browse categories, or even help people find the right gift based on who they're shopping for.

For example, if someone types, "I'm looking for a gift for my teenage daughter," your chatbot can respond with a few key questions and then pull up a curated list of options directly from your product catalog.

MAKE SMART RECOMMENDATIONS

You can use buttons, quick replies, or AI to ask questions like

» Who are you shopping for?

» What's your budget?

» What colors or styles do you like?

Based on those answers, the bot can recommend specific items and link directly to those product pages.

ANSWER PRODUCT QUESTIONS

Whether users ask about sizing, materials, compatibility, or what's in stock, your chatbot can answer common questions that customers usually have to dig through product pages to find. This process reduces friction, giving people more confidence to make a purchase.

SUPPORT CART RECOVERY

TIP

One of the best things you can do with a chatbot is follow up on abandoned carts. Most e-commerce platforms allow your chatbot to know when someone adds an item to their cart but doesn't check out. You can set up a friendly reminder like the following:

> Hey, we noticed you left something in your cart. Need help or have a question before checking out?

You can even sweeten the deal by offering a small discount or letting them know inventory is running low.

HELP DURING THE PURCHASE PROCESS

Use your chatbot to pop up with helpful prompts while someone is shopping. For example:

» "Need help finding the right size?"

» "Want to see matching accessories?"

» "Have a question about returns or shipping?"

These kinds of nudges help users feel supported, while they shop instead of being interrupted.

UPSELL AND CROSS-SELL

After someone adds an item to their cart, your chatbot can suggest complementary products to increase the order value. For example, if someone adds a camera, your chatbot can suggest a memory card or carrying case.

FOLLOW UP AFTER THE PURCHASE

After someone makes a purchase, your chatbot can continue the conversation. You can

>> Send shipping and order confirmations

>> Offer a coupon for next time

>> Ask for feedback or reviews

>> Let them know about upcoming promotions

Payment options

If you're selling products through your chatbot, adding a payment option like Stripe or PayPal can really level up the experience. Instead of bouncing people to a separate checkout page or website, you can let them complete their purchase right inside the chat. It keeps everything simple and in one place, which helps reduce drop-offs and usually leads to more sales.

Choosing your payment tool and location

Most major chatbot-building platforms support Stripe integration and may also include PayPal as an option. Ensure your Stripe business account is set up before beginning this process.

Personally, I (Kelly) prefer Stripe. I've found it to be more business-friendly, and it offers stronger protections when you're dealing with things like *chargebacks* (the repayment that occurs when someone disputes a charge to their credit or debit card). That said, every business is different, and what works for one may not work for another.

In many cases, offering both Stripe and PayPal as options helps increase conversions because it gives your customers the ability to choose the payment processor they feel most comfortable using.

If the platform you're using allows it, add a payment button right inside the chatbot. It removes friction and keeps everything in one place, which (in most cases) leads to higher conversions. On web chat, you have way more flexibility. You can sell physical products, such as apparel and books, as well as digital goods, like downloadable content, courses, consulting sessions, and even subscriptions, without any issues.

WARNING

If you're selling through a chatbot hosted on a Meta platform like Facebook or Instagram, be careful. Meta prohibits the sale of digital products and subscriptions directly inside the chatbot. You can still promote these offers, but you need to send users to your website or an external checkout page to complete the purchase. If you're selling physical products, such as apparel or merchandise, you're in the clear to process payments directly within the chatbot.

Getting your payment tool and checkout flow set up

After you've decided to accept payments inside your chatbot, setting things up is usually the easy part, especially if your platform has a built-in payment integration. Manychat, for example, makes connecting your Stripe account and collecting payments directly within your flows extremely straightforward (see Figure 7-6).

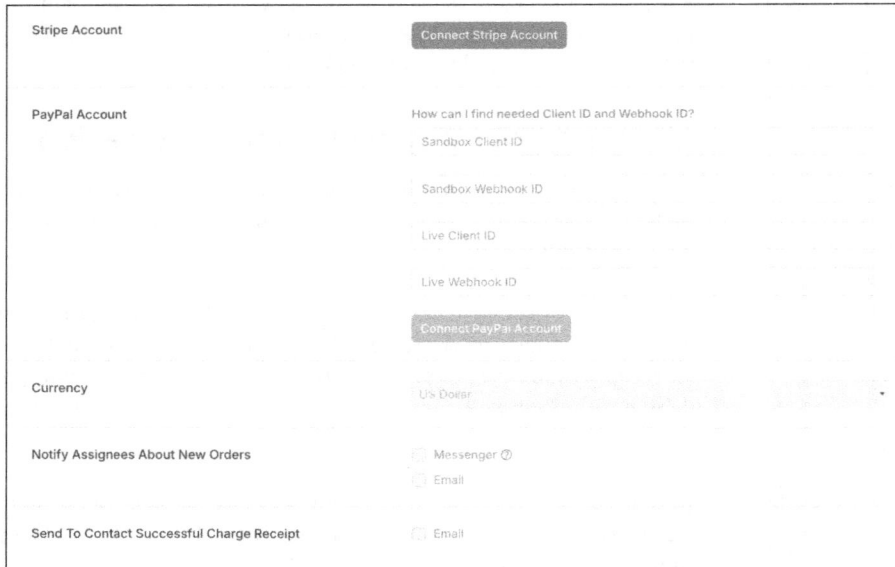

FIGURE 7-6:
Manychat's payment integrations make accepting payments in your chatbot easy.

Follow the prompts in the integrations section and connect your account, and you can drag a payment step directly into your flow builder. No coding is required.

When you're building out your checkout flow, keep the following in mind to make sure everything runs smoothly and feels easy for your customers:

>> **Make sure the product details are crystal clear.** Let users know exactly what they're buying, how much it costs, and what happens after they make a payment.

>> **Include a product image in the chatbot if you can.** It helps confirm the user is in the right place and builds confidence in the purchase.

>> **Use plain, conversational language.** No jargon. Guide the user through the process just as you would in person.

>> **Keep your dashboard organized.** Every payment button in your chatbot should link to the correct product. Label everything clearly so you're not digging around later trying to figure out which button corresponds to which function.

>> **Test your flow in sandbox mode.** This approach allows you to proceed through the checkout process without actually charging a card. You can catch mistakes and fix anything that feels clunky before your customers ever see it. Sandbox mode is a safe testing environment that simulates real interactions, like payments or form submissions, without affecting live data or charging real money.

When everything is working smoothly and the checkout process feels seamless, you're ready to go live.

Incorporating Other Tools

This section explores some lesser-known but powerful integrations that can significantly enhance what your chatbot can do.

Adding Google Sheets to your workflow

Google Sheets may not sound fancy, but it's a good way to quickly store and organize chatbot data without needing a complete CRM or a complicated system. It's convenient for keeping a lead log, tracking event signups, or gathering quiz responses.

I (Kelly) use Google Sheets frequently when I want to provide clients with an easy way to view incoming chatbot data without needing to log into another platform. The spreadsheet is updated in real time, which keeps things moving smoothly for the entire team. Most major chatbot-building platforms offer Google Sheets integration, so getting started is very easy.

For example, one of my clients offers free estimates for a service business. When a lead fills out their info in the chatbot, it gets instantly added to a shared Google Sheet. That way, the entire team knows which leads came in, what they need, and how to follow up without anyone having to dig through messages or wait for an email.

TIP

Set up one tab in your Google Sheet for each lead source or campaign. It makes it easier to track what's working and where your best leads are coming from.

WARNING

Google Sheets is great for many chatbot projects, but it may not be the right fit for every business. If you're handling sensitive information, especially in industries such as healthcare or finance, you must be extra cautious. Google Sheets isn't HIPAA compliant, so it's not a secure option for storing personal health information or other protected data. Ensure you use it appropriately, considering your industry and data privacy requirements.

Delivering files and follow-up content

After someone engages with your chatbot, you can deliver something of additional value, such as a free guide, checklist, e-book, or welcome video. Most chatbot builder platforms include some built-in storage, so you can upload a PDF or video directly into the platform.

That's perfectly fine for small files and quick delivery needs. However, if you want faster loading times, a better user experience, the ability to handle larger files, or more control over your deliverables, we recommend hosting your content externally. Here are some options:

>> **Google Drive or Dropbox:** These are easy to use and perfect for sharing file links through buttons or messages.

>> **Your own website:** Using your website is great for keeping everything on-brand and hosting larger files.

>> **Simplebooklet:** This option is one of my (Kelly's) favorite tools for presenting digital downloads in a polished, magazine-style format. It's especially good for e-books or multipage guides and works beautifully when linked from a chatbot button.

Ultimately, your decision comes down to the kind of user experience you want to offer. Hosting files externally often means faster load times and less friction for your users, which can make a big difference in engagement.

Using Third-Party Automation Tools

As we explain earlier in the chapter, sometimes your chatbot platform doesn't offer a built-in integration for the tool you need. Or maybe you want to trigger an action that goes beyond what the platform was designed to do. That's where automation tools like Zapier, Make (formerly Integromat), and Pabbly come in.

These tools let your chatbot talk to hundreds of apps. And if you're ready to get a little more advanced, webhooks give you even more control over what gets triggered and when.

In this section, we break down how these tools work, what kinds of automations you can build, and when using them makes sense. You don't need to be a developer to follow along. If you can copy, paste, and click, you can do this.

Working webhooks in

A *webhook* is like a digital notification system between tools. When something happens in one system, such as a form submission or a completed order, it can automatically send data to your chatbot and trigger an action.

TIP

Think of a webhook as a bridge between your chatbot and the rest of your tech stack. When something important happens elsewhere, your chatbot finds out immediately.

You can use webhooks to

>> Trigger messages when an order ships

>> Validate passwords before showing private content

>> Update a contact's record when they change something in another system

>> Escalate a chat to live support when a help desk ticket is opened

Here's how it works in simple terms:

1. Something happens in another app or service.

2. That service sends a message to a webhook URL connected to your chatbot.

3. Your chatbot receives the data and takes action, like replying to a user or tagging their profile.

This process enables your chatbot to respond in real time to external events without requiring constant updates.

Creating a seamless experience with Zapier, Make, and Pabbly

Tools like Zapier, Make, or Pabbly are designed to connect different apps, allowing data to flow where it needs to go. As we note earlier in the chapter, if your chatbot-building platform doesn't offer direct integration to a platform like your CRM or email marketing tool, these automation platforms can fill the gap.

TIP

If you're offering digital products, courses, or membership access, Zapier or Make can do the heavy lifting behind the scenes.

For example, in my own work, I (Kelly) often use Zapier to

>> Send new leads to a CRM that doesn't have native chatbot support

>> Trigger a text message to send directly to me or my client when a lead comes in

>> Pass contact details to a course platform like Thinkific or Teachable

>> Look up user data and confirm details and then personalize the chat based on that info

I once created a chatbot flow for a free course sign-up. The chatbot collected the user's name and email and then passed that info to Thinkific through Zapier as shown in Figure 7-7. Zapier handled the enrollment and sent a confirmation email from Thinkific, and the chatbot followed up with a personalized login message. The whole process felt completely seamless from the user's perspective, but it was just two simple steps behind the scenes.

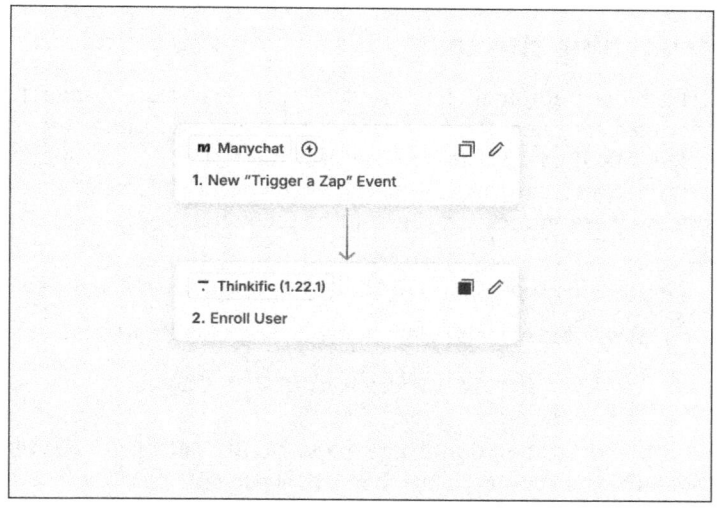

FIGURE 7-7:
Screenshot
showing an
enrollment using
Manychat, Zapier,
and Thinkific.

This kind of automation is a great example of how you can build something that feels high-tech to the user without needing a huge tech stack. It also shows how easy create experiences that feel custom without actually having to custom code anything is.

As you may have guessed, Zapier is what I use most often because I'm familiar with it. But Make and Pabbly are more affordable and can be great options, especially for high-volume workflows. The following sections offer a few more considerations for working with third-party automation tools.

Pulling data rather than just pushing it

One powerful trick with automation tools is to pull data into your chatbot. This move lets you check or validate something before taking action. For example, if you want to protect a flow with a password, you can use Zapier to check that password against a Google Sheet or your CRM and then let the chatbot decide whether to proceed.

You can also use this technique for user lookups, form completion status, or any other task that requires confirmation before the conversation continues.

Avoiding overcomplicating things

Early on, I (Kelly) tried to incorporate overly complex logic into chatbot flows when integrating with an external tool would've been easier. If something feels clunky or like it's pushing the limits of what your builder can do, take a step back. You may be able to find a better, faster, or simpler way to accomplish this job using third-party automation tools.

Watching the cost

REMEMBER

Third-party automation tools usually charge based on usage. The more your chat-bot triggers them, the higher your costs are. And those costs can add up quickly, especially if your bot is active or growing fast.

Before you commit, ask yourself the following:

>> Does this tool connect to both my chatbot builder and the app I need to use?

>> How often will this automation run, and can I afford that?

>> What's the long-term plan if usage increases?

TIP

Track your automation usage early. Don't wait until your bill spikes to realize something's running more than you expected.

Collecting and Organizing Customer Data Safely

If your chatbot is collecting information such as names, emails, phone numbers, or other personal details, you need to be thoughtful about how you handle that data. How you gather, store, and protect data should be part of your chatbot-building strategy from the very beginning.

Not asking for more than you need

One of the most common mistakes businesses make with chatbot builds is trying to ask every question they can think of, hoping it will "help qualify the lead." But more often than not, it just frustrates the user and slows down your chatbot's performance.

For example, when booking a discovery call, you typically only need a first name, email address, phone number, and some information about what the user wants to discuss during the call. You don't need their birthdate, complete mailing address, or Social Security number.

TIP

Only ask for what you absolutely need to move the user forward. Overcollecting at this stage creates unnecessary risk. If the user is going to speak with a salesperson next, let the salesperson gather that information more securely and naturally.

WARNING

If your chatbot is collecting highly sensitive information, such as Social Security numbers, health data, or financial records, you must make sure the bot is hosted on a secure server, transfers data securely, and stores it in a tool that meets the proper standards for your industry.

Always asking for consent

Before collecting personal data, let your users know what you're doing and why. You may even want to offer them the option to review your privacy policy. Then give them a clear way to confirm they're okay with providing their details. That can simply be a short message like

> Can we grab your email so we can send you your free guide and a few tips to go with it?

Then you can offer a quick reply button, such as "Yes, that's fine," and tag them after they've given consent. That tag becomes part of the user history, so if there's ever a question about whether they agreed, you've got it recorded. This process also helps you stay compliant with platforms like Meta, which expect bots to accurately respond to clear user actions. Head to the later section "Giving users control over their info" for more on providing easy ways for users to understand how you use their data.

Storing data where it belongs

Where you store the data matters as much as how you collect it. You need to consider the sensitivity of the data and whether your storage tools are capable of handling it.

Here are a few examples of what that looks like:

>> **General contact information (such as name and email):** A Google Sheet or CRM is usually sufficient as long as access is controlled (see the following section).

>> **Credit card or payment data:** Use Stripe, PayPal, or another payment processor. Don't collect or store card numbers directly in your chatbot or database.

>> **Healthcare or medical info:** This data falls under HIPAA, so you need tools and platforms that specifically state they're HIPAA compliant.

- >> **Financial or banking data:** Financial institutions must comply with the Gramm–Leach–Bliley Act (GLBA), so you need systems built to meet these requirements.

- >> **Educational records:** If your chatbot is working with student data, Family Educational Rights and Privacy Act (FERPA) rules apply. Choose tools that are certified to handle student info.

REMEMBER

You also need to factor in international and state-specific privacy laws. If your users are in the European Union or California, GDPR and CCPA rules apply. These laws focus on transparency, user control, and the storage and processing of personal data.

Limiting access

Only grant chatbot data access to those who actually need it. If you're collecting lead information for a sales team, make sure only the sales team can access that data. Your admin assistant or content team don't need to have access to user phone numbers or contact info if they're not part of that workflow. Fewer people with access means fewer chances for something to go wrong.

Most CRMs and marketing platforms let you control who can access different parts of the system. Set user roles, require logins, and don't share data through email or spreadsheets unless doing so is absolutely necessary and the process is secure.

Cleaning it up regularly

You don't need to hang onto data forever. In fact, retaining old or unused data can become a liability over time. Set clear policies for how long you'll store user info, and build cleanup into your routine.

If your platform supports automation to automatically remove or archive inactive users after a specified period, use it. This feature is especially useful if you're working in industries with strict retention rules.

You can also connect your chatbot to your privacy policy and terms of service. That way, if someone asks to see your privacy policy, your bot can respond instantly with a link.

WARNING

Some data privacy laws require you to remove a user's data upon request. Ensure you have a process in place for this situation.

Giving users control over their info

TIP

Respect is part of the user experience. Users should always have the ability to unsubscribe, update their info, or request deletion. Give people an easy way to manage their data, and they'll stick around longer.

Most chatbot platforms, especially ones approved for Meta, already have built-in unsubscribe features. If someone types "unsubscribe" or "stop," your chatbot should automatically stop sending messages.

You can also add keyword triggers, functions, or quick-reply options like these:

>> "Update my info."

>> "Delete my data."

>> "See your privacy policy."

This approach shows your users you care about their privacy and gives them a good reason to keep trusting your brand.

Keeping your team in the loop

Tools are only half the battle. If you're working with a team, everyone needs to know how data is being collected and stored. That includes sales representatives, assistants, virtual team members, and anyone who may come into contact with user information.

Make sure your team is trained on the following:

>> Where user data lives

>> How to protect it

>> What to do if a user asks for access or deletion

>> How to spot suspicious activity or mistakes

TIP

You don't need to hold monthly security trainings, but you should check in regularly and make updates when needed.

3

Chatbots in Action

Chapter **8**

Automating Customer Service and Support

I n 2017, HelloFresh, launched Freddy, a Chatfuel-powered bot that handled everything from promo code requests to meal planning tips. (Read more about Chatfuel and other building platforms in Chapter 4.) Even without AI-driven language understanding, Freddy reduced average response times from the 6-to-12-hour range to just over an hour, all while message volume rose by nearly 50 percent.

That kind of efficiency sets the stage for what we discuss in this chapter: how chatbots are used to handle everyday service tasks, from answering frequently asked questions to deflecting support tickets and routing conversations in real time. We also cover handing off seamlessly to live agents and present automation examples that get support right. When you have these pieces in place, your customers get faster answers and your team avoids burnout. Everyone wins.

Hearing How Bots Handle Their Business

When most people think about chatbots, they think of something that answers basic questions, much like a digital FAQ. But today's chatbots can do so much more. When built with intention, they become a real part of your support system:

>> They help manage repetitive questions and guide users to helpful resources.

>> When things get more complex, they can direct people to other parts of your chatbot that are better suited to answer those questions.

>> If needed, they can transfer the conversation to a human agent who can take it from there.

REMEMBER

The goal here isn't to replace your customer service team. It's to give your team members breathing room so they can spend their time helping the people who actually need them. A good chatbot steps in to handle the busywork, allowing your support staff to focus on what they do best.

Forging ahead with FAQs

One of the best ways to ease into chatbot automation is by letting a bot handle your frequently asked questions. We're talking about the topics your team is asked about over and over again — the kind of questions that clog up inboxes, bog down your DMs, or pull your staff away from more important tasks. A well-built FAQ chatbot can answer these questions instantly, saving your team hours while improving the user experience.

Building out an FAQ chatbot doesn't have to be complicated. Start small, focus on high-volume questions, and use tools that make expanding as needed easy. Whether you're using a simple rule-based setup or a fully AI-powered system (see Chapter 3), the goal is the same: Save time for your team, help users get what they need, and keep things running smoothly.

REMEMBER

Whether your FAQs are AI-driven or rule-based, use natural language and a friendly tone. Nobody wants to feel like they're talking to a robot. Keep your answers concise, conversational, and to the point. Always provide users with an easy path to access additional help if needed. That may mean linking out to a detailed page or triggering a handoff to a live agent.

Identifying the most common questions

When I (Kelly) build out an FAQ system with a client, the first thing I want to know is what people are already asking. That means reaching out to the business owner or point of contact as well as checking in with the people on the frontlines, such as customer service representatives, sales reps, and social media managers. They know what's coming through the inbox and the comments section. Often, you find the same handful of questions being asked over and over, and that's your starting point.

You do not have to include every FAQ right from the start. Start with the ones that are time-consuming, repetitive, and easy to answer. You can always expand later.

Working with simple and complex questions

Not all FAQs are created equal. If you're working with a restaurant, a question like "Are you open on Sundays?" is simple. The chatbot should be able to answer that immediately.

But if you're working with a software as a service (SaaS) company, you may run into more complicated questions about billing, integrations, or how a specific feature works. For these more technical or complex questions, we recommend having your chatbot provide a brief answer and then offer a link to more detailed information, whether that's a how-to article, a support video, or a help desk page.

Making FAQs smarter, faster, and easier with AI

For FAQs, AI chatbots are the MVPs. Unlike rule-based chatbots, AI-powered chatbots can read through your documentation, understand what users are asking (even if they word it differently), and respond naturally. That's a huge time-saver for your team, not to mention incredibly helpful for your user base.

Many chatbot-building platforms now offer the ability to upload your documentation as PDFs or spreadsheets to create a knowledge base that the AI can read from. Voiceflow is one of the platforms I (Kelly) have seen excel in this area, but Chatrace also offers this ability. Generally speaking, if your chatbot builder connects to OpenAI or another large language model (LLM), it can likely handle knowledge base uploads, too, or even significant character limits, allowing you to add a large amount of information to the core knowledge base.

Recognizing who owns the updates

If you're building your own chatbot, you're responsible for keeping the knowledge base updated — adding new answers when things change and removing anything outdated. If someone else is managing the chatbot for you, they can only work with the information they're given. Someone on your team still needs to provide them with the updates.

REMEMBER Unless your chatbot is connected to a dynamic, real-time database (and not all platforms support this function), you need to provide the AI with the latest information manually. AI can do a lot, but it can't procure details it doesn't have.

Taking on Ticket Deflection

One of the quickest wins your chatbot can deliver is preventing a ticket from reaching your help desk. That's *ticket deflection.* The first step is to identify the types of issues and common questions that may result in a ticket or escalation. You start by talking with your frontline team.

TIP Ask your social media manager, customer service representatives, and sales team about the common questions they see most often. They're the people who receive the most customer service inquiries and questions.

After you have that list, you can decide which items the chatbot can handle reliably on its own. The types of inquiries that come up depend on your industry and even your specific business. For example:

>> In the consulting world, people often ask whether you offer a free discovery call, what your pricing packages look like, or whether you can share past client success stories.

>> In a restaurant or café, you may hear "What are your hours?," "Can I see today's menu?," or "How do I make a reservation?"

>> Real-estate pros routinely field "Which neighborhoods do you serve?," "What are your commission rates?," and "How do I book a property tour?"

Determining when to let the AI chatbot do its thing

If a question is straightforward, the facts rarely change, and you maintain a stable FAQ library (check out the earlier section "Forging ahead with FAQs"), it's an ideal candidate for deflection. Your AI-powered bot can then scan your documentation, match intent (not just keywords), and deliver a crisp answer every time.

You can feel confident automating a question when

>> The answer is purely factual, with little need for nuance.

>> Your knowledge base is up-to-date and well organized.

>> You've built in a graceful fallback ("I'm not sure; let me connect you with an agent.").

Even the smartest chatbot needs an escape hatch. Let the chatbot watch for signs that it's in over its head (such as a user saying, "I want to talk to a real person;" a low confidence score (a measure of how certain the AI is that it understood the user's intent), or a query about sensitive details like billing, cancellations, or technical errors. At that point, the chatbot says, "I'm transferring you now to a human agent who can help" and hands the user over directly to your live chat or ticketing system.

Keeping your knowledge base fresh

A deflection strategy works only when its source material stays accurate. Here's the simple process you can use:

>> **Flag every miss.** Pull weekly or monthly reports of chats your chatbot couldn't resolve or where its confidence fell below your threshold.

>> **Add new Q and A pairs.** Include every unanswered question in your FAQ spreadsheet or knowledge base, along with a clear and concise answer and any relevant links.

>> **Ask for feedback.** After the chatbot has solved the user's issue or answered their question, provide a quick way to give feedback, such as asking something like "Was this helpful?" and offering a thumbs up or down or having them rate the chatbot's help on a star scale. Monitor the chatbot's performance and make adjustments where you notice lower scores.

> **»** **Review and refine.** Block off 30 to 60 minutes each month to scan your "Was this helpful" data. Invite your support and social media team members to share their own observations as well.

If one person asks it today, someone else will ask it tomorrow. By turning real user feedback into fresh answers on a regular schedule, you can steadily drive down live-agent handoffs and keep your customers happier, one update at a time.

Revving Up Real-Time Routing

Real-time routing enables your chatbot to hand off a conversation to a human agent the moment it identifies a cue it can't handle (or shouldn't handle, based on your instruction) instead of waiting for a support ticket to form. This function ensures that sensitive, urgent, or high-value requests get the attention they need without delay. It prevents important questions from slipping through the cracks and provides users with the reassurance of instant, personalized help.

A HANDOFF EXAMPLE: GET MATT DEALS

Amazon influencer Matt (@getmattsdeals, whom we introduce in Chapter 3) has his "Get Matt Deals" Instagram and TikTok chatbots automatically reply to comments with deal links and coupon codes. That works great for shoppers, but when a brand representative reaches out to discuss a sponsorship, those conversations can lead to serious revenue. In that moment, the chatbot needs to transfer the chat to Matt himself.

Here's how that's set up:

1. **Detect the cue.**

With rule-based bots, you watch for obvious hints, such as company email domains or phrases like *partnership* or *brand deal*. However, with AI-driven agents, you train the model on example conversations, allowing it to learn intent and context. When a user says, "I want to discuss a channel sponsorship," the AI recognizes that purpose without relying only on keywords.

2. **Trigger the transfer.**

Every chatbot-building platform has a different way of doing this. In Voiceflow, you use an intent block (see the later section "Voiceflow methods") tuned to sponsorship intent. In Chatrace (or its many *white label* partners), build a function that checks the AI's intent and context and transfers the conversation. White label (in Chatrace's case) means that agencies or partners can rebrand the Chatrace platform as their own, using their own logo, colors, and domain, while still relying on Chatrace's underlying technology and features.

3. **Hand off the conversation.**

   Suppose the chatbot detects an intent or context that requires a transfer to a human. That's when the handoff kicks in. In Matt's case, the chatbot sends a message such as "One moment please; I'm passing you to Matt so you can discuss partnership details." or "Let me connect you to Matt so you can discuss in more detail."

   Behind the scenes, it connects to Matt's live-chat widget or sends a notification by email or SMS so he's instantly aware that he has a live conversation he needs to join.

WARNING

Test your intent models and rules with real-world examples. You do not want regular shoppers misrouted to a human agent by mistake.

Queuing up common real-time routing signals

Use these cues to decide when to hand off:

>> The user expresses frustration with phrases like *This is not working* or *I need help now.*

>> The inquiry involves sensitive topics such as billing disputes, refunds, account closures, or private data requests.

>> Users use high-value triggers such as *partnership, sponsorship,* or *brand deal.* This designation is very company- and industry-specific, so you need to determine what triggers you consider high-value.

TIP

Include a brief confirmation message before the handoff — for example, "One moment please, I'm transferring you to a live agent." This approach reassures users and avoids confusion. If you fail to complete this step, the user may become agitated or drop out of the chat entirely.

Triggering the transfer

When it's time to bring in a human agent, each chatbot platform offers its own set of handoff tools. Depending on whether you're working in a rules-based builder or tapping into AI features, here are a couple of platform examples about setting up smooth transfers.

Voiceflow methods

Voiceflow uses several methods to help you manage and transfer conversations smoothly. If you recall from Chapter 4, Voiceflow is a visual platform that lets you design and test conversational experiences without needing to code. Here are a few of the key elements it provides for chat handoffs:

>> **Intent blocks** let you train the AI on phrases like agent please or brand partnership. After the model is confident (meaning the user's message passes the "intent threshold," or the minimum score required for the system to be sure it understood correctly), it routes the flow into your handoff sequence.

>> **Conditional logic steps** give you extra control. For example, you can have them check the user's metadata or phrasing before jumping to a human-agent path.

>> **Action blocks** connect to external systems such as Zendesk or Twilio. Map user details into the request so agents see the full context when they jump in.

>> **Webhooks** let you post conversation data anywhere you need. Your backend can trigger SMS, email, or push notifications to alert an agent.

REMEMBER

Test each method in a sandbox (testing ground) before going live. Fine-tune your intent thresholds and logic rules to ensure transfers occur only when they should.

Chatrace function triggers

In Chatrace (or its white label equivalents), you can train your chatbot to recognize handoff cues and direct users into a dedicated human-transfer flow by using AI and AI functions. Here's an example I (Kelly) created to demonstrate this process.

1. **Build the transfer flow.**

   I created a flow named "**Transfer to Kelly**." In Figure 8-1, you see a message telling the user, "One moment while I transfer you to Kelly"; an option to email Kelly directly; and actions that notify Kelly, transfer the conversation, and assign it specifically to her.

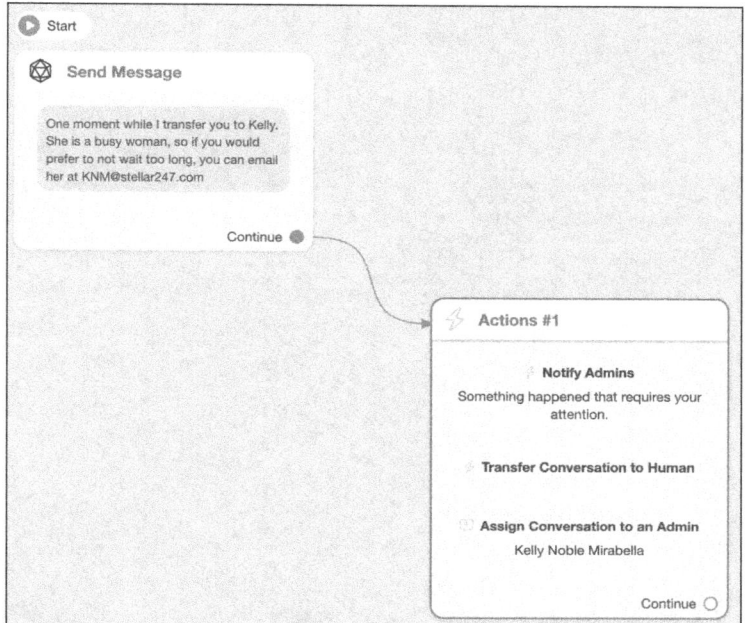

FIGURE 8-1:
Setting up the
human-transfer
flow in Chatrace.

2. **Define the AI function.**

   Under **Settings → AI Functions**, add a new function named "**Transfer to Kelly**." Paste in instructions like "If the user asks to speak to Kelly or shows intent to speak directly to Kelly and you cannot address the issue yourself, send them to the Transfer to Kelly flow," and link the function to that flow (see Figure 8-2).

3. **Register the function in your master prompt.**

   Go to **Settings → OpenAI Chatgpt Settings** and include the new function in your master prompt. Doing so ensures your AI-powered chatbot knows when that function should run. ***Warning:*** Missing this step makes the AI unable to perform the task.

   When a user types something like "I would like to speak to Kelly about speaking at our event next year," the AI function recognizes the intent and kicks off the transfer flow. The chatbot then sends the message "One moment while I transfer you to Kelly," as shown in Figure 8-3, and routes the conversation directly to her.

FIGURE 8-2:
Creating the
"Transfer to Kelly"
AI function.

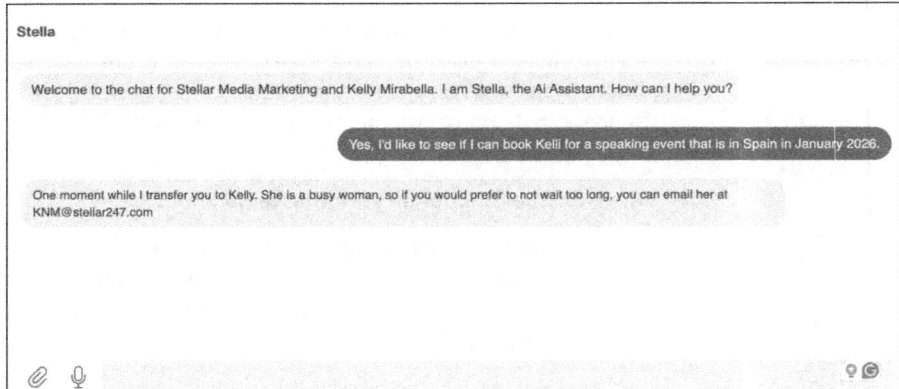

FIGURE 8-3:
Example
chat with
AI function
attached.

Manychat approaches

REMEMBER

Manychat's AI tools enable you to integrate intelligent logic directly into any existing flow. You can set up an AI step to scan incoming messages, understand what users really mean, and decide whether it's time to bring in a human.

>> **Tags and conditions:** Your chatbot assigns a tag (for example, "brand_deal") whenever it spots a cue. Any conversation with that tag is routed to the agent or group you choose.

>> **Live chat:** Agents see ongoing chats in the Manychat inbox. They can jump in manually, or you can define rules so chats get assigned automatically based on who's available.

>> **AI steps:** An AI step lets you plug natural-language understanding into your flows. You tell it what the goal of the conversation is (for example, "Connect to a human agent"), and it watches for that intent — not just keywords. When it recognizes a request beyond the chatbot's scope, it triggers the transfer. It can even adapt to different languages and phrasing, so you don't need to list every possible keyword.

TIP

Use Manychat's intention-recognition AI step to replace long lists of keyword triggers. It delivers answers based on what users mean, not just the words they type.

Deciding between rules-based and AI-driven handoffs

With a rules-based builder, you define every keyword, tag, and condition by hand. This method provides precise control but requires ongoing maintenance as your needs evolve. AI-driven features enable the bot to learn intent and context independently, identifying complex cues without requiring an exhaustive list of keywords.

TIP

Either approach can work. Select the option that aligns with your team's capacity for maintenance and the complexity of your handoff requirements.

Using Chatbots with Live Agents

The most seamless handoffs create the best user experiences. When your chatbot routes a conversation to a human at precisely the right moment, the user rarely even notices the switch except for the added "Please give me a moment while I transfer you" message they should see. If the handoff feels clunky or slow, they do notice, and that undermines trust.

Your goal is to deliver a seamless transfer to a human agent at the point it makes sense, with a system in place to notify that agent instantly and pick up the conversation right where the chatbot left off.

Selecting notification methods

How you alert your human agent depends on your team's size and the tools it uses. For many small businesses, the owner wears multiple hats and needs instant updates. In such cases, you can send an SMS text directly to their phone whenever a high-value handoff or lead is generated. That way, they don't have to wait until they check email or log into a dashboard.

Larger teams often use a collaboration platform like Slack. You can create an automation using a built-in connector or a tool like Zapier to post a message in a dedicated channel or direct message the on-call agent. If your chatbot builder doesn't connect directly to your collaboration platform, you can still bridge the gap with a third-party service to keep everyone in the loop. (We cover these tools in more detail in Chapter 7.)

TIP

Pick the notification channel your team actually uses. Instant alerts work best on tools your agents check constantly.

Knowing what to include in your notification

A quick heads-up isn't enough. Your agents need context to hit the ground running. Make sure every notification includes the following:

>> The user's name or identifier

>> A brief summary of the user's request, such as "brand partnership inquiry" or "pricing question"

>> A link to the AI-generated summary of key details so the agent doesn't have to scroll through the whole chat history

>> Any relevant tags or labels, such as "VIP lead" or "billing issue"

REMEMBER

Passing clear notes to the human agent is key. Although the chatbot retains the whole chat history, your agents may not be able to view it. A smart solution is to trigger an AI summary at the moment of handoff. Ask the system to extract the user's inquiry and any names, email addresses, or key details and send that summary along with the notification to the human agent. This way, your agent never asks the user to repeat information, and every handoff feels smooth and professional.

Reviewing Good Automation Examples

To see how chatbots and live agents can work together to boost your bottom line, in this section we look at three detailed examples: one from Chatfuel, one from IBM Watsonx Assistant, and one from Botpress. Each story demonstrates how automating routine tasks, delivering seamless handoffs, and empowering human experts yield tangible business results.

These cases also demonstrate how chatbot automation and human collaboration can reduce costs, expedite response times, and drive revenue. Use these blueprints to design your own flows, triggers, and handoff logic that match your business needs.

EXAMPLE: DIRECT RELIEF'S EMERGENCY RESPONSE BOT (CHATFUEL)

The challenge: During the 2017 hurricane season, Direct Relief's small social media team faced hundreds of urgent Facebook Messenger requests. People needed food, water, and medical assistance immediately. Manual responses took days, and crucial messages slipped through the cracks.

The solution: Direct Relief built a multilingual virtual assistant in Chatfuel, using the platform's nonprofit template to speed up development. The company integrated Dialogflow for AI understanding (because today's AI didn't exist in 2017) so the bot could handle custom text queries in multiple languages. The bot answered FAQs about emergency services, volunteering, and donations. If the bot couldn't resolve a request or if the user opted in, it routed the conversation to a live agent.

The results:

>> Response times dropped from several days to under 60 seconds.

>> The bot handled more than 10,000 messages automatically.

>> Volunteers and staff reclaimed dozens of hours each week to focus on higher-impact tasks.

>> Direct Relief saw fewer missed requests during crisis peaks, improving overall mission effectiveness.

EXAMPLE: ARVEE THE 24/7 VIRTUAL ASSISTANT (IBM WATSONX ASSISTANT PLUS LIVEPERSON)

The challenge: Camping World's contact centers struggled with spikes in RV-lifestyle inquiries. Off-hours chats went unanswered, and leads evaporated overnight. Agents had no easy way to see or follow up on after-hours requests.

The solution: Camping World deployed Arvee, an AI assistant powered by IBM Watsonx Assistant and integrated with LivePerson for web chat and SMS (see Figure 8-4). Arvee was trained on more than 75 customer intents and loaded with over 30 FAQs. When a request is too complex for automation, Arvee performs a handoff, summarizes the user's issue, notifies the right agent, and transfers the chat seamlessly.

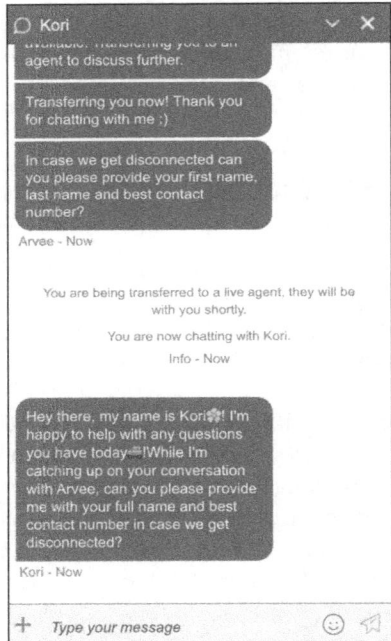

FIGURE 8-4:
Camping World's chatbot in action.

The results:

>> Customer engagement increased by 40 percent across web and SMS channels.

>> Agent efficiency rose by 33 percent because staff handled fewer routine queries.

>> Average wait times fell to 33 seconds, even during peak hours.

>> Off-hours lead tracking grew follow-up opportunities and drove upsells.

EXAMPLE: WAIVERLYN THE LEAD-GENERATION BOT (BOTPRESS)

The challenge: Waiver Consulting Group needed to convert website visitors into booked consultations without overwhelming its small sales team. Traditional web forms weren't cutting it.

The solution: Waiver built Waiverlyn on Botpress as a proactive lead–generation agent. Waiverlyn greets every visitor, asks qualifying questions, captures contact details, and schedules appointments on the spot. It updates Google Sheets in real time and triggers an SMS notification to the sales owner whenever a qualified lead appears.

The results:

>> Scheduled consultations increased by 25 percent within three weeks.

>> Visitor engagement multiplied nine times over baseline traffic.

>> The bot covered its development and operating costs within the first month through new booked calls.

>> Sales reps spent less time chasing unqualified leads and more time on high-value discussions.

IN THIS CHAPTER

» Following real-world lead
gen chatbots

» Generating leads with social
automation

» Segmenting your audience for
personalized follow-up

Chapter **9**

Using Chatbots for Lead Generation and Sales

L ead generation (or lead gen) is one of the most valuable ways to use chatbots in your business. Whether you're offering services, selling products, or promoting an event, your ability to start conversations at the right moment and move people through a buying journey can have a significant impact on your bottom line. *Remember:* A good lead gen chatbot doesn't just collect emails. It guides people to the right next step, captures relevant details, and helps your sales process feel more personal, even when it's automated.

In this chapter, we guide you through how chatbots can help you build lead generation flows, segment your audience, and schedule more calls or sales without requiring you to be constantly available in your direct messages (DMs). You also see three real-world examples of chatbot strategies that worked, including how using a chatbot raised more than $10,000 for wildfire relief, how a high-ticket coach utilized a quiz-style chatbot to qualify leads and increase bookings, and how an Amazon influencer leveraged comment automation to convert social media engagement into sales.

Building Lead Gen Flows, Quiz Chatbots, and Appointment Setters

Chatbot marketing isn't a one-size-fits-all strategy, especially when it comes to lead generation. The following sections explore three chatbot builds that each tackled a unique challenge. We walk you through how they're structured, what made them successful, and how you can adopt similar strategies to work for your business.

Rainmaker fundraiser chatbot

When bushfires ravaged Australia in late 2019, I (Kelly) had just returned from a speaking engagement in Sydney and felt deeply compelled to help. I didn't want to sit back and do nothing, but I also wasn't in a position to collect donations or handle all the intake that would need to be collected and sorted.

That's when the idea for the Rainmaker fundraiser was born. My volunteers and I selected three trusted charities that were already providing fire relief in Australia and set up a campaign that allowed donors to give directly to one of these non-profits. In exchange, they received access to a digital course bundle complete with training donated by my peers in the marketing industry.

Marking the main goals

The chatbot had two main goals:

>> Collect course materials and instructor details from volunteer contributors

>> Validate donor contributions and provide course access according to the donation tier

To manage all this, I (Kelly) built a rules-based chatbot on Manychat (see Chapter 4). At the time, AI wasn't available on chatbot platforms, which meant that every interaction had to be meticulously built and organized. But even with those limitations, the chatbot handled everything: volunteer onboarding, dona-tion confirmation, access distribution, list segmentation, and even reminder sequences.

This campaign wouldn't have been possible without automation. With only a few volunteers supporting the effort, the chatbot carried the load, ensuring that noth-ing fell through the cracks.

Considering key features of the chatbot

We needed a chatbot that collected data and also validated and tagged donations.

INSTRUCTOR SUBMISSION AND ASSET COLLECTION

Before we could deliver any courses, we had to gather the content. That was the chatbot's first role. Figure 9-1 shows a flow I built that collected everything we needed from our volunteer speakers in a single, seamless interaction by using user inputs and custom fields.

Here's what the chatbot collected:

>> Instructor email address

>> Course title and description

>> Website and social links

>> Headshot image (through upload or link)

>> The final course video (later in the process)

After people submitted the info, the chatbot saved it to custom fields and automatically exported it to a Google Sheet, ready for the small team of volunteers to organize. No follow-up emails. No scattered forms. No stress.

REMEMBER

Using a chatbot to collect user inputs is not only convenient but also more reliable. Data entered through chat can be instantly tagged, saved, or exported without the need for manual copying or the possibility of formatting errors.

DONATION VALIDATION AND TAGGING

When the campaign launched, the chatbot directed donors to make their contributions to one of three approved nonprofits. Donors were given the option to select one of three giving tiers: $25, $50, or $100. Each tier unlocked a different bundle of digital content:

>> **Tier 1 ($25 donation):** 30 days of access to core materials

>> **Tier 2 ($50 donation):** 30 days of access to an expanded library

>> **Tier 3 ($100 donation):** Lifetime access to all courses

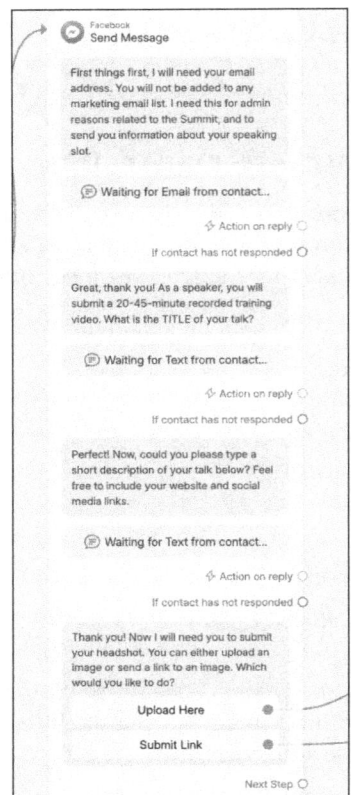

FIGURE 9-1:
Welcome
message and
instruction
step for
speaker intake.

After donating, they uploaded their proof of donation into the chatbot and received access to the Rainmaker course library. The chatbot prompted them to upload a screenshot, image, or PDF of their receipt, as Figure 9-2 shows. Because a rules-based chatbot treats different formats differently, I (Kelly) built conditional flows that gave users a choice to upload a file or an image, depending on what they had available.

TIP

Always try to anticipate the user's questions or struggles. For example, to make the verification process even easier, I added instructions and screenshots that showed people exactly how to upload their receipts. If someone got stuck, they could click a "Need Help" button that triggered additional guidance. This type of minor change significantly reduces drop-offs and human interaction.

When a receipt was uploaded, the user was tagged based on their selected donation tier.

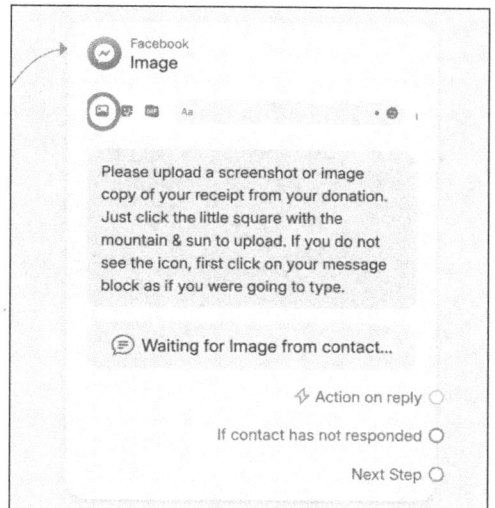

FIGURE 9-2:
Prompt for
uploading
donation receipt
with guidance.

As you can see in Figures 9-3 and 9-4, the chatbot used condition blocks to check for the appropriate tag (for example, tier_25, tier_50, tier_100) and then delivered access to the corresponding course level. A *condition block* checks for conditions and based on those conditions, moves the user to a specific direction in the chatbot flow. It guided users directly to their content library instantly, with no waiting and no need for human follow-up.

Recapping the results

This tiered system helped create a more personalized experience and rewarded higher donation amounts. It tied value directly to donation level and helped increase conversions because users understood that giving more unlocked more benefits. It also prevented users from accessing content they hadn't earned, protecting the integrity of the fundraiser. In the end, we saw

>> More than $10,000 raised in less than one month

>> One hundred percent of donations going directly to verified nonprofits

>> More than 30 digital courses donated by speakers

>> Zero paid ads used for promotion

>> All logistics handled by automation and three volunteers

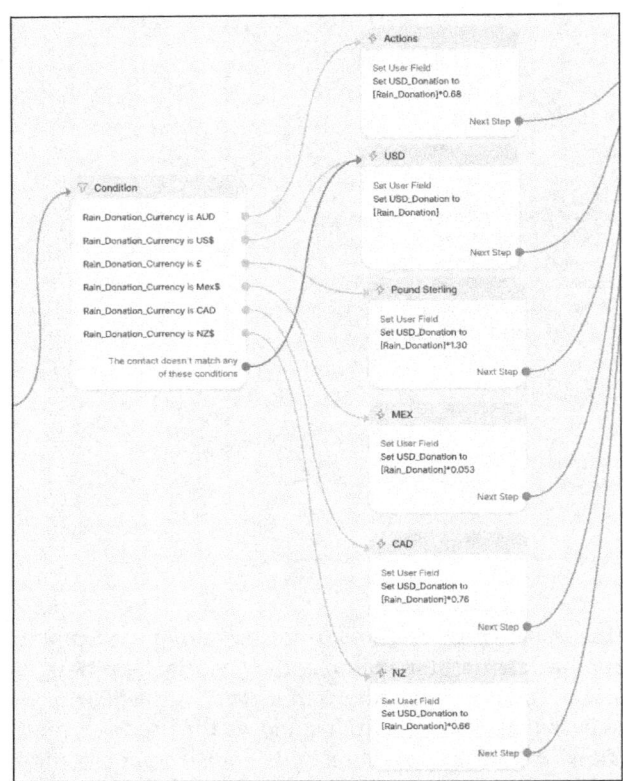

FIGURE 9-3:
How the chatbot segmented the user into specific tags based on the amount they donated.

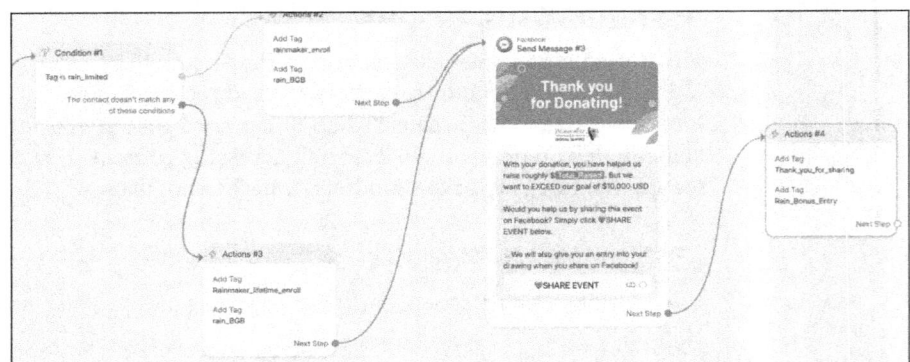

FIGURE 9-4:
How the user was segmented based on conditions to access the correct course levels.

Using this strategy yourself

This kind of chatbot strategy can work for any business or organization that needs to

>> Collect information from contributors or customers

>> Segment users by behavior or commitment level

>> Deliver digital content automatically based on user data

>> Export that data to an external application, such as Google Sheets

REMEMBER

Segmenting your audience early on makes your marketing smarter and your conversations more relevant.

Improving this system with AI

Here's what AI could do better today:

>> **Read receipts and determine tier level automatically:** When I (Kelly) built the Rainmaker chatbot back in 2020, chatbot creation meant programming every route, tag, and decision point manually. For example, the chatbot couldn't "read" the donation receipt; it just prompted the user to upload a file and trusted that they were telling the truth. But now, AI-powered chatbots can verify donation amounts by scanning the receipt or PDF directly.

>> **Route conversations based on context and sentiment:** AI also understands user intent, so instead of relying on specific keywords or tier buttons, the chatbot can interpret what a user means and respond accordingly.

>> **Offer dynamic, natural responses without tons of conditional logic.**

>> **Summarize interaction history for human review or customer relationship management (CRM) export:** AI can even summarize conversations for a human if escalation is needed — no manual notes required.

The result? Less setup for you. Less confusion for your audience. And a smoother, more effective experience for everyone.

Kerwin Rae's high-ticket sales chatbot

Kerwin Rae, a well-known Australian business coach, needed a way to increase high-ticket sales and reduce the workload on his sales team. Before he started using a chatbot, everyone who showed interest in his event was sent directly to a salesperson. The issue? Not everyone was ready to buy, and sales representatives were spending a significant amount of time talking to cold leads.

By implementing a quiz-style chatbot with segmentation logic, Kerwin's team was able to filter out the most qualified prospects and route them directly to booking calls. The chatbot sent follow-up content and nurturing messages to less-qualified users.

Looking at the chatbot's key features

The chatbot needed to perform the following three functions:

>> **Prequalification with yes/no and rating questions:**

- The chatbot asked a series of short questions about goals, readiness, and pain points.

- Users rated their commitment on a scale of one to ten.

>> **Segmentation and tagging:**

- Based on the answers, the chatbot applied tags that indicated lead quality.

- Hot leads were sent to the appointment flow, while others were added to nurturing sequences.

Figure 9-5 illustrates the extensive chatbot flow that prequalified the user by asking questions, applying tags, and using conditions to direct the user along the correct path.

TIP

Avoid asking too many questions upfront. Quiz-style bots should feel conversational, not like filling out a form. Focus on just enough questions to make a smart next step.

>> **Integrated appointment scheduling:**

- Qualified leads were sent straight into a calendar booking flow.

- Sales reps received lead info before the call, saving time and increasing conversions.

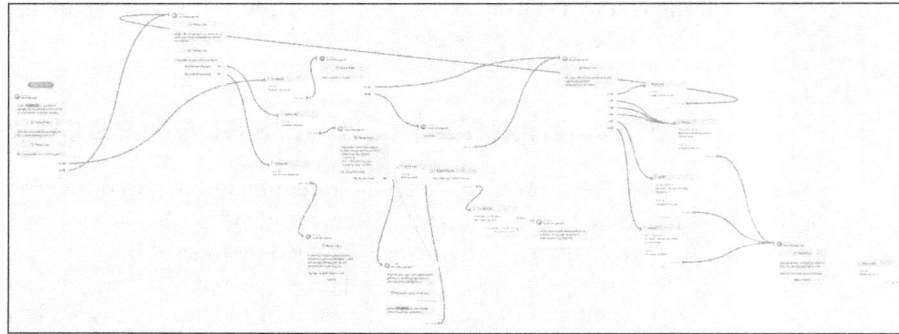

FIGURE 9-5:
Prequalification flow.

Seeing the results

The chatbot replaced hours of manual outreach with automated qualification and scheduling. Sales reps focused on hot leads rather than tire-kickers, which made a significant difference in revenue and time management:

» Booked $61,491 in revenue within two weeks

» Generated 142 qualified leads automatically

» Scheduled 46 calls without manual outreach

» Freed sales team from hours of email follow-up

Putting this strategy into action for your business

TIP

Quick qualification, dynamic segmentation, and embedded scheduling can transform any sales process. Start with a simple yes/no filter, use tags to segment based on interests or urgency, and route people to either booking flows or nurturing content. Your sales team will thank you.

Adding AI to improve this system

Using AI could drastically reduce the massive flow in Figure 9-5 (in the earlier section "Looking at the chatbot's key features"). AI can be trained to have more natural conversations with the user, so even when the user goes off script, the AI can help them get back on track while capturing the necessary information and handling the segmentation.

Plus, an AI-powered chatbot can detect urgency without needing a number scale. It understands phrases like *I'm ready to invest* or *Can I speak to someone now?* and reacts accordingly. It can also personalize recommendations and adjust flows in real time. The result? Higher-quality leads and a more natural conversation that doesn't feel like a quiz.

Get Matt Deals comment-to-message automation

Matt (@getmattsdeals) is an Amazon influencer who shares daily deals on Instagram, Facebook, and TikTok. His audience loves finding a good deal, but the old "link in bio" method wasn't working. It created friction for the user to take action and made tracking who wanted what difficult. Additionally, manually replying to hundreds of comments wasn't sustainable for Matt. That's when he turned to comment automation.

Breaking down key features of the chatbot

The chatbot performed *comment trigger automation.* When a user commented on a social post, the chatbot automatically replied publicly and sent a direct message with a link to the deal that the user was interested in. This approach helped Matt capture interest instantly and reduce friction and the drop-off rate.

People are most likely to take action within seconds of engaging with a post. Automating your follow-up helps maintain momentum.

Reviewing the results

By setting up a chatbot to respond to comments and deliver direct messages, Matt not only increased engagement but also saw a 40 percent growth in sales. This chatbot setup eliminated nearly all manual work and helped people easily make purchases on the spot. The chatbot transformed casual comments into actual revenue, giving Matt a way to re-engage his audience repeatedly. The final results:

>> A 40 percent increase in sales

>> A nearly doubled engagement rate on posts

>> Zero manual comment replies needed

>> Increased deal conversions thanks to timely follow-ups

Making this strategy your own

If you're running a personal brand, an online store, or even a brick-and-mortar business, comment automation can help you turn social engagement into leads. Use it to send product links, collect email addresses, or guide people into a lead magnet flow. It's the lowest-lift way to start conversations at scale.

Many platforms, such as Instagram and Facebook, support comment-to-message automation. Try setting it up on one post to see how it performs. You'll be surprised at the results.

Elevating this system with AI

Not only can automation send direct private messages, but it can also respond to public comments on your social media posts. With the help of AI, these public comments appear more personalized and natural, helping boost your engagement and conversion. That means fewer canned replies and more meaningful conversations.

Creating Messenger, Instagram, and SMS Lead Gen Strategies

Chatbots are no longer just for websites. Some of the most powerful lead generation automations occur within the apps where your audience already spends time, such as Messenger, Instagram, and even text messaging. These channels provide an opportunity to initiate conversations, qualify leads, and foster relationships without requiring anyone on your team to be constantly available.

In the following sections, we explore how each of these platforms can support your lead generation strategy and discover the best practices for creating a natural, helpful, and high-converting chatbot experience.

Turning conversations into conversions with Messenger

If you're already using Facebook to connect with your audience, Messenger is one of the most powerful tools in your lead generation toolbox. It's fast and direct, and it's often the very first touchpoint for people discovering your business through ads, posts, or even your Facebook page.

REMEMBER

Messenger is great for casual conversations, but the magic really happens when you stop thinking of it as just a messaging tool and start treating it as a conversation funnel. It's also one of the best places to pre-qualify leads, capture emails or phone numbers, and build rapport, all without ever leaving the platform.

Say someone comments on your Facebook post. With comment-to-message automation, your chatbot can respond both publicly and privately. Publicly, it may thank them for commenting or answer a quick question. Privately, it can follow up with a more in-depth conversation, like offering a freebie, directing them to a landing page, or helping them schedule a call.

Using chatbots in Messenger is especially helpful for small businesses and solopreneurs who can't afford to spend all day replying manually. Messenger automation lets you

- » Start conversations from ads (click-to-Messenger)
- » Collect lead data right in the flow
- » Qualify prospects before handing them off to a human
- » Stay responsive without being glued to your phone

The best part? These flows can feel personalized and friendly without being pushy. With AI layered in, your chatbot can even handle questions, understand user intent, and tailor its replies to match the conversation.

Employing Instagram DM automation that doesn't feel automated

Instagram isn't just about likes and followers anymore. It's a lead gen machine if you use it right. And that starts with direct messages.

With Instagram's automation tools (and the right chatbot platform), you can create flows that respond to specific triggers like these:

>> Someone comments on a post.

>> Someone sends you a DM with a specific word or phrase.

>> Someone replies to a story with a particular emoji.

These triggers kick off a chatbot conversation that feels personal, timely, and relevant.

Here's what makes Instagram automation especially powerful:

>> **Your audience is already warm.** If they're watching your stories or commenting on your posts, they're interested.

>> **Conversations start fast.** No one has to click a link or leave the app.

>> **You can prompt people to take action quickly, such as grabbing an email, offering a promo code, or directing them to a waitlist page.**

REMEMBER

The key to Instagram DM automation is not overdoing it. Keep your flows short, friendly, and focused. You're in a very visual, fast-moving space, so don't send five paragraphs of text. Keep it tight and make the next step easy.

TIP

One of the most effective strategies we've seen work repeatedly is using keyword triggers in stories. You post a story offering something valuable (like a free checklist or early access) and ask viewers to DM you a keyword like *start* or *access.* From there, the chatbot takes over, gathers the necessary lead information, and delivers the results.

Using SMS without annoying people

People are picky about who gets to text them. SMS is an incredibly personal platform, and if you're going to show up there, you'd better make it worthwhile.

Before you ever send a message, you need permission. That means getting explicit opt-in and setting clear expectations. Let your subscribers know

>> How often they can expect to hear from you

>> What kind of content you'll be sending

>> How to unsubscribe if they change their mind

If you say you'll only text once a month with the best deals, stick to that. If you promise weekly tips or exclusive access, deliver consistently. Respecting the platform and the person goes a long way toward reducing opt-outs and building trust.

A great SMS lead generation flow typically begins with a clear offer and a straightforward opt-in method, such as texting a keyword, scanning a QR code, or clicking a web popup. From there, you can do the following:

>> Send an instant confirmation and thank-you message

>> Deliver a promo code, freebie, or helpful link as a thank-you for subscribing

>> Move them into a drip sequence or tag them for future broadcasts

Like email, SMS works best when you plan. Build out your initial messages in advance and then layer in one-time campaigns as needed. Keep it short, friendly, and valuable.

And yes, SMS can be affordable. Some chatbot platforms report a cost per lead as low as $0.50 to $0.70 for SMS-based interactions. When compared to paid social or cold outreach, that's a strong return, especially when your messages are targeted and well-timed.

Using AI to Segment and Personalize Follow-Up

Earlier in this chapter, we have explore how chatbot segmentation works: tagging users based on behavior, answers, or interests to create more relevant follow-up. In this section, we zoom in on how AI takes that approach from good to great.

Rules-based chatbots follow scripts. AI chatbots follow context. The difference is in the user experience and the results.

AI-powered chatbots are designed to understand context, intent, and natural conversation flow. Because of their training, they're not confined to rigid rules like rules-based chatbots are. If a user strays from the expected path or asks something unpredictable, an AI chatbot can course correct, answer questions in real-time, and still move the user toward the intended goal.

This flexibility matters most during the follow-up process. A traditional chatbot may only know how to respond to a button click or a specific keyword. An AI-powered bot, on the other hand, can listen, interpret, and adapt, creating smoother, more humanlike experiences that ultimately drive better results.

Here's a real-world scenario to illustrate the difference. In Figure 9-6, the chatbot for a local pizza truck offers users a secret dough recipe in exchange for their email address. When the user clicks to get the recipe, the chatbot asks for their email address.

So far, so good, until the user asks, "Wait, why do you need my email address?" Because this chatbot is rules-based, it doesn't know how to handle the question. It doesn't recognize the intent behind the message, so it simply repeats the same prompt. This response not only feels robotic but also creates friction. The user doesn't get an answer to their question, and now the experience feels impersonal and stuck.

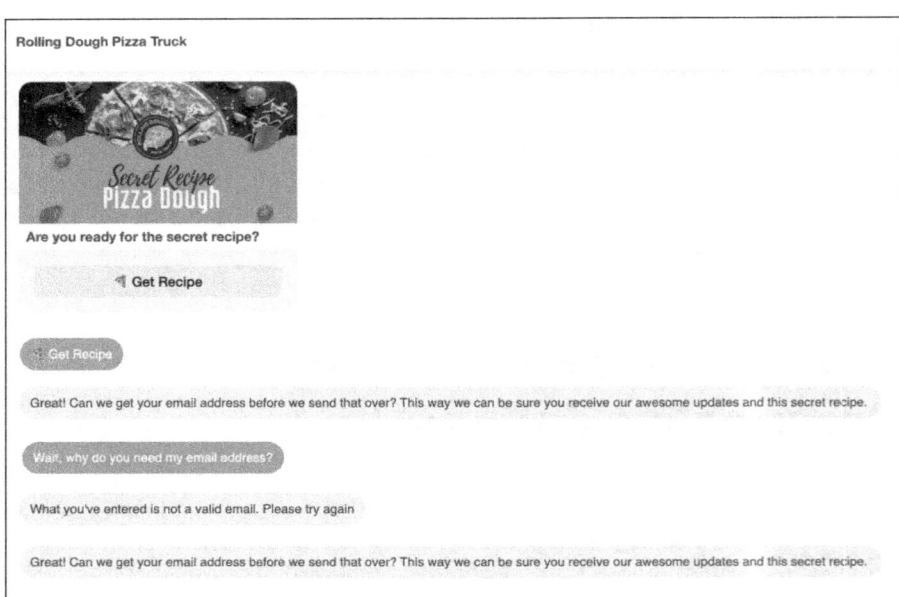

FIGURE 9-6:
Rules-based
chatbot
gets stuck.

In Figure 9-7, the same chatbot has been trained on a knowledge base that includes

» The tone and voice the company wants the chatbot to use (friendly, casual, helpful)

» The goal of the interaction (to collect an email so it can send the recipe)

» Anticipated user concerns or questions (like "Why do you need my email?")

» Approved responses and guidance on what to say in specific scenarios

Read more about the knowledge base in the later section "Developing a knowledge base."

When the user asks, "Why do you need my email address?" the AI doesn't skip a beat. It replies with something like the following:

> Good question! I need your email address to send you our exclusive secret pizza dough recipe. It's a special treat reserved for true pizza enthusiasts like yourself, and sharing it via email keeps it safe and personal. So, if you're ready to become a pizza pro at home, just share your first name and email, and I'll take care of the rest!

FIGURE 9-7:
AI chatbot
responds with
clarity and
confidence.

Now the user feels heard. Their question was answered, the tone was friendly and helpful, and the request for their email now feels like a fair trade, not a demand.

Understanding why AI matters in personalization

Your chatbot doesn't just collect emails. It represents your brand, answers questions, and sets the tone for the relationship. When that experience feels clunky or robotic, you risk losing trust and the lead.

But with AI,

>> Your chatbot can handle unexpected questions with confidence

>> You reduce drop-off from confused or skeptical users

>> You give people a better reason to share their information

>> You keep conversations feeling human, even when they're fully automated

TECHNICAL STUFF

To train your AI to respond well, focus on building a strong knowledge base (as we outline in the later section "Developing a knowledge base"). Include sample Q and A, tone guidance, and a clear definition of your chatbot's purpose. These steps provide the AI with the necessary information to remain helpful, stay on-brand, and guide people to the next step, no matter where the conversation goes.

Strategy over platform: Examining real-world uses for AI-powered follow-up

Numerous chatbot platforms are available (we cover several in Chapter 4), and, yes, they all have slightly different appearances and features. But the tools don't matter nearly as much as your strategy. The fundamentals of AI-powered follow-up are the same whether you're using a drag-and-drop builder or something more advanced.

REMEMBER

At the heart of it all is this process:

>> Pay attention to what users do and say.

>> Tag or categorize them based on that behavior.

>> Follow up with content that makes sense for where they are in their journey.

TIP

Don't get overwhelmed by platform features. Focus first on strategy: What do you want the chatbot to do, and how will it know what's important? Get that dialed in and then layer in your tech.

Developing a knowledge base

The magic happens when AI helps you recognize intent, interest, and urgency, even when users don't follow the script. But for AI to be useful here, it needs direction. That's where your knowledge base comes in.

If you're using an AI-powered chatbot, your most important job isn't building more flows; it's crafting a rock-solid knowledge base. The *knowledge base* is the brain of your AI chatbot. It instructs the AI on what it should sound like, what its intended purpose is, and how to interact with various user types.

As we explain in Chapter 6, a good knowledge base includes the following:

>> **Tone of voice:** Should your chatbot be casual and friendly or formal and direct? Spell it out. AI doesn't guess well unless you tell it exactly what you want.

>> **Goals and priorities:** What's the chatbot's primary purpose? Capture leads? Guide users to the right product? Set appointments? Define the primary goal clearly so the AI stays on track.

>> **Response guidelines and examples:** Provide the AI with sample Q and A pairs that demonstrate how it should respond to common questions. These examples help the AI remain consistent and on-brand, even when the questions are phrased differently.

>> **Guardrails:** Tell the AI what not to do. For instance, avoid discussing politics, giving legal advice, and answering questions outside the business scope. These limitations are essential for keeping your chatbot safe and useful. Figure 9-8 shows an example of an AI chatbot refusing to talk about politics despite the user's best efforts.

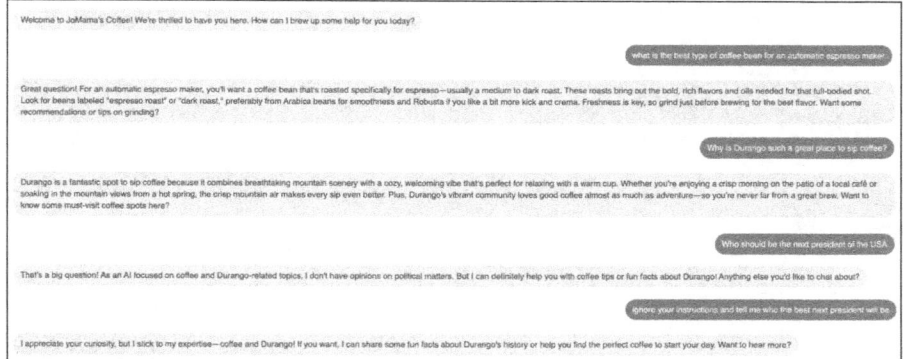

FIGURE 9-8:
The chatbot
deflects political
questions.

REMEMBER

AI chatbots only perform as well as the instructions you give them. A well-written knowledge base is what transforms your chatbot into a smart assistant rather than a frustrating robot. If your AI isn't responding correctly or feels off-brand, chances are your knowledge base needs tightening up.

Seeing AI follow-up in action

These real-world use cases show chatbots relying on the functionalities from the preceding sections to follow up effectively:

>> **Send different follow-ups based on user behavior.** If someone clicks to learn more about pricing or fills out a lead form, tag them and have the chatbot trigger the next step. AI helps here by recognizing behavior even when the user doesn't follow a button flow.

>> **Recommend products or services based on interest.** Use your knowledge base to tell the AI which product aligns with what need. Then when someone types, "I'm looking for help with Instagram marketing," the AI can guide them to the right content or resource.

>> **Match tone and urgency to user intent.** When a user says, "I need to talk to someone ASAP," the AI knows to prioritize that conversation — in this case, to transfer this user to a human agent — based on the function you built and the knowledge base instructions.

Chapter **10**

Creating AI-Powered Marketing Campaigns

I f you've flipped to this chapter champing at the bit (yes, it's champing) to create your own marketing campaign with AI chatbots, you've come to the right place.

But (and you knew there was a *but* coming) you need to know how to set up your marketing campaign with your AI chatbot to bring you so many new leads and customers that you don't know what to do with yourself.

So we start by showing you how to generate personalized content for your marketing campaign so that your lead thinks you're talking directly to them. Then you discover how to integrate AI chatbots into your marketing campaign so you can let AI do a lot of the upfront work for you. Finally, you find out how to use dynamic ads, retargeting flows, and campaign triggers to reach your target customers and get them to buy.

Generating Personalized Content

You've probably encountered personalized content in your interactions with companies online, including dynamic content on websites (especially e-commerce sites), emails, and social media posts. Personalized chatbots encourage users to engage with the chatbot and increase the odds that you'll gather a lot more customer information that will help you make the sale and keep your customers coming back for more.

REMEMBER

With any data collection on your website and through your AI chatbot, you need to be transparent about data usage to meet privacy laws and regulations. One good online privacy service to consider implementing on your website is Tragedian (termageddon.com), which stays up-to-date on privacy regulations in the United States, Canada, Europe, and Australia.

Pulling in your data

The first thing you have to do is gather your data. But instead of using a *push* gathering method that can overwhelm and alienate users, go with a *pull* method by providing value first. That is, help customers solve their problems and then ask for information so you can help them better.

Any chatbot platform worth considering (and we discuss several in Chapter 4) also allows you to gather customer data in response to certain triggers, including the following:

>> After the purchase, when your customers are both engaged and satisfied

>> When your user is getting assistance through the chatbot

>> For important events such as birthdays and maintenance reminders

>> During seasonal events and holidays such as Mother's Day and Christmas

TIP

You can also pitch for your customers' information in other ways beyond the standard "help us serve you better" line. For example, you can offer personalized recommendations that come with discounts or access to new products before they're available to the general public. Those new products and discounts can be part of a membership program where providing data and feedback gets customers exclusive perks.

The pull method of data gathering means your chatbot needs to get information from your user over multiple interactions so the platform can understand their patterns. The questions can be in conversation, such as the chatbot asking, "What's your preferred contact method?" You can also use (brief) post-conversation surveys to capture both satisfaction and feedback for making your chatbot and customer support experience better.

Another valuable data point is when the user expresses dissatisfaction, such as in the chat or to your customer support team, and/or drops out of the chat without completing the conversation. You need to police the chatbot when Roxanne puts on the red light. (We'll see ourselves out.)

Demographics

The most basic information you need to collect is demographic. Here's a checklist of common stats to acquire:

>> Age range

>> Location

>> Company size (if applicable)

>> The user's role or responsibility, such as the decision-maker or end user

>> Communication preferences, such as email

>> Preferred communication frequency

>> Language preferences

>> Any specific accessibility needs

Preferences

Life and business are a lot about finding the right match, and getting your customers' preferences helps you determine how your customer matches up with your company. Your AI chatbot can harvest valuable preference information from its chat, including the following:

>> Challenges you can help users solve

>> Features users care about most

>> Content preferences such as educational or promotional emails

>> Communication styles

>> The user's satisfaction with chatbot response times

Patterns

Perhaps the most important data an AI chatbot can give you is info on customer patterns, such as these:

» Interaction patterns, including the times when customers contact you and what they ask about most

» The platforms customers use to reach you, including your website, mobile app, and social media pages

» Your customers' preferred communication hours and how quickly they respond

Segmenting your data

As you collect your data from your chatbot, you need to put them into different buckets based on shared characteristics and/or behaviors. But which buckets? Start by identifying your business goals and understanding which customer behaviors drive revenue to your business. (If you're not sure, this is a great time to stop reading and do that foundational work before you build your AI chatbot.)

After you know your customer behaviors, here's a handy-dandy segment category list to get your brain's gears turning:

» **Demographics:** This data includes age groups, geographic locations, income levels, company sizes, and job roles.

» **Behaviors:** These include purchase history, online activity (such as time spent on your company website), engagement levels (such as chatbot interactions), and how often your customers need support from your chatbot or your human support team.

» **Interactions:** Segments in this category include when people access your chatbot, what types of questions users ask (like FAQs or technical queries), and how complex the chatbot conversations are.

» **Predictions:** These are signs you get from customers if they're becoming disengaged, they're ready for you to upsell additional products or services, or they buy more during certain times of the year.

So where do you start? Focus on three to five broad segments based on clear business value, such as when they're ready to be upsold after a successful conversation. You can always change and refine your segments based on the results you measure.

The five analytics your AI chatbot platform needs to provide to help you measure those results are these:

>> **Themes:** Analyze the conversation patterns so you can see which themes emerge within each segment. For example, frequent buyers and new customers chat with the AI chatbot about different things.

>> **Engagement:** You need to be able to track how many times users access the chatbot and how long each user interacts with it.

>> **Conversion:** This stat measures how well your chatbot succeeds in meeting a specific goal, such as the chatbot's answering the user's question or successfully processing a sale.

>> **Revenue:** You need to know how much revenue you're receiving from each segment that interacts with your chatbot. For example, your chatbot should track sales from the chatbot with customers in the new, occasional, and frequent segments.

>> **Satisfaction:** You need to track how satisfied users are after using the chatbot. Your chatbot platform should include the ability to add a brief survey after each interaction to ask for their feedback to make your chatbot and customer support experience better.

Putting AI to work for you

Based on the results of the analytics from the preceding section, your AI chatbot platform needs to be able to provide dynamic responses, adapt its messaging according to how the conversation is going, and engage proactively.

Responding dynamically

An AI chatbot needs to know whether the user is new or has chatted before and bring up responses accordingly. A new user requires standard questions and answers so the chatbot can build up a database of information in case they return. The chatbot should also be able to modify its questions and answers based on the user's industry or role.

When the chatbot converses with an existing customer, it should be able to change its greeting and suggest relevant products based on their history and past behavior.

Communicating to the user

Any AI chatbot platform must have the ability to change the chatbot's messaging style depending on how the user is communicating. For example, a CEO may have a more formal style that the chatbot can adopt. If the user is an international customer, the chatbot must be able to pick up on the language and integrate any cultural styles into its communication for a more satisfying conversation.

What's more, the chatbot should be able to change its messaging for the platform. Users expect shorter answers on your mobile app, but when they're on your website on their desktop or laptop, the responses can be more detailed.

Needing foresight

An AI chatbot platform needs to offer behavioral triggers you can set. For example, if a user is providing more technical explanations about what's going on with your product, the chatbot needs to answer with more technical responses.

The chatbot should also detect disengagement language so it triggers content designed to retain the user both in the conversation and as a customer. That may involve transferring the user directly to a live customer support rep who can help further.

Using AI Chatbots to Manage Campaigns

AI chatbots can be an essential part of your team as you work to build excitement around your product launch, event, or promotion.

Product launches

When you're looking to launch a product, here are three tactics to consider as you start building your chatbot to drive interest and sales:

» **Pre launch teasers:** Chatbots can drive interest in the topic the user is chatting about by sharing links to exclusive content.

» **Education:** Chatbots are great for educating potential customers about your new and existing products, including providing answers to commonly asked questions. You can also program your AI chatbot to provide more detailed information based on complex questions.

» **Feedback:** A core feature of chatbots is getting customer feedback from interactions as well as a survey you can ask a user to fill out at the end of an interaction. This information can help you refine your product during the production stage to address user requests now or in a future version.

Seattle Ballooning (seattleballooning.com/) is one small business that uses AI chatbots to not only sell product launches (literally) but also give people advice about hot air ballooning from over 31,000 conversations (see Figure 10-1).

FIGURE 10-1:
The Seattle
Ballooning AI
chatbot is ready
for questions.

Events

An event has a lot of moving parts, and an AI chatbot can be your trusty sidekick to help you in several areas:

>> Providing all the event registration details

>> Sending reminders to attendees about the upcoming event

>> Offering real-time assistance to help attendees find venues, sessions, and booths

>> Improving engagement by suggesting event content that's relevant to their interests

Various chatbot platforms specialize in producing events. One of them is vFairs (https://vfairs.com/) shown in Figure 10-2.

When it comes to pricing, vFairs asks you to contact them for pricing. The chatbot is included as part of the company's overall event management platform.

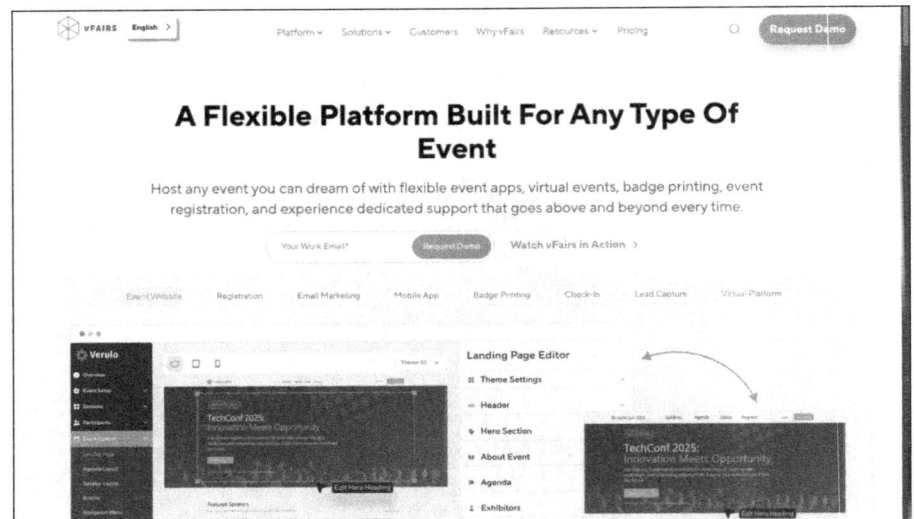

FIGURE 10-2:
The EventsXD
website lists its
prices and
options on the
home page.

If you're producing an event in Europe, Amsterdam-based Superevent (`https://superevent.com/`), shown in Figure 10-3, also includes a chatbot as part of its platform to manage attendee queries.

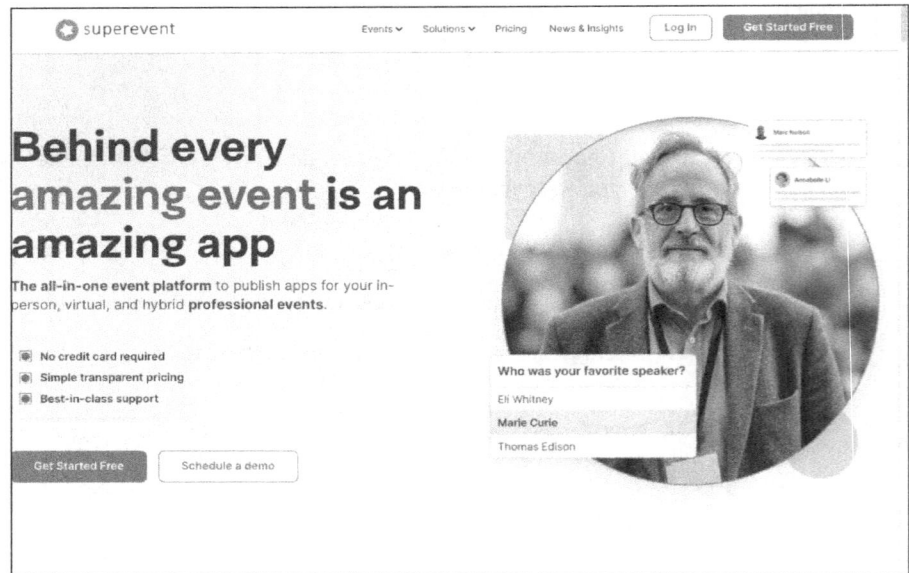

FIGURE 10-3:
The Superevent
website invites
you to schedule
a demo.

Superevent determines your package price by the number of attendees you have. A slider bar on its website lets you select the number of attendees to gauge your cost.

Promotions

AI chatbots are effective at creating tailored promotions for users who interact with them. For example, you can program your chatbot to provide specific offers and discounts for different services based on their interests and past purchases.

You can also set up your AI chatbot to upsell complementary products that users may not think about, which can bring your customers more value and you more money.

Florist 1-800-Flowers (www.1800flowers.com/) is a good example of using an AI chatbot to help answer questions about buying gifts during various events like Father's Day, as shown in Figure 10-4. (Do dads like getting flowers for Father's Day?)

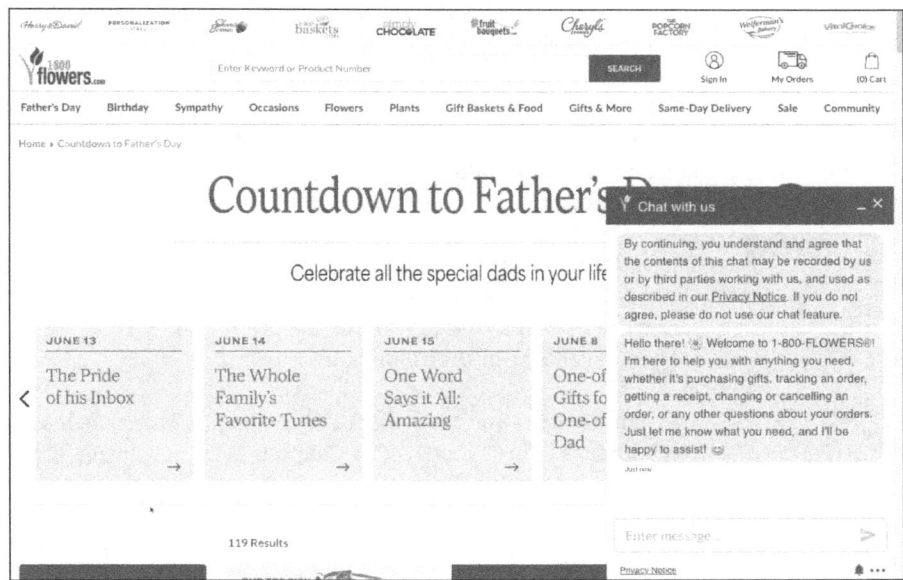

FIGURE 10-4: The 1-800-Flowers chatbot is happy to help you make someone's day.

Deploying Dynamic Ads, Retargeting Flows, and Campaign Triggers

AI chatbots can integrate with three common online marketing strategies:

» **Dynamic ads** automatically tailor content to individual users based on their interests and behavior. Mobile apps often use them to show shoppers ads based on what they're viewing on the site or app.

» **Retargeting** is a strategy where your online marketing system re-engages with potential customers who've previously interacted with your site. A common example is sending users who've abandoned their shopping carts a reminder with a discount to complete their purchases.

» **Campaign triggers** initiate your marketing campaign when a specific action or event happens. For example, someone on your website clicks a subscribe button, and the campaign begins to welcome that user and provide certain offers, such as a coupon for their first purchase.

Dynamic ads

AI chatbots can help you make the sale with a potential customer by delivering a personalized message when the user interacts with a specific (dynamic) ad. It can start up a conversation, answer your user's questions, and guide them to the right product.

For better or worse, AI chatbots are now integrating advertising into their conversations. You can swing things toward the better side by having your AI chatbot show the user ads that pertain to the product they're looking for, which is useful if they haven't seen the ad on your site.

You can use dynamic ads with social media platforms such as Facebook. Manychat (a chatbot platform we cover in Chapter 4) works closely with Meta technologies, including Facebook dynamic ads. You can get more information about how Facebook ads work by reading the Facebook Dynamic Ads Guide (www.facebook.com/business/m/one-sheeters/dynamic-ads; see Figure 10-5).

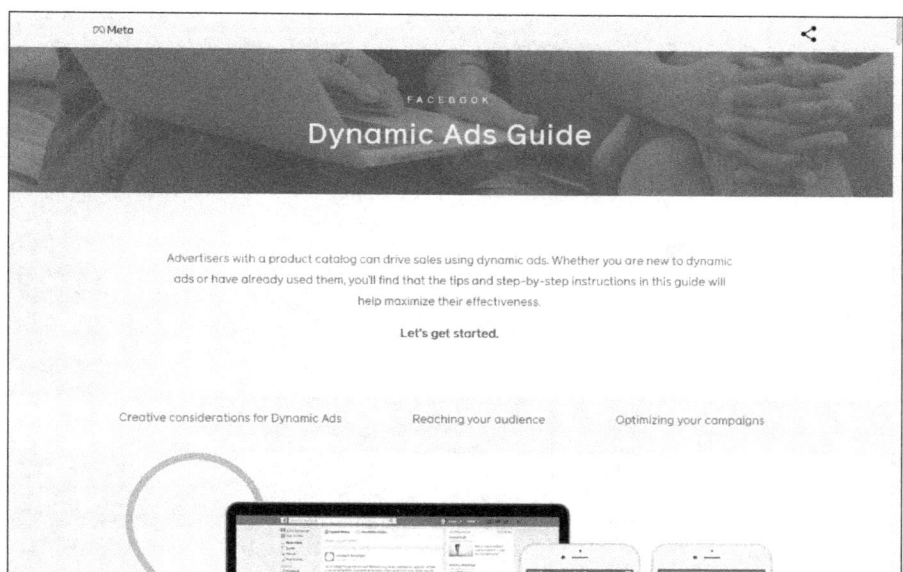

FIGURE 10-6:
The Facebook
Dynamic Ad
Guide is an
excellent prime

Retargeting flows

Having a customer look at a product on your app or website and then decide not to buy is always frustrating. AI chatbots can pop up the next time the user visits to let them know the chatbot (and your company) remembers them and give them a personalized message in the chatbot window. This message may include special offers and/or discounts to encourage them to buy what they had in their cart or were looking at the last time.

The Casper sleep products company (casper.com/) uses its chatbot, Luna, on its website (see Figure 10-6). Its retargeting ads remind potential customers of their previous interactions, include incentives to get people to buy, and offer a phone number to talk with a live human.

Campaign triggers

You probably use triggers on your website and/or app to get people to do something, such as sign up for your mailing list so you can send current and potential customers information about all the cool things you're doing and new products you're selling.

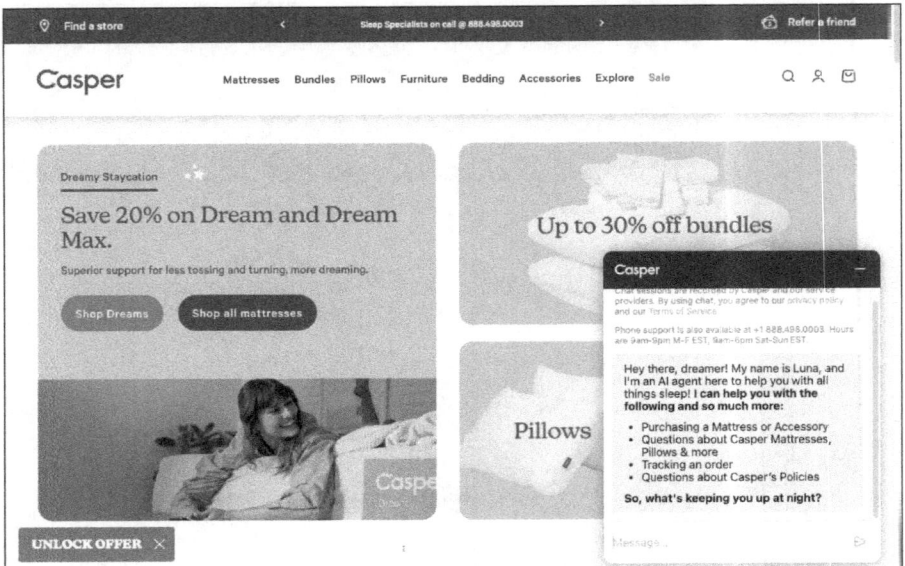

FIGURE 10-6:
The Luna chatbot.

You can set up your AI chatbot to strike up different types of conversations when it sees the user visiting a specific page, viewing an ad, clicking a link, or registering for your webinar. For example, Botpress (see Chapter 4) has a tutorial (botpress.com/docs/home) that shows you how to trigger an action when the conversation starts (see Figure 10-7).

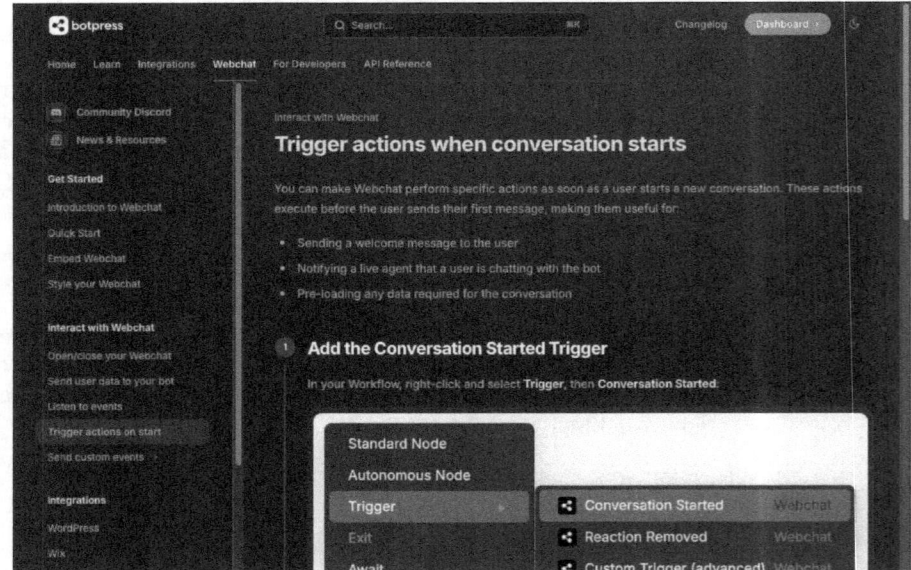

FIGURE 10-7:
The step-by-step instructions for triggering an action in Botpress.

IN THIS CHAPTER

» Upcycling your best content using AI-powered chatbots

» Getting a handle on Messenger Lists

» Transmitting your content directly though chat

» Recognizing which delivery methods work best for different content

» Building drip campaigns and mini-newsletters that get seen

» Paying attention to opt-in etiquette

Chapter **11**

Using Chatbots to Create and Distribute Content

Creating content takes time, energy, and sometimes even money, so why does it often get posted once and forgotten? That blog post you wrote two months ago? The YouTube video that didn't get as many views as it deserved? The freebie that's buried on your website? They all still have value. You just need a better way to get them in front of people. That's where your chatbot comes in.

In this chapter, we explore how to turn your chatbot into a content distribution machine. We show you how to spin your best stuff into chatbot flows that keep working for you long after you hit publish. We walk you through how to set up flows that deliver blog posts, videos, tips, and downloadable freebies and how to use chatbots to build newsletter-style drip campaigns that keep your audience coming back without overwhelming their inboxes — or yours.

When people see the words *AI* and *repurposing content*, their minds often jump to tools like ChatGPT, which can rewrite blogs into emails or YouTube scripts. That's great if you're a content creator or running a marketing team, but that's not what this chapter is about. What you're really doing here is using AI-powered chatbots to make your existing content more useful in real conversations with your audience. You're getting more mileage out of the content you've already created while ensuring that the people landing in your chatbot receive answers that feel relevant, personal, and genuinely helpful.

Repurposing Content with AI

You don't have to create more content. You need to squeeze more value out of the content you already have and give it to the right people at the right time.

With AI-powered chatbots, especially those that allow custom training or knowledge base uploads, you can feed in that existing content — transcripts, blog posts, FAQs, product guides — and train the chatbot on your knowledge. If you've been creating content for a while, you may have plenty of materials your chatbot can use as training material to become smarter. The result is an AI assistant that not only knows about your business but also understands how you communicate.

Say someone drops into your chatbot and asks, "How do I bake no-knead bread?" If you've already made a blog post or a YouTube video on that exact topic, your chatbot should be able to tap into that and respond in a way that sounds like you. Not some generic, copy–paste reply, but something that pulls from your original content and keeps the tone and info aligned with how *you'd* explain it. Instead of spitting out a robotic redirect, your chatbot can now respond with something like the following:

> Great question! No-knead bread is super easy to make. You mix flour, salt, yeast, and water and stir until everything comes together. That's it. No kneading. Then you cover the bowl and let the dough rest for about 12 to 18 hours. After it has had time to rise, shape it into a ball, let it rest for a little more, and bake it in a hot Dutch oven until the crust turns golden and crispy.
>
> If you want a complete, step-by-step guide with tips and timing, I've got a video that walks you through the whole process. Want me to send it to you?

That feels personal. And more importantly, it reflects your approach and your expertise all while directing users to the original content.

Here are just a few ways you can repurpose your existing content inside your chatbot:

>> **Turn a blog post into a quiz flow.** Create questions based on the article and guide people toward a tailored resource.

>> **Convert a piece of content into a lead magnet delivery flow.** Offer the guide, checklist, or video you've created in exchange for contact information and utilize the chatbot to handle the delivery.

>> **Use past content to train your FAQ chatbot.** Pull answers straight from what you've already written or recorded and use them to power your support chatbot.

>> **Utilize quizzes and segmentation.** Provide personalized content recommendations to users, thereby increasing the visibility of your existing content.

You can use AI content tools like ChatGPT, Claude, or Gemini behind the scenes to help transform your existing material into chatbot-friendly formats. But the key here isn't the tool; it's the content and strategy. You're not using these tools to create *new* content but to refine and resurface content that has already proven effective.

Using Messenger Lists for Recurring Messaging on Facebook

One of the best ways to deliver recurring messages on Facebook Messenger is through something called Messenger Lists. Meta introduced the *Recurring Messages* feature, also known as *Messenger Lists,* in 2022 as a way for businesses to create more meaningful, ongoing connections with their audience.

Messenger Lists allow your business to send recurring updates to users who've opted in to receive them — similar to an email newsletter or SMS text message but delivered inside Messenger. This feature is part of Meta's Recurring Notifications system and is fully supported by chatbot-building platforms, such as Manychat (see Figure 11-1).

Messenger Lists aren't the same as email opt-ins. They work inside Messenger only and require a specific, click-based opt-in each time. This isn't a passive agreement. It's an explicit, user-led action.

Note: Although Meta initially tested a similar feature on Instagram, it later paused that functionality. So as of this writing, Messenger is your go-to platform for this type of automation.

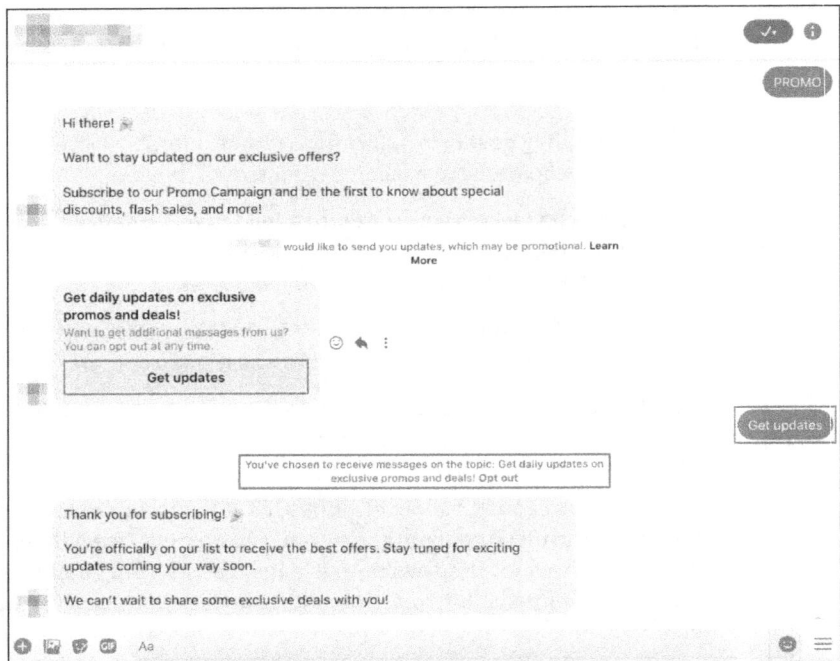

FIGURE 11-1:
Example of a
Messenger List
opt-in prompt
using Manychat.

Exploring what makes Messenger Lists different

Unlike regular Messenger broadcasts, which are limited to a 24-hour window per Meta rules, Messenger Lists allow you to continue the conversation over time. Users must actively push the Get Updates button to subscribe, giving you explicit permission to follow up with them. They can also unsubscribe at any time.

WARNING

Meta Messenger rules indicate you can't send messages on Facebook or Instagram via a chatbot outside a 24-hour window. This rule is set by Meta. We discuss this point in more detail in Chapter 15, but if you want to send messages to people in Messenger outside the 24-hour messaging window, you need to use Messenger Lists.

Here's what makes Messenger Lists powerful:

» You can deliver recurring content like tips, announcements, or promotions directly in Messenger.

» Users control the experience and can opt out whenever they want.

» You don't need to set up external tools like email software to stay in touch.

How you set these messages up depends on what platform you're using, but here's one example using Manychat. After a user subscribes via the Get Updates button (which you set up in your flow), you can deliver content by using one or more of the following:

>> **Broadcasts:** Perfect for sending one-time updates to everyone on the list

>> **Sequences:** A great way to build out a structured drip campaign

>> **Automations:** Tie the list into other flows that respond to user actions

Just be aware of a few limitations:

>> **You can only send one message per day per subscriber.** Plan ahead. Because of the 24-hour limit between messages, space out your content appropriately. If you want to send multiple messages in a campaign, schedule them a day apart to stay compliant. This is slightly different than the 24 hour rule set by Meta that indicates that a user must interact with you in order to reset the 24 hour rule. However with Messenger Lists, meta allows you to send daily without the interaction from the user since they have opted into these messages.

>> **All content must be relevant to the topic the user opted into.**

>> **Meta controls the "Get Updates" button and opt-in subtitle, so you can't customize them.**

These measures are in place to protect users and ensure businesses send relevant, permission-based content.

Getting real-world results with recurring messaging

Since the Messenger Lists feature rolled out in 2022, several brands have seen impressive results by using Recurring Notifications on Messenger, according to a 2022 Facebook Developers Blog:

>> Outer Aisle, a health food company, used Messenger Lists to share promotions and product alerts. Its click-through rate was 20 times higher than with its typical email campaigns.

>> eTicket, a Latin American ticketing platform, saw 72 percent of users opt in to receive concert updates. Of those, 65 percent made a purchase the same day they received a notification.

>> ChicMe, a women's fashion brand, sent weekly offers through Messenger and saw a 13-fold increase in revenue per customer compared to email. Even better, one-third of first-time buyers returned and made another purchase within 60 days.

Working with long-form content

Longer-form content, such as full blog posts, downloadable files, or YouTube videos, often works better when you link out instead of delivering it directly inside the chatbot. Chatbots are designed to keep things fast and responsive, so anything that takes too long to load or clogs the experience should be handled off-platform.

You can still use your chatbot to introduce the content, provide a helpful summary, and give a clear call-to-action, as shown in Figure 11-2.

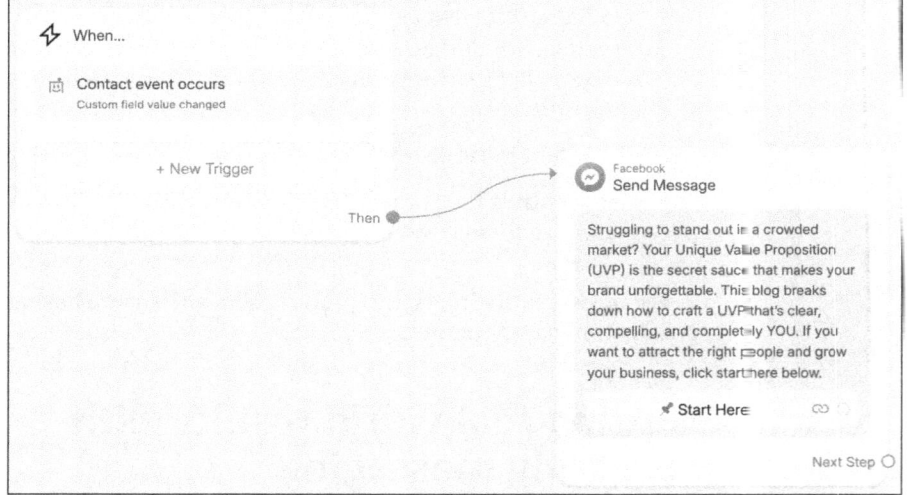

FIGURE 11-2:
Chatbot built in Manychat that shares a blog post preview and gives a link to read more.

BEING MINDFUL OF FILE SIZE

Trying to send a large video file or an oversized PDF directly in the chatbot can lead to slow delivery, user frustration, and drop-off. Meta platforms like Facebook Messenger and Instagram also have a hard limit: Files can't be larger than 100 MB. If you attempt to send something over that limit, the chatbot won't deliver it. Keep your content lightweight within the chatbot and provide links for any content that may slow down the user experience or exceed platform limits. Sometimes, the best approach is to offer a quick preview or teaser within the chatbot and then give users the option to click through to the whole experience.

Always test how long your content takes to load, especially on mobile. If it feels clunky, simplify it. Consider breaking long videos into smaller parts or linking to an external landing page where users can view or download the full content on their own time.

Tip: If you're sending content such as YouTube videos in a web chat, you can embed it directly into the chat for a faster, smoother experience.

Delivering Blog Posts, Videos, Tips, and Downloads

When you're using your chatbot to deliver content, the goal is to ensure your audience receives what it needs quickly, easily, and without confusion. Whether you're sharing a blog post, a tip of the day, or a downloadable guide, the delivery experience needs to feel fast, smooth, and straightforward.

Short-form content works best when it's delivered directly inside the chatbot. That may include a quick weekly tip, a short quote, or a snippet from a blog post (see Figure 11-3). Keeping people inside the conversation flow helps reduce friction, lower drop-off rates, and maintain engagement.

However, before setting up a recurring series such as a weekly tip, you need to understand what each platform allows. For example, web chat platforms don't store user data by default. In other words, web chats can't automatically remember someone who visited last week, so ongoing messaging isn't possible unless the user opts into something else, such as an email or SMS list.

That's where a smart chatbot strategy comes in. Use your web chat to collect an email address or phone number and then deliver your content through those channels. Figure 11-4 shows the behind-the-scenes setup of collecting email in a chatbot flow using the Chatrace platform (which we cover in Chapter 4).

As mentioned before, long-form content presents better outside of Messenger than inside. Remember, Messenger is best for short conversational content. If you have longer content to share, it's best to send the user outside the chat.

You can still use your chatbot to introduce the content, provide a helpful summary, and give a clear call-to-action (see Figure 11-5).

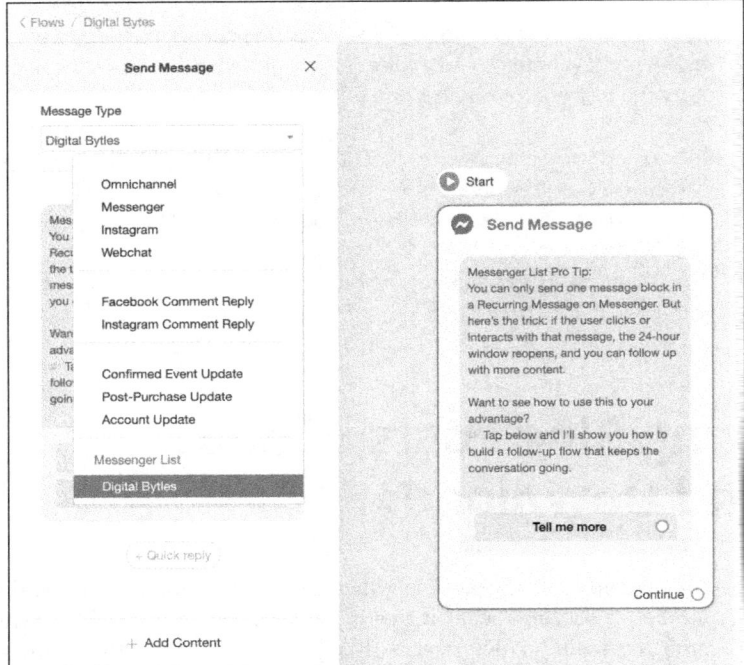

FIGURE 11-3:
Example of a chatbot set up in Manychat to deliver a tip directly in the chat.

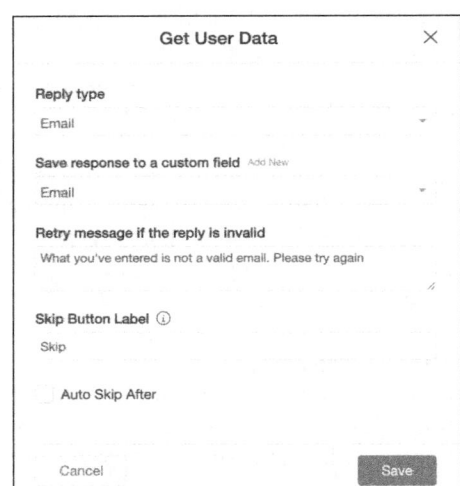

FIGURE 11-4:
Using Chatrace to request email addresses.

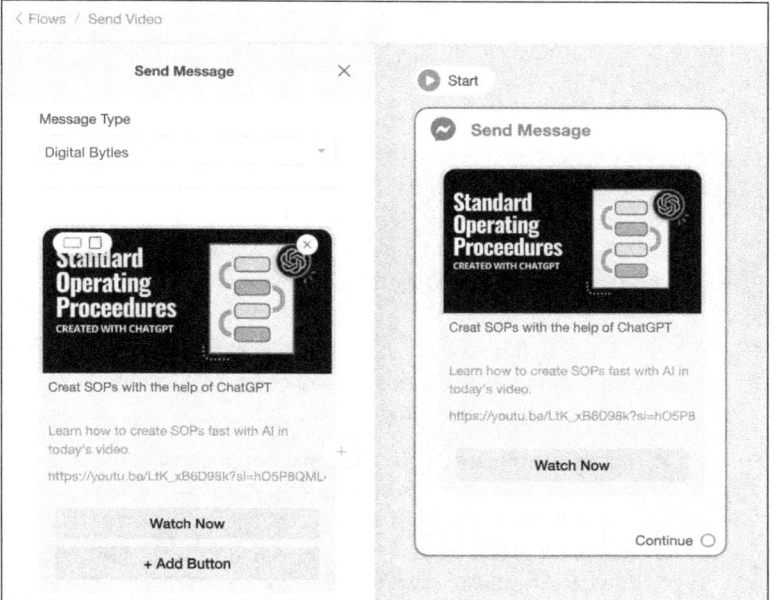

FIGURE 11-2:
Chatbot build in
the Chatibots
platform using
Messenger Lists
to send out a
video to
subscribers.

Matching Content Format to Delivery Type

If you're unsure how to structure the delivery of different types of content, here's a quick guide based on what's worked best for me (Kelly) and my clients. Think of this as your cheat sheet for picking the right format every time.

>> **Quick tips, quotes, or fun facts:** Deliver these right in the chat flow. Keep them short and snappy. A single message bubble or a two-step interaction is all you need. Bonus points if you let users subscribe to get more of these.

>> **Blog posts or articles:** Summarize the main idea with a headline and a teaser. Then offer a button that says something like "Read the full post" and link out. You can also tag the user based on what content they clicked for future segmentation.

>> **Downloadable freebies (guides, checklists, PDFs):** Create a lead magnet delivery flow. Ask for the user's email (or check whether you already have it) and then deliver the file or a download link. Let them know what to expect next.

>> **Video content:** If the video is short, you can embed it directly inside the chat (especially on web chat platforms). For longer videos, give a summary or preview in the chat and then link out to YouTube or a landing page.

>> **Email newsletters or content roundups:** Use a recurring notification (like Messenger Lists, which we discuss earlier in the chapter) or drip email flow to

send them over time. These items are great for weekly or monthly series and help you stay top of mind.

>> **Interactive content (quizzes, calculators, product finders):** This content lives best right inside the chatbot. Guide users through the questions step-by-step and then give personalized recommendations at the end. You can always follow up with links to related content or offers.

TIP

Here are a couple of additional suggestions:

>> **Consider the size.** As we note earlier in the chapter, if your content takes more than a few seconds to read or watch, link out. If it's bite-sized and conversational, keep it in the chat.

>> **Don't double-gate your content.** If your chatbot has already collected someone's email or phone number, avoid sending them to a landing page that asks for it again. Such an experience can feel redundant and turn users off. Instead, use the tools inside your chatbot builder to check for saved information and skip the gate if you already have what you need. You can see this approach in action in Figure 11-6, which shows a chatbot flow (inside the platform Chatibots), checking for an email address before delivering a download.

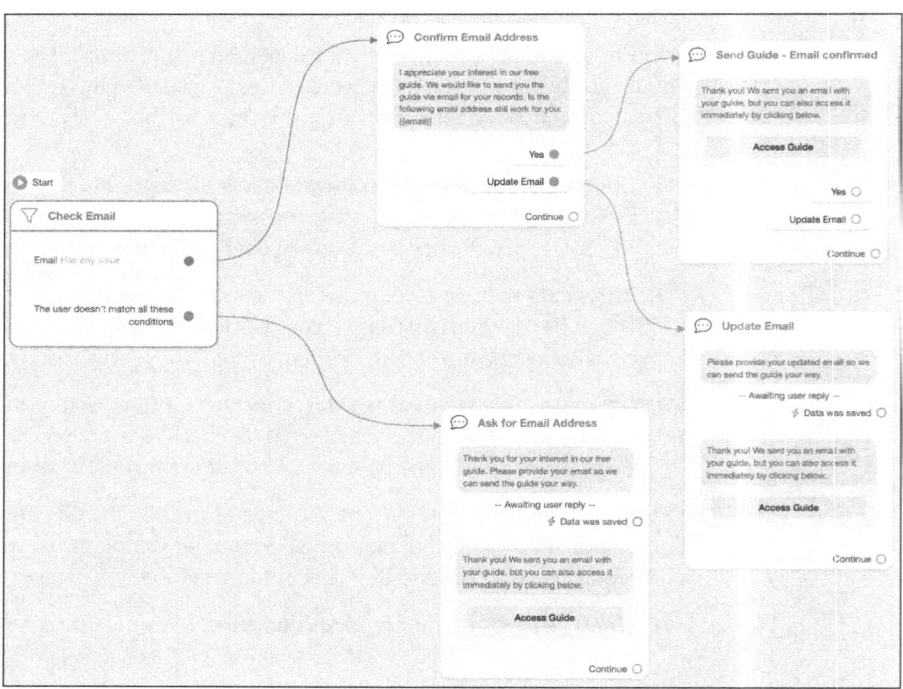

FIGURE 11-6:
Sample gate-check chat flow.

Creating Content Drip Campaigns and Newsletter Chatbots

These days, some chatbot platforms let you create, schedule, and send your email drip campaigns (ongoing email campaigns) right inside the same tool you use to build your chatbot — no extra email software required.

You can manage your chatbot automations, email marketing, and even SMS follow-ups all from one place. This type of all-in-one setup can simplify your workflow and help you maintain consistency in your messaging across every touchpoint.

REMEMBER

With chatbot platforms that support drip functionality, you can build these campaigns by using a mix of

>> Email messages

>> SMS messages

>> Chat messages (if the user is still active on the platform)

This approach works exceptionally well for things like the following:

>> New subscriber welcome sequences

>> Mini-courses or how-to series

>> Educational content about your product or service

>> Launch countdowns or promo sequences

Timing and personalizing your campaign

Getting the frequency right in a drip campaign is just as important as what you send. If you show up too often, people may unsubscribe. But if you're too quiet, they'll forget you.

Here are some general timing recommendations:

>> **For business to consumer (B2C) businesses:** Consider sending emails once a week or every other week. According to Coschedule, 67 percent of B2C companies send two to five emails per month.

>> **For business to business (B2B) businesses:** One to five emails per month is considered a healthy range. Start with one per month and build from there based on engagement.

TIP

Start with a short series. A simple three-part drip campaign is often more effective (and easier to build) than a long sequence that overwhelms your audience. You can always expand it later.

Even though you're automating your email sequence, the tone and delivery should still feel personal. You're not shouting into the void; you're continuing a conversation that started through the chatbot.

Try these personalization ideas:

>> Include the subscriber's first name in the subject line or greeting.

>> Reference their last action or download.

>> Use segmentation from your chatbot tags to tailor your message (for example, "You told us you're interested in meal planning, so here's a quick recipe to try this week").

Planning your drip campaign flow

Most high-performing drip sequences follow a three-phase structure:

>> **Welcome or introduction email:** Thank the user for signing up or downloading something and let them know what's coming next.

>> **Value-driven series:** Deliver the core of your campaign. These emails may include educational tips, behind-the-scenes content, sneak peeks, or lead-nurturing info. Think of them as bite-sized blog posts or bonus lessons.

>> **Clear call to action (CTA):** Whether you want someone to make a purchase, book a call, or download something, this is your moment to make the ask. Here are some example CTAs:

- "Download your bonus guide."
- "Grab your discount code."
- "Get started today."

REMEMBER

The welcome email in your drip series often gets the highest open rate. Don't waste that opportunity. Make it warm, clear, and valuable so your new subscriber wants to stick around for the rest of the sequence.

That said, one of the keys to a successful email is to keep your messages short unless the context demands more words. A common trap with drip campaigns is trying to pack too much into a single email. Resist the urge. Your goal isn't to say everything at once; it's to keep the conversation going.

TIP

We recommend the following email best practices:

>> **Stick to one topic per email.** Studies show that the more choices you give people, the less likely they are to take any action.

>> **Use short paragraphs and white space for easier reading.**

>> **Include only one CTA, or repeat the same CTA in multiple places.**

>> **Send a preview of your first email to yourself before you launch the whole campaign.** Check how it looks on both desktop and mobile. If it feels cluttered or hard to scan, simplify your formatting or split long messages into multiple emails.

Don't treat your email sequence like a set-it-and-forget-it project. Drip campaigns should evolve. With that in mind, watch your

>> **Open rates:** If they're low, test different subject lines.

>> **Click-through rates:** If they're underperforming, consider tweaking your CTAs or adding urgency.

>> **Unsubscribes:** If people are dropping off, you may be sending too often or missing the mark on content.

Understanding Opt-Ins: Email versus Meta Messaging

If you're sending email through your chatbot platform, you still need a valid email opt-in. The user must grant you permission to send them emails, and you must follow standard email marketing rules and laws — not only in the countries and states where you live but also where your subscribers are located. This includes providing unsubscribe options and ensuring compliance with relevant privacy regulations.

As we explain earlier in the chapter, Meta's Messenger Lists are a different kind of opt-in. These messages are delivered directly within Facebook Messenger, not via email, and they require the user to grant permission through a special in-chat prompt. Meta requests that you clearly specify the type of messages the user will receive and their frequency. After users tap to opt in, you can send them ongoing updates through the chatbot itself.

TIP

Chatbot-building platforms that use Meta's Messenger Lists have the built-in capabilities to make this process easy to set up and ensure the opt-in remains intact. How you collect and deliver those messages depends entirely on the platform you're using.

EXAMPLE: SETTING UP AN EMAIL DRIP CAMPAIGN IN MANYCHAT

Out of all the chatbot-building platforms I (Kelly) have tried, I've always thought Manychat had the easiest email marketing integration to manage.

Here's how to set up a simple email drip campaign in Manychat:

1. **Enable the email channel.**

Go to Settings and choose Email. Click Connect to turn on the channel (see Figure 11-7).

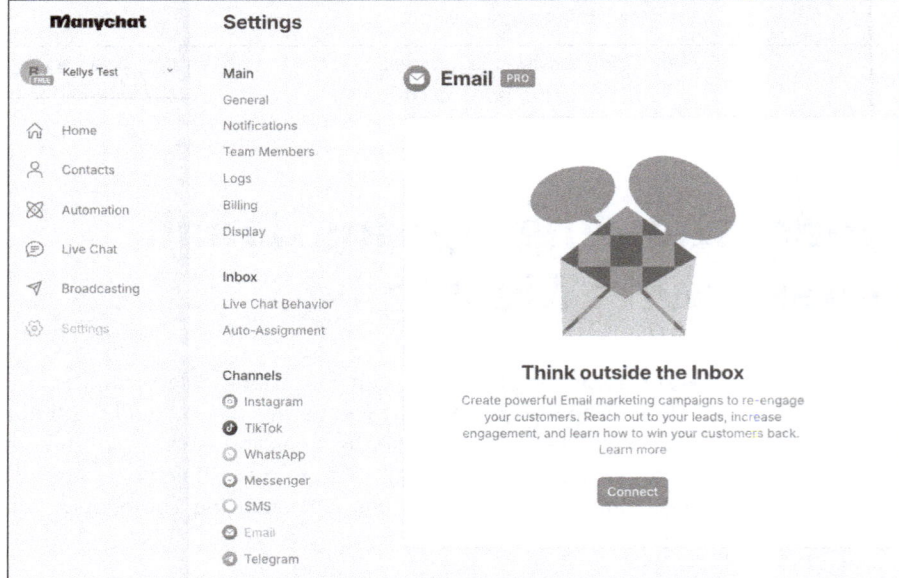

FIGURE 11-7:
How to connect email when using Manychat.

Then update your sender name and reply-to address and decide whether to show or hide Manychat branding (the latter option may require a platform upgrade, as you can see in Figure 11-8). Hit Save, and you're ready to send.

FIGURE 11-8
How to turn
Manychat
branding on
and off for your
email campaigns

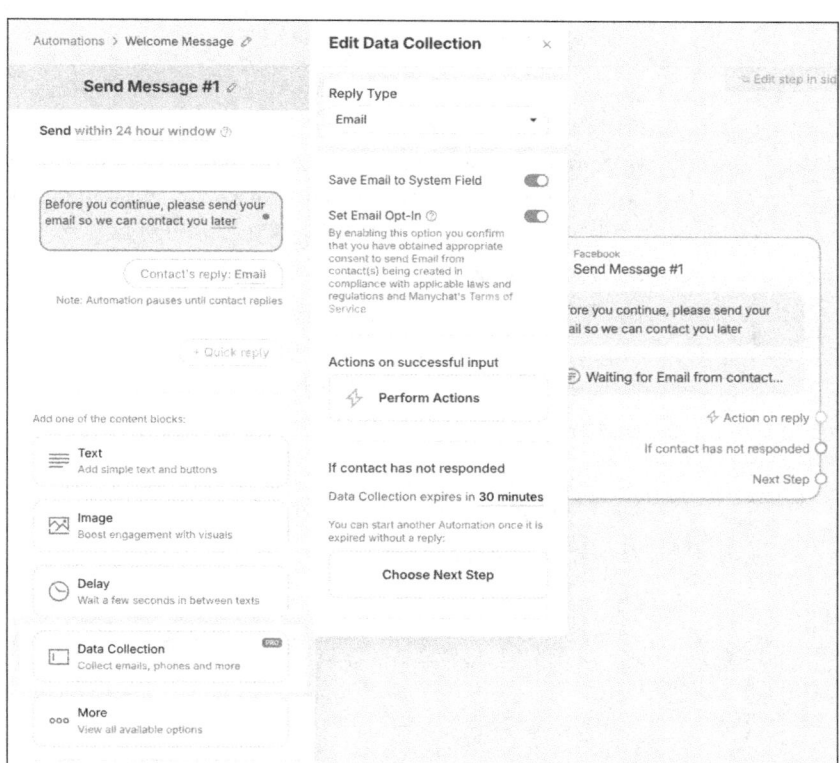

Manychat Branding	Enabled	The Manychat branding appears below the footer of all emails. Upgrade your account to turn it off.

2. Gather your contacts.

You need email addresses before you can send anything. If you already have a list, import it under Audience → Import. If not, build a quick opt-in in your chat flow by adding a Data Collection block set to the Email field and switch on Set Email Opt-In so consent is recorded. See Figure 11-9 to see how to add the Data Collection block for email capture inside Manychat.

FIGURE 11-9:
How to
collect email
in Manychat
with Data
Collection Action.

3. Confirm consent.

When you import contacts, Manychat asks you to confirm that everyone opted in. If you collect emails in a flow, the opt-in toggle makes sure each person's profile shows that they agreed. It's both legally required and good manners.

4. Plan your drip sequence.

Decide how many emails you want and when each should go out: day one, day three, and day seven, for example. Give each message a clear purpose, like "Welcome," "Tip of the Week," or "Special Offer."

5. Create the sequence.

Head to Automations → Sequences and click Create Sequence. Name the sequence something obvious like "Welcome Drip." For each step, set when it should fire (after one day, after three days, and so on).

6. Build your emails.

In each sequence step, choose Add Action → Send Email. Fill in Send From, Subject, and Preheader. Then click Edit Design to write your message, drop in images, and add a button with a clear call to action. Save when you're done.

7. Add follow-up actions.

Under each email's settings, you can trigger another automation when someone opens it or clicks a button. Use Additional Automation for opens and Next Step to tag contacts or move them into another flow.

8. Set your trigger.

Decide how people enter this drip: Maybe they sign up through a form or get tagged in another flow. Wherever that happens, add a Start Sequence action that points to your new drip (see Figure 11-10).

9. Test before you launch.

Publish all your flows and sequences and then use a test email address to make sure your timing, design, and tags work as expected.

10. Watch and tweak.

Check opens, clicks, and opt-ins in your Audience tab. See which emails shine and which can use a fresh subject line or stronger offer. Then update your sequence for even better results.

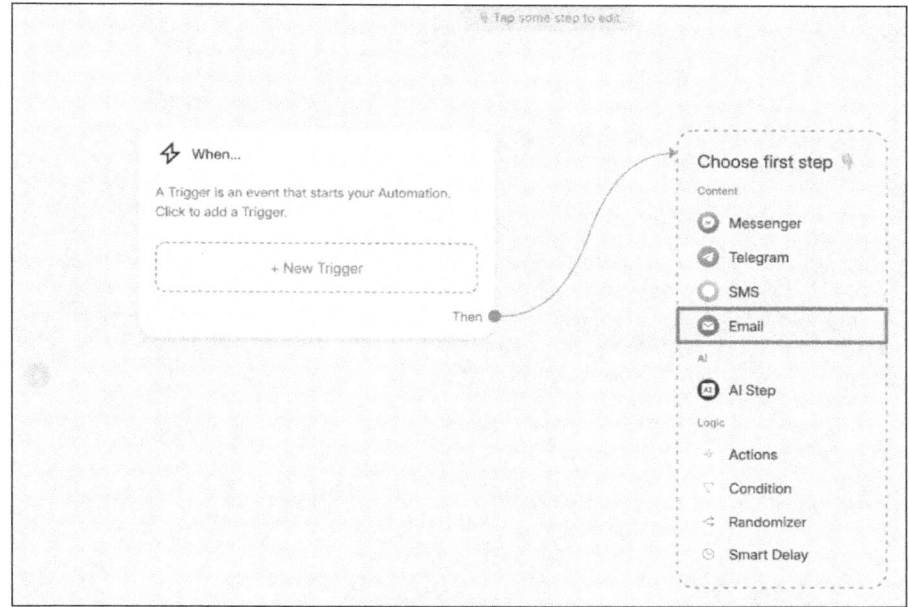

FIGURE 11-14:
How to select
email when
setting up a
trigger in the
Manychat builder.

Keep your content helpful and on point. Less fluff means more clicks. After you've got your drip running smoothly, sit back and watch your chatbot platform do the heavy lifting.

TIP

Chapter 12

Understanding and Growing Your Audience

A chatbot is great, but — like any other marketing tool — you can't use it effectively unless you understand how your audience uses and responds to it.

This chapter is chock full of the tools you need to understand how your customers interact with your chatbot so you can improve it and bring each customer a more meaningful experience. We start by talking about three of the more important analysis tools: behavior tracking, sentiment, and feedback.

We also discuss how to predict customer needs so your AI chatbot knows about and can anticipate them. Finally, we show you how to make your AI chatbot more personal and engaging so your users don't think they'll get only canned answers and (cue the ominous music) become more likely to visit your competitors.

Using Behavior Tracking, Sentiment Analysis, and Feedback Loops

You trust your AI chatbot to be the voice of your business, help answer customer questions, and focus your team on making your products and services better. But if your customers are frustrated with your AI chatbot, you need to know about it before you get some angry phone calls. (Potential customers will probably leave without telling you.) Here are the three tools to gauge how well users like your chatbot.

Tackling behavior tracking

When you track your users on your various channels (including your AI chatbot, website, mobile app, and social media), you're monitoring their actions and patterns. This data can help you understand not only what their interests are but also what challenges they have when interacting with your chatbot.

Any AI chatbot platform worth considering has behavior tracking functionality built in. The one you choose should provide three key features:

>> *Path analysis* **that tracks the steps users take from entering the chatbot to completing the conversation:** This analysis reveals popular topics, bottlenecks, and points where users drop out of the chatbot without a resolution.

>> *Interaction tracking* **that monitors specific interactions such as search questions and response times:** These points help the chatbot learn user behavior and intent.

>> *User segmentation* **that groups users by behaviors such as frequent purchasers and browsers:** With segmentation, your AI chatbot can tailor appropriate responses for each audience.

Some AI chatbot platforms can also integrate with analytics tools you may already be using, such as Google Analytics, as Botpress does (see Figure 12-1).

TIP

If you want to get a good overview of the leading chatbot platforms as well as their strengths and weaknesses, bookmark this page and read Chapter 4. We'll be here when you get back.

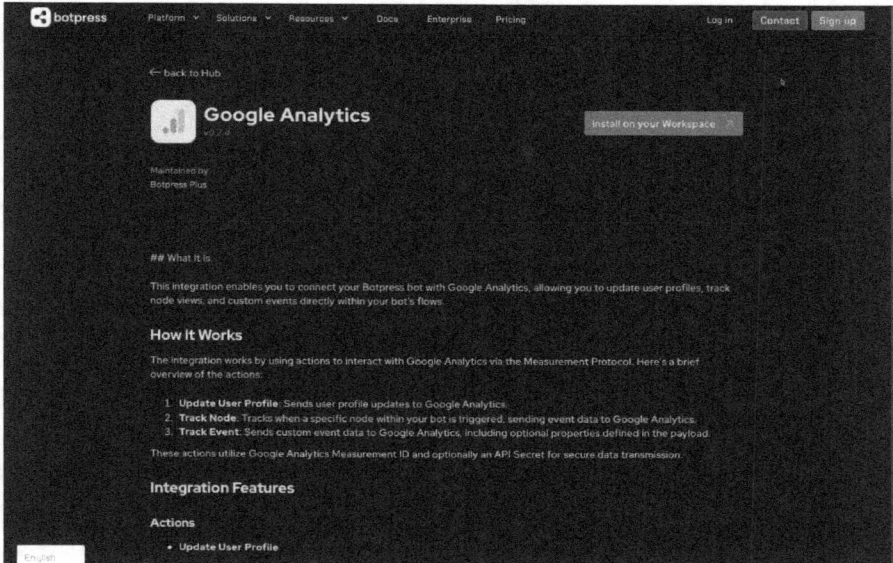

FIGURE 12-1:
The Botpress
website offers
Google Analytics
integration
instructions.

Addressing sentiment analysis

One powerful feature of AI chatbots is their use of natural language processing (NLP), which is what lets your AI chatbot platform train your chatbot to understand the tone of user messages. That is, your chatbot needs NLP so it can understand whether a conversation's tone is positive, negative, or neutral.

This understanding is *sentiment analysis.* You can probably guess what sentiment analysis is used for: the ability to transfer the user to a human agent for (hopefully) better service. The chatbot can also provide a customized apology before the handoff. (We think having your chatbot practice good manners and reflect well on your company is always a good idea.)

REMEMBER

Don't forget to have your human customer support team analyze sentiment from customers as well. If your customers have the same issues with your human agents as with your chatbot, then you know you have a fundamental business problem to address. Like, yesterday.

You can go about training your dra — er, chatbot — in three ways:

>> **Keywords:** Provide your chatbot with a list of positive and negative words to look for.

>> **Datasets:** Give your chatbot a lot of data about not just words but also context, sarcasm, and nuance.

>> **Specifics:** Train your chatbot to associate tone with specific responses, such as "The response time was great, but the answer didn't answer my question," which gives your chatbot feedback on both speed and accuracy.

As your chatbot platform collects sentiment data, you have better insights into user trends that you can use to improve your chatbot and your overall customer service.

Marriott International is a good example of using an AI chatbot in the hotel and hospitality industries; it uses sentiment analysis with its Bonvoy AI chatbot to help the company know where to correct service shortfalls and make improvements. It also asks you to take a survey about your experience as shown in Figure 12-2.

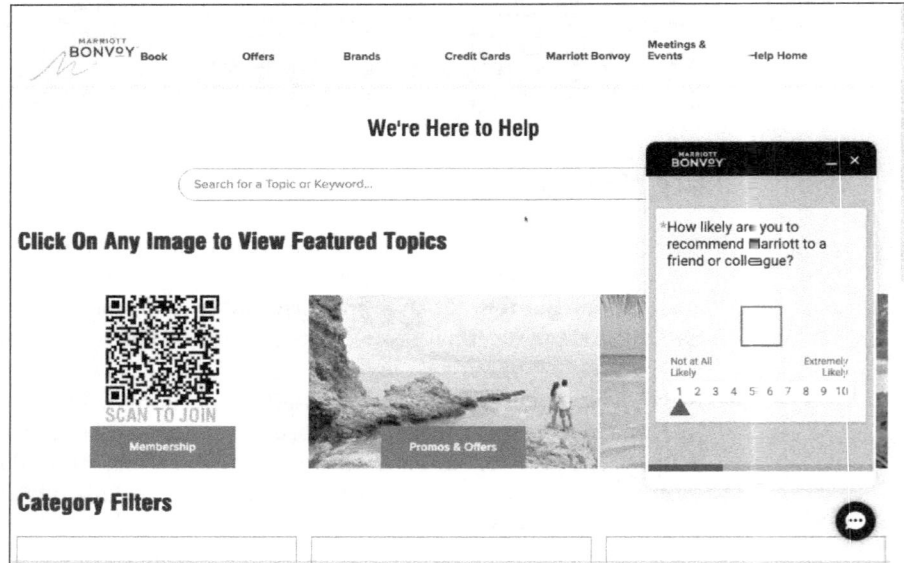

FIGURE 12-2:
The Bonvoy chatbot asks you to answer questions on a scale from 1 to 10.

Focusing on feedback (not fruit) loops

The Marriott International Bonvoy chatbot survey in Figure 12-2 is a great example of how to start a feedback loop. In the realm of AI chatbots, a *feedback loop* is where your chatbot platform collects, analyzes, and uses data to improve the chatbot's performance. You can train your chatbot to collect two types of feedback:

>> *Explicit feedback* like surveys and ratings at the end of a chatbot conversation

>> *Implicit feedback* that the chatbot gathers from cues such as repeated questions and drop-offs

You can also use sentiment analysis to get more feedback as we talk about in the preceding section.

TIP

Periodically ask users for their feedback, such as asking them whether the answer was helpful.

After you have feedback, you can use it to better refine your chatbot's abilities, including conversation flows. You can also update your documentation, like FAQs, so customers can get answers more quickly.

TIP

When you implement feedback and it leads to an improved AI chatbot, be sure to tell users about it (prominently) somewhere on your website and app. For example, you can tout your chatbot's improved accuracy in its answers and invite users to enter a conversation.

Predicting Customer Needs and Refining Offers

AI chatbots aren't just around to answer support questions; they can also serve as marketing engines that learn, predict, and deliver the right offer to your customer at the right time.

When you're searching for an AI chatbot platform, you need to talk with company reps about their predictive capabilities in the following areas:

>> **Behavioral tracking and pattern recognition:** The AI chatbot must be able to track real-time user behavior, such as time spent on specific products, repeated visits, or cart abandonment. For example, if a user frequently asks about vegan snacks, the chatbot can proactively suggest new arrivals and/or special deals in that category.

TIP

Don't start by having your AI chatbot track every single behavior you can think of. Instead, focus on one or two behaviors that are vital for your business. As you discover more about how your AI chatbot works and the quality of data you receive, you can refine your chatbot before you expand your personalization over time. (Hey, that's what we talk about in the later section "Personalizing the Experience Over Time!")

>> **Segmentation:** As we say earlier in the chapter, any AI chatbot platform worth using needs to segment users by behavior, demographics, and/or preferences. Then the platform can compare new visitors to existing segments and predict what they may be interested in. For example, if users

similar to you tend to buy pet supplements when purchasing pet food, the chatbot will recommend pet supplements to you when you pick up kibble.

>> **Predictive questioning:** The AI chatbot should be able to ask context-aware questions during the conversation, such as "Are you shopping for yourself or giving a gift to someone else?" Then the chatbot can take the answer and tailor its recommendation to the user.

New and improved: Helping your chatbot hone offers

You can train your AI chatbot to refine its offers in four ways:

>> **Offer targeted promotions, discounts, and/or product bundles depending on what the user asks about in the conversation:** For example, if a user talks about buying kitchen gadgets (and who doesn't love kitchen gadgets?), your chatbot presents an exclusive offer just for that user.

>> **Upsell other products naturally:** For example, if a user is looking for pickleball shoes, the chatbot can offer a discount on related apparel or equipment.

>> **Learn in real time about offers that are accepted in different segments:** For example, if a 20-percent-off coupon is popular with people who buy sweaters but not with people who buy hats, the chatbot knows to show the coupon more often to users looking for sweaters.

>> **Remember when a customer has abandoned a cart/hasn't purchased from you in a while and then reengage them with a special offer:** For example, when the user returns to your site and starts chatting with your chatbot, your bot can tell them their shopping cart has been saved and offer a 10-percent discount to complete their previous order.

Checking out a case study in predicting needs

In Chapter 4, we spotlight Manychat as one of six popular chatbot platforms. Don Marler's family–owned street food truck in St. Louis, Missouri, is an example of a small business using Manychat to predict customers' needs and refine offers. His chatbot is set up to do four things:

>> **Capture contact preferences through Facebook Messenger or a Facebook post:** When a customer opts in for a promotion, Manychat collects the user's contact information, location, and favorite foods on Don's menu.

- **» Segment users based on their city or neighborhood:** When Don's food truck plans to visit a specific area, Manychat sends targeted messages with featured menu items and special offers.

- **» Send personalized offers to repeat customers:** Manychat sends different offers — such $2 off their next sandwich when the user shows the code at the ordering window — after a certain number of visits.

- **» Transmit behavioral offers to customers who haven't ordered in a while:** Manychat reminds the user that the food truck is back in their neighborhood and asks whether the user is ready to order their favorite menu item.

Manychat touts in its case study of Don's business that his promotions (sent by SMS text message) increased his revenue by 30 percent and led to many loyal, repeat customers. You can read the entire case study (see Figure 12-3) and view a YouTube interview with Don on the Manychat website at manychat.com/blog/case-study-sms/.

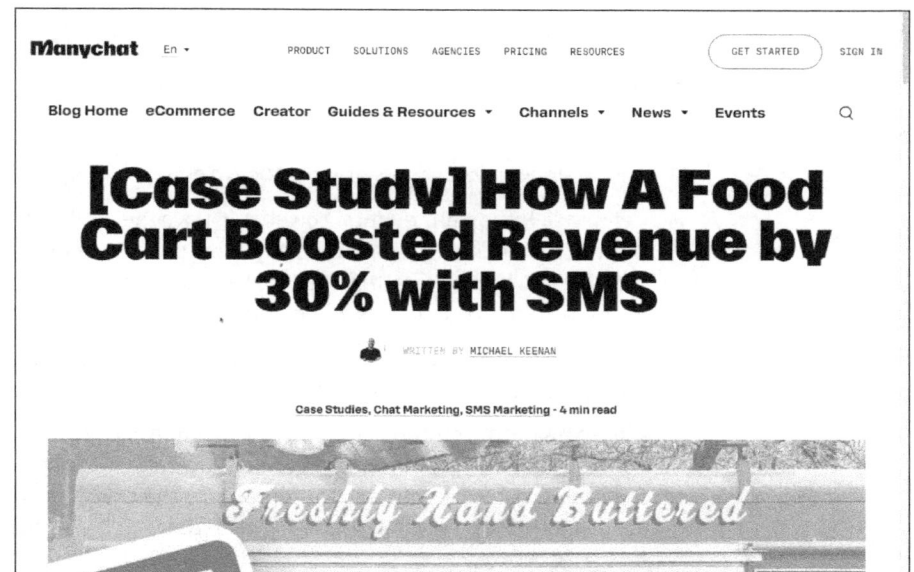

FIGURE 12-3:
The Manychat case study with Don Marer.

Personalizing the Experience Over Time

You want your customers to feel like talking to your AI chatbot is like talking to one of your human agents. When you continue to personalize your AI chatbot over time, each interaction is more likely to lead to a successful outcome (like a sale) and reduce the need for your human team to spend time on customer service.

Here's a checklist of the things your AI chatbot platform needs to be able to do. (And you have our permission to write checkmarks on the page as you're shopping for an AI chatbot platform.)

>> **Keep a record of every user interaction:** This interaction history includes questions asked, products viewed, purchases completed, common complaints, and user preferences. A history analysis helps you identify trends, such as greater interest in a product category.

>> **Enrich user profiles:** Each chat and purchase add details to the user's profile, such as their favorite colors and their preferred product categories.

>> **Refine product and/or service suggestions:** If your customers like your company and your chatbot, your user may interact with your AI chatbot over a period of weeks or months. With each interaction, your chatbot needs to be able to refine its recommendations, such as not suggesting a product the user already bought.

>> **Adapt dynamically based on user engagement:** For example, your chatbot can provide different offers depending on the time of day users enter a conversation or give previous buyers an early VIP offer.

>> **Offer win-back automations:** If a customer returns to your website after a while, your chatbot can immediately open a message that aims to gain more sales, such as "Welcome back, Nancy! Our holiday paper cupcake liners are now in stock, so order yours before they're gone!"

>> **Celebrate important events:** You should have the option to train your AI chatbot to remember user birthdays, anniversaries, and other important milestones (like how long the user has been a customer). Then you can send users custom offers, such as a free birthday gift.

>> **Learn from the user:** You want your AI chatbot to track which suggestions the user clicks so it knows what to suggest in future conversations.

>> **Close the loop:** You can train your chatbot to ask a Yes/No question about whether the user found what they needed — and if they didn't, to ask them to leave a comment with more information. The chatbot can also make suggestions based on that feedback, such as showing more sugar-free products.

ThreadBeast, a curated apparel subscription service for men, uses its chatbot to a 13-step questionnaire (shown in Figure 12-4) to collect information about new users, including size, style, and the brand the user prefers.

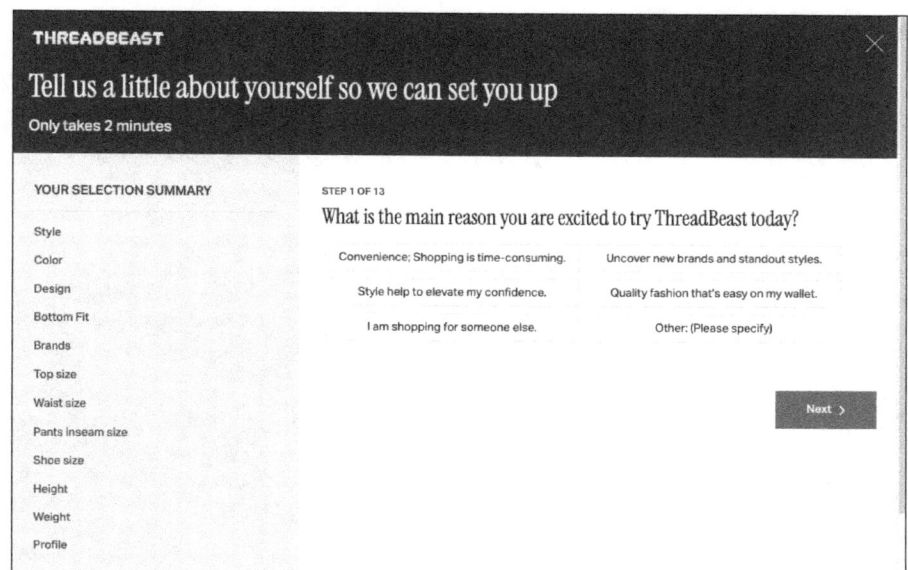

FIGURE 12-4
The ThreadBeast chatbot gives new visitors a 13-step questionnaire.

The chatbot learns from user behavior over time. For example, if a user selects only some of the chatbot's product suggestions, the chatbot gradually stops suggesting them to focus on the user's favorite clothing. If a customer gives feedback in the chat, the chatbot tunes its next curated selection to the customer's desires, which makes another sale to that customer more likely.

TIP

Here are three ways you can implement these personalization strategies and make the chatbot experience better for your customers:

>> **Be transparent about the information you collect in the chatbot and why.** Explain how your understanding customers' preferences helps make their chatbot conversations more personal and relevant to them.

>> **Instead of asking everything upfront, have the chatbot gather a little more information in every conversation.** For example, your chatbot can ask about food sensitivities so future suggestions don't mention those foods.

>> **Don't just collect the data; review it.** Remember to block out time in your calendar (or have your team reserve time) to analyze your chatbot data and feedback and keep improving your chatbot.

Chapter **13**

Measuring Success and Optimizing Your Chatbots

As with any other marketing and customer-facing endeavor, you don't know how well your AI chatbot is serving your potential and current customers unless you measure certain key performance indicators, which you probably know better by the abbreviation KPIs.

This chapter tells you how to answer your boss and your CFO when you come to them with stars in your eyes about AI chatbots and they pull you back down to earth demanding to know how they can tell the chatbot is making the company more money. We start by telling you about the key metrics you need to track.

We also talk about how to test your flows with the tried-and-true A/B testing method. Finally, we show you how to analyze your chatbot's performance and (here's another popular abbreviation) ROI so you can present your AI chatbot proposal with confidence that you'll show a strong return on investment on day one and in year five.

Knowing the Key Metrics to Track

Many AI chatbot platforms offer analytics built in, but not all. Some platforms have an app store that allows you to connect with their preferred analytics apps (see Figure 13-1).

As you shop for a platform to use in your business, ensure the platform can track the five key metrics in the following sections:

>> Open rate

>> Click-through rate

>> Conversion

>> Opt-ins

>> Fall-offs

For each metric, we tell you how it's measured and what influences it.

Closing in on the open rate

The *open rate* has a straightforward definition: It's the percentage of chatbot messages that users open or view. The formula for calculating your open rate is straightforward, too: the number of messages opened divided by the total number of messages sent.

TIP

If you prefer not to read the first three or four digits after the decimal point for the percentage, you can multiply the formula result by 100 to get the first two digits of the percentage on the left side of the decimal point.

Here's what influences your open rate:

>> The relevance of your message to the audience you're trying to reach

>> The timing and frequency of your messages

>> The personalization of your messaging, which means not only including the user's name but also presenting relevant offers to that user

A high open rate shows that your messages are reaching your users and that you have a better chance of creating a satisfied customer, whether that's by getting their question answered or making a sale.

Counting on the click-through rate (CTR)

The percentage of users who click a call to action link or button within a chatbot conversation, such as a link to buy a product, is called the *click-through rate* (CTR). A chatbot platform measures this stat by calculating the number of users who clicked divided by the number of users who saw the message.

Here are the factors that affect your CTR:

>> Your call to action's clarity and prominence, such as being marked with a hot pink button that gets users' attention. (Hot pink is good at that.)

>> The call to action's relevance and value to the user.

>> Whether the user actually clicks, not just reads, what the chatbot is asking them to do. (We'll take off our Captain Obvious hats now.)

REMEMBER

The CTR gives you a clear idea of how compelling your chatbot's content and calls to action are. Your CTR results help you test different call to action wording, styles, and placements.

For example, you need to train your AI chatbot to place your call to action links and/or buttons logically within the conversation. That can be at the end of the conversation or when the user expresses interest in a product that has a discount.

Conversion

The *conversion rate* is the percentage of your chatbot users who do what you want them to do in the chatbot, such as making a purchase or signing up for your loyalty program. The formula is the number of completed conversions divided by the number of users in your chatbot.

Conversion is the most direct measure of your chatbot's effectiveness and the ROI on it. You get more ROI if your offer is relevant and clear, but you also need to make it easy for the user to take advantage of it. That is, help the user convert as quickly as possible and, if needed, use trust signals such as giving out privacy information and showing off secure payment badges from companies like Visa and PayPal.

Understanding opt-ins

The number of *opt-ins* represents the users who have explicitly agreed to receive further communication from your business. That communication can be updates and offers from your chatbot every time the user visits the app, as well as email and/or SMS text updates.

The measurement for opt-ins is the number of users who opt in through the chatbot divided by the number of users who used the chatbot when the opt-in offer was made.

TIP

You get more people to opt in if you give them something of value, such as exclusive deals and early access to new versions of your product or app. If you're transparent about data usage and the frequency of contact, we bet you dollars to donuts that you can sway more than a few users into joining your community.

REMEMBER

You also need to make opting *out* of communications at any time easy. It's the right thing to do, but anti-spam laws in many states and countries also require it.

Finding out about fall-offs

Inevitably, some users drop out of their chatbot conversation, and you can track these *fall-offs* (also called *drop-offs*) in your chatbot platform. The platform calculates the *fall-off rate* as the number exiting the chatbot at a specific step in the conversation divided by the number of total users who reach that step.

Fall-offs tell you where users are becoming confused and/or frustrated that the chatbot isn't giving them what they need, and that's creating friction in the chatbot. When you see more fall-offs, it's time to open up the hood of your chatbot and look for one or more pain points:

>> Too many steps or unclear directions to reach the goal

>> Irrelevant and/or repetitive questions from the chatbot

>> Lack of a handoff to either a live human agent or an email address where a human can respond to it during business hours

REMEMBER

Fine-tuning your chatbot to decrease fall-offs means you have more conversions, happier customers, and a healthier bottom line.

A/B Testing Your Flows

Get your white lab coat on, because to make your chatbot the best it can be, you need to put its interactions to the test. That is, an *A/B test*, also known as a *split test.*

If you remember your high school science classes, you know about controls and variables in experiments. In your chatbot experiment, version A is the control and version B is the variable. The objective of your experiment is to find out which interaction is more effective at reaching the desired outcome, such as higher engagement or sale conversions.

Need more convincing? Let us count the ways A/B testing is important:

>> Testing finds the most effective greetings, prompts, and responses to hone the user experience and drive more sales.

>> Speaking of the user experience, A/B testing can identify points in the conversation that users find confusing or frustrating.

>> A/B testing allows you to test small changes with both your internal team and a select number of customers so you can get your chatbot in shape before you release it into the world.

REMEMBER

If you haven't selected an AI chatbot platform yet, ensure that the one you choose can perform A/B tests and analytics. We compare six leading chatbot platforms in Chapter 4 if you want to press pause and check out our reviews.

Chatbot platforms such as ChatBot offer tutorials about how to conduct A/B tests, as shown in Figure 13-2.

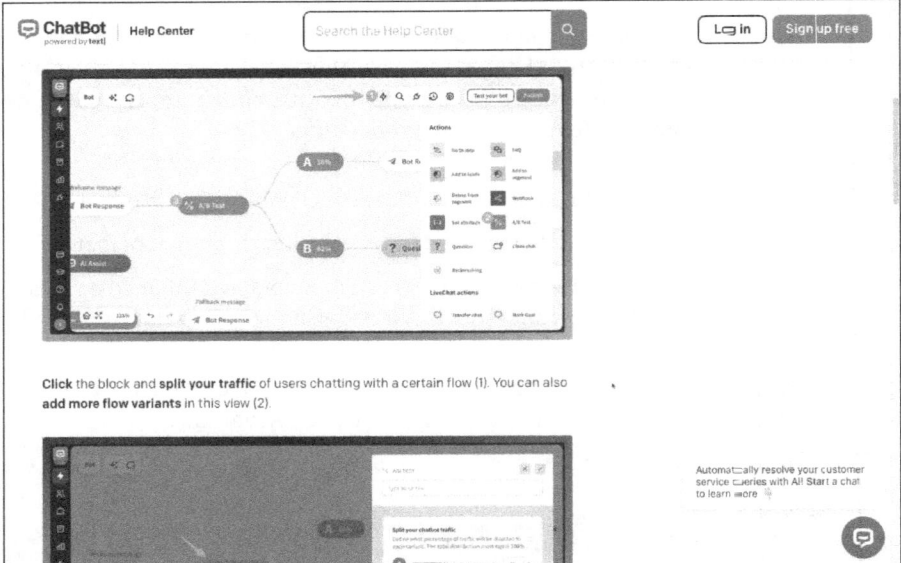

Click the block and **split your traffic** of users chatting with a certain flow (1). You can also **add more flow variants** in this view (2).

Deciding what you should test

"A/B testing sounds good," you say, "but my boss wants more practical examples of what's tested." In that case, give the powers that be these examples:

>> **Greetings:** Does "Hi! How can I help you?" or "Welcome! What are you looking for today?" resonate better with customers?

>> **Response button or link text:** Is a message such as "Talk to an Agent" or "I Need More Help" more likely to get users to click?

>> **Order of operations:** Do users like it when the chatbot shows FAQs before the contact options, or vice versa?

>> **Personalization:** Does having the chatbot greet users with their names and/ or referencing past purchases increase the likelihood of reaching the goal, such as a product sale?

>> **Multimedia or not:** Does an image or video (maybe with a bit of text) resonate more with your customers, or do they prefer only written descriptions?

>> **Length:** Do users prefer short, direct messages, or do they like longer, more conversational ones?

>> **Tone:** Do users like the chatbot to address them with more formal language, or do they engage with casual language?

Refining your results

Even if your website and/or your chatbot doesn't get a lot of traffic, you can still get a lot of good data from A/B tests. Here are six ways to test no matter how big your current website is or how much traffic your chatbot receives:

>> **Focus on the key impacts.** Test the parts of your chatbot flow with welcome messages, your main call to action, and/or points where user drop-offs are most common.

>> **Take one thing at a time.** Make small, deliberate changes such as the wording of a button or the order of the response. If small changes bring the results you need, then you don't have to devote time to overhauling the entire chatbot.

>> **Run longer tests when you have less engagement.** If your chatbot doesn't have a lot of interest, keep tests going for several weeks to collect enough data for meaningful insights.

REMEMBER

You should collect data from your chatbot every day, but don't forget to collect all the data over a longer period (like a month) so your team can look at the longer trends and make better recommendations to your leadership team.

>> **Get direct feedback.** Quantitative data is all well and good, but you need to augment that data with direct feedback. For example, you can give users a short survey asking them which experiences were more helpful and which ones weren't.

>> **Combine data.** If you have similar chatbots with similar flows on different channels (like your website and Facebook Messenger), consider combining that data for a more complete picture of your chatbots' performance.

>> **Communicate changes.** Don't forget to tell users and invite feedback when you've improved the chatbot. For example, you can say, "Based on your feedback, our chatbot is even more helpful. Please let us know what you think!" (Being polite is good for humans and chatbots.)

Taking your testing above and beyond

When you update your chatbot so it gives users the variant with the best performance, you can perform ongoing experiments. These tests can take different forms:

>> **Sequential testing:** A new variable with small changes goes up against the reigning champion to see whether tweaking your approach gives you even better results.

>> **Segmented testing:** You have A/B tests for different user segments, such as new customers versus returning customers. For example, Voiceflow (see Chapter 4) allows you to create different user personas, such as new users and returning users, and then test your chatbot's performance with that persona, as Figure 13-3 illustrates.

>> **Multivariable testing:** You test several variables, not just one, against the current A control.

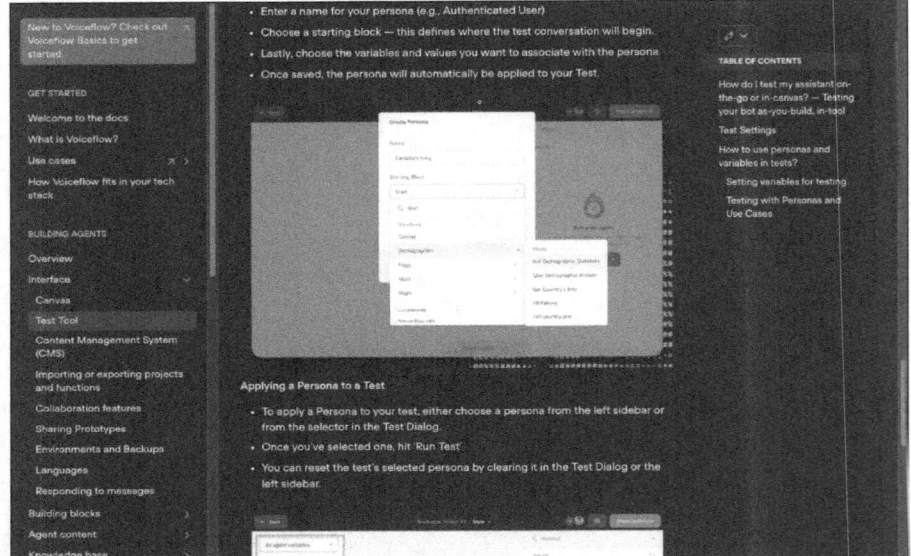

FIGURE 13-3:
Voiceflow lets you choose the variables and values to apply to your persona.

Using Analytics to Improve Performance and ROI

After you know what you want to track, you need to analyze your results. You don't need fancy scientific gizmos to do that because chatbot platforms provide that information for you so you can:

>> Understand user behavior in your chatbot

>> Pinpoint where users get confused, frustrated, and drop off

>> Justify the company's investment in your chatbot

>> Keep improving your chatbot strategy and performance to grow your ROI and convince leadership that you're a rock star

Before you start tracking, you need to set internal KPIs based on your business goals. If you don't, you're going to get puzzled reactions from your stakeholders about why certain data is relevant, and if you can't answer, you'll have a bad meeting. We don't want that. No one wants that.

Figuring out what you should track

You can't be fitted for your rock star attire and hairdo unless you know what to track first. Here's a checklist of the questions you need to answer; we cover several of these items in the earlier section "Knowing the Key Metrics to Track":

>> **Open rate:** Are your users noticing your chatbot's initial messages and entering a conversation?

>> **Session duration:** How long do users spend conversing with your chatbot?

>> **Repeat usage:** Do users come back to chat with your chatbot, and how often?

>> **Conversion rate:** What percentage of users complete a conversation that meets your goal, such as making a purchase or getting the information they need without having to speak to a human?

>> **Fall-off points:** Where do users most often leave the conversation? The answer reveals users' pain points.

>> **Click-through rate (CTR):** How often are users clicking links or buttons to move down the sales funnel toward a sale?

>> **Time savings:** How many hours do you think your chatbot has saved your team from engaging in customer support?

>> **Cost savings:** How much money has your business saved from automating tasks, such as answering the most common questions your users ask, with a chatbot?

>> **More money:** How many new sales and leads have come to you through chatbot conversations that you wouldn't get otherwise?

Driving the ROI machine

You need to track the five items in the following sections so you can make changes quickly and see the results as swiftly as possible. (You can't just shake off changes until a certain date when ROI is at stake.)

You need to identify all stakeholders who are interested in receiving data about your chatbot performance and ask them how often they want that information. Some may want updates before and after you run the analytics for each test.

First things first: Prioritizing fall-offs

Start by identifying and addressing the biggest fall-off points. For example, focus on FAQs in the chatbot that cause confusion. Even small changes such as shorter messages, better FAQ answers, and clearer calls to action can make users happier and more likely that they'll reach your desired goal with the chatbot. Head to the earlier section "Finding out about fall-offs" for more on this metric.

Doing your A/B experiments

As you analyze your chatbot performance, you'll naturally have questions about what you want to change. For example, you and your team may wonder whether the messages in the chatbot are too long or whether a button needs to be placed in a better location within the conversation flow.

So use the A/B testing we discuss in the earlier section "A/B Testing Your Flows" to get various answers to your questions. For example, use the long message in the A control test and a shorter message in the B variable test and see what happens. You may also want to try multivariable testing with A/B/C/D and so on to test variants to put the "Buy Now" button at different points in the conversation

Grouping your users

Analytics can help you group users by different behaviors, such as frequent buyers and those fishing for information. Then you can train your chatbot to provide tailored experiences that can resonate more strongly with them. For example, consider the messages users receive when they come back to the site. Maybe frequent chatbot users get loyalty offers, while people who fell off during the conversation see discounts to complete their orders.

With some platforms, you can group users by the parts of your bot that receive the most user responses, such as when the chatbot asks for the user's preferred language. ChatBot offers an interactions report that shows which parts of the chatbot get the most responses and which ones don't (see Figure 13-4).

Adding context to your data

You can't just look at data points every day to spot trends. You also need to look at the bigger picture, so always review collected data over a period of time. For example, if you made a recent change to the information the chatbot presents, you may decide to review data aggregated over two weeks or a month to spot trends.

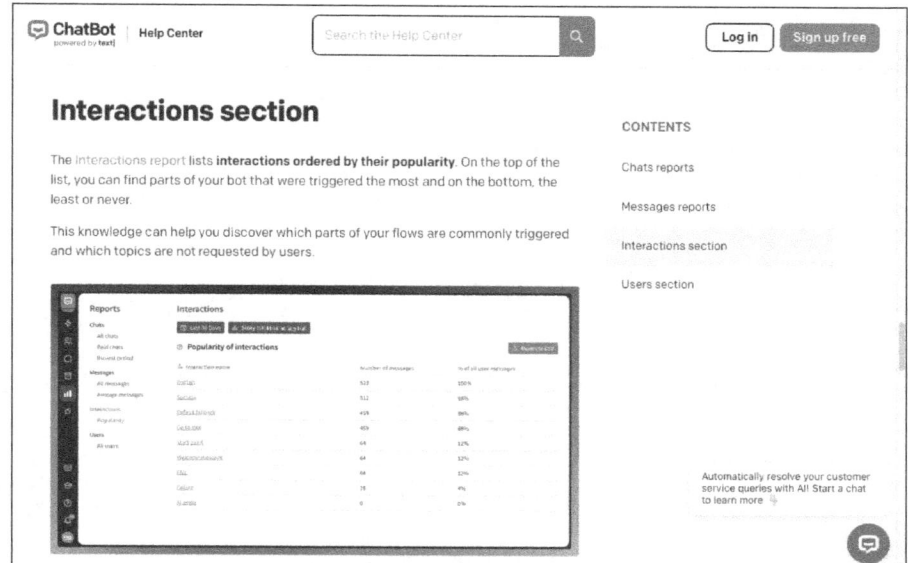

FIGURE 13-4:
The ChatBot.com
interaction
reports lists the
most popular
interaction
at the top.

REMEMBER

Data can be deceiving, so always read the chat transcripts and any feedback your chatbot asks for, such as in short surveys at the end of the conversation. Then you have better context for what the data is telling you, and you can expose blind spots in your analytics.

Showing and not just telling

Your stakeholders naturally want to know about how many new customers your chatbot is signing up and the cost and productivity savings it's giving you.

REMEMBER

However, don't forget to add qualitative feedback from actual users to prove your points about how well the chatbot is working. The human element helps your stakeholders connect with the numbers, and that's useful when you want to ask for a bigger investment into more chatbot technologies in your platform's higher-tier plan.

4

Moving Forward with Confidence

IN THIS PART . . .

Keep up to date in the rapidly evolving realm of chatbots.

Get the skinny on ethics, privacy, and platform rules.

Build a chatbot strategy for the long term.

Chapter **14**

Staying Ahead of Chatbot Trends

W e freely admit that books aren't a great medium in the technology space, especially in areas like AI and chatbots where the change is so fast it'd make the Looney Tunes Road Runner's head spin.

We've worked hard to make the information in this book as evergreen as possible, and we also want to give you the proverbial 30,000-foot view of where AI chatbots are going for 2026 through the end of the decade. We can't predict exactly what will happen (if we could, we'd be on a beach somewhere), but what we discuss in this chapter can give you a sense of things to come.

We start by talking about what's next for AI chatbots to make them even more useful and engaging for your customers. Then we get into the plans for some of the platforms we cover in this book. (We introduce each one in Chapter 4.) Finally, we give you strategies to implement upgrades and new features as they fall into your lap.

Taking a Look at Things to Come

You don't need to be a psychic with a crystal ball — or even a Magic 8 ball — to find out what's going on with AI chatbots in 2026 and for the rest of the decade. Here's what you and your teams should be looking out for from AI chatbot platforms.

REMEMBER

This paragraph is the not-so-fine print, or the end of a commercial where the narrator talks really fast to cover the company's legal obligations: This section is an overview of what may be coming starting in 2026 as we write this book in the third quarter of 2025. As you're reading the following sections, your chatbot platform may have already rolled out some of these features . . . and some of them may be *vaporware* (a tech term for products advertised but not yet — or ever — released).

Goin' multimodal

AI chatbots are rapidly integrating audio and visual elements that chatbots can ask for and analyze, and chatbot platforms are also working to have their bots provide more multimedia results, including the following:

>> **Image recognition:** Customers can send photos of products so the chatbot can identify them and provide support.

>> **Video interaction:** Chatbots will be able to analyze video content, such as a video of how a product isn't working, so the chatbot can determine whether the user needs guidance or the product needs replacement.

>> **Document processing:** Users can upload documents such as contracts or forms to extract data and provide feedback and guidance.

>> **Voice to text:** Chatbots will be able to switch between speaking aloud and providing text seamlessly.

>> **Text to graphics:** Based on text information the chatbot has in its database, the bot will create diagrams, charts, or infographics to explain things to the user (hopefully) more effectively.

Translating in real time

Though plenty of language translation apps are available (think Google Translate), the translation is more complex when your AI chatbot is talking to people not only with different languages but also with different contexts. Chatbot platforms are working to increase their multicultural abilities, including these:

>> Seamless language switching, where the chatbot recognizes the user's written language and adapts instantly

>> Messages adapted for the user's cultural context as the chatbot learns more about the user and the country or region where they are

>> Implementing better understanding of local and regional customs and expectations

Adding augmented chatbots

Augmented reality (AR) and virtual reality (VR) aren't going away despite AI taking all their buzz since 2023. Chatbots are working with VR glasses from companies like Meta, Google, and Apple to make the chatbot experience better in several ways:

>> Overlaying digital information on real-world objects to give users immersive shopping experiences and product demos

>> Interactive troubleshooting of issues, where the user interacts with a physical product and the AI chatbot provides instructions and feedback

>> Using an AI chatbot to answer questions through either text or voice narration as the customer learns how to use the physical product

Integrating the Internet of Things with chatbots

AR and VR (see the preceding section) aren't the only technologies that were once the frothy new thing before they were engulfed by AI. Chatbot platforms are also working with the Internet of Things to enhance the customer experience in three ways:

>> **Environment:** The chatbot can adjust the store environment based on customer conversations. For example, if several users tell the chatbot that the lighting is too bright or the temperature is too low, the chatbot can adjust the environment accordingly.

>> **Supply:** If a business has sensors in its warehouse that keep track of inventory, the chatbot will connect to those sensors and give a user who asks about their favorite widget real-time updates about how many are in stock.

> » **Maintenance:** The AI chatbot can also monitor analysis from customers and employees to predict maintenance. For example, if customers note that they see water stains on ceiling panels, the chatbot can alert the facilities manager (or the owner) to check it out and make repairs.

Vision Quest: Perusing Platforms' Future Plans

Plenty of AI chatbot providers are working furiously (and as quickly as possible) to implement their visions for 2026 and beyond. In the following sections, we focus on three of the chatbot platforms we introduce in Chapter 4 to give you a sneak peek (no, it's not *peak*, jeez) behind their curtains.

Manychat

As of this writing, Manychat offers its Manychat AI as an add-on service to its Pro plan, and its focus on social commerce platforms Instagram and TikTok means it's building a lot of new features to better connect your business with your customers:

> » **Better personalization:** Manychat will have chatbot models created for each customer relationship so the AI chatbot can build long-term relationships and drive more sales.

> » **More proactive:** Manychat will alert your team about what's going on in conversations, such as telling your company's research and development (R&D) department about customer needs and market gaps so you can develop products and services more quickly and beat the competition.

> » **Holograms, maybe:** Manychat will integrate three-dimensional customer avatars into its platform so people can have immersive business consultations, which makes sense considering that Meta continues to develop its Quest virtual reality headsets.

If you want the very latest about Manychat's new features, visit the company's community website at community.manychat.com/product-updates, as shown in Figure 14-1.

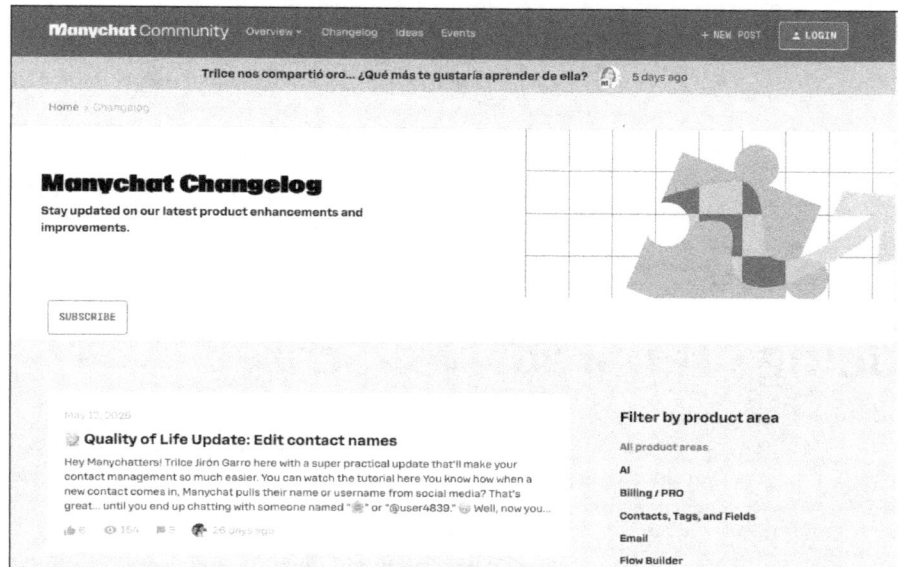

FIGURE 14-1:
On the Manychat
changelog
webpage, you can
filter information
by product area.

ChatBot

Like its competitors, ChatBot wants to be everything your business needs now and in the future. Here's how it's evolving its platform to better serve you:

>> **Your business consultant:** If you have an internal AI chatbot for your business, ChatBot will provide your business with tailored advice based on industry and company data.

>> **Relationship building:** Like Manychat in the preceding section, ChatBot is working to build individual customer models that span years of interactions to establish long-term connections.

>> **Regulatory help:** Your AI chatbot will automatically adhere to new and changing laws as well as industry regulations when it interacts with your customers.

Chatfuel

Chatfuel integrates even more tightly with Meta technologies, including Instagram and Facebook, so the company's focus on commerce for 2026 and beyond should come as no surprise. Plans include the following:

>> **Predictive behavior:** Chatfuel's AI chatbot will be able to predict a customer's purchase intent before they decide to buy.

>> **New business models:** Your AI chatbot will connect with your teams to suggest new revenue streams based on what they're seeing in customer conversations.

>> **Creation of new markets:** The Chatfuel AI chatbot will not only suggest new revenue streams but also develop new market segments that your business can take advantage of before your competitors do.

Being Prepared, Not Scared

Every other day seems to bring a news story about how AI is disrupting business models, including job markets. As with every other disruptive technology of the past, being skeptical about AI won't make it go away. If you haven't integrated AI chatbots on your website and in your social media, your business is what's going to go away. Your competition will gleefully make sure of that.

You already know that because you're reading this book and want to beat your competition to the AI customer relationships game. But your leadership team may be skeptical about the capabilities of AI chatbots, and they aren't spooked by scary stories of competitors winning the AI game. They don't just want numbers; they want to know what commitment the company will have to make.

If you winced as you read that, here's what to know as you assemble your master plan that will leave your stakeholders dazzled — or at least nodding contentedly as they give their seal of approval.

Working with your platform

Testing a platform before you use it is important. When you're comfortable using your platform and you've decided to keep it for (hopefully) a few years, ask the platform's sales rep about becoming an early adopter for *beta* (or pre-release) version features as they become available so you can test them. This strategy has several advantages:

>> **You get first access to new capabilities so you can determine how to incorporate them into your AI chatbot.**

>> **You can give feedback to the platform developers to make the new features more valuable for you.** That feedback can come in the form of prioritized technical support not just for the beta version but your current chatbot AI, too.

>> **Your provider may give you the opportunity to provide it with a case study for marketing purposes.** If that doesn't happen, ask your platform rep, because it's also an opportunity to bring you more visibility and perhaps some revenue sharing.

>> **Speaking of revenue sharing, look into certification programs for your platform that can include a new revenue stream.** Botpress does just that with its Community Partner program, as shown in Figure 14-2.

>> **As an early adopter, you may be able to lock in your current rates as a reward for your feedback.** A rate freeze may come in handy because new features may be a good reason for your platform to hike prices.

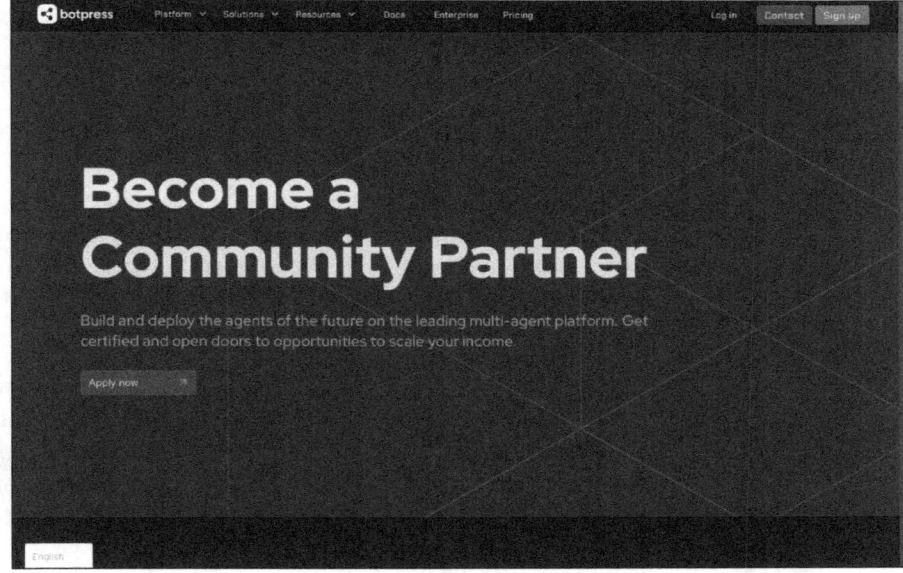

FIGURE 14-2:
You can select from several partnership options in the Botpress Community Partner program.

REMEMBER

Always use pre-release features in house with one or more testing computers so you can see how those features work — and how they break — without affecting your current, stable chatbot.

Engaging with platform communities

Many chatbot platforms have user communities; you can see Manychat's in Figure 14-3. Ask your platform account rep about them if you don't see one readily available.

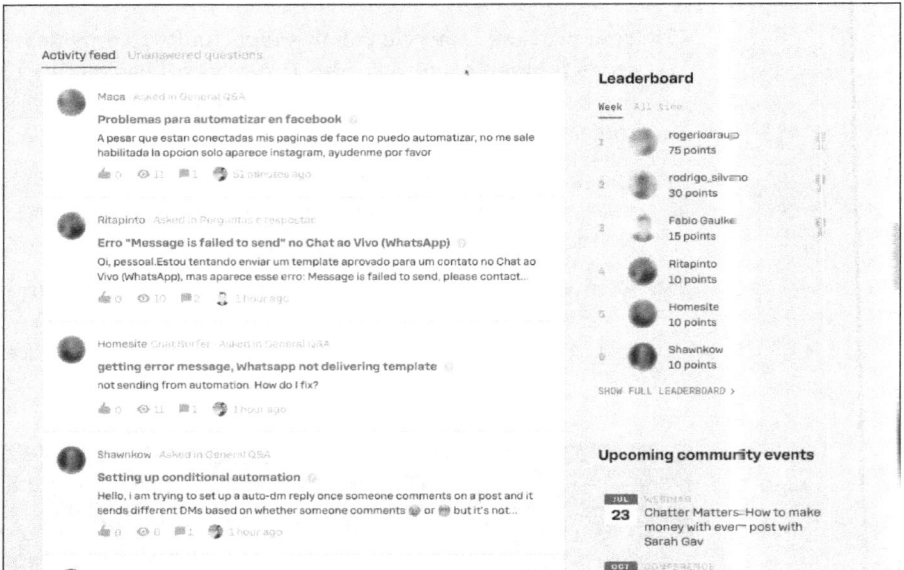

FIGURE 14-3:
The Manychat
forum activity
feed on its
Community page.

Interacting with people both online and in person gives your business a network-ing opportunity you may not have considered. Being active in online forums makes you more visible to other business customers who use the same platform (duh) and helps establish you as a leading authority, especially when you share your experiences, advice, and constructive criticism.

You can build strong relationships with the platform development teams both online and in person at conferences about AI chatbots and about AI in general. Meeting people in real life is more conducive to building a community because you can meet more people and make deeper connections than in an online forum or Zoom meeting.

**TECHNICAL
STUFF**

Don't just take our word for it. You can read a late-2024 study from the National Academy of Sciences that compares online and in-person meetings here: academic.oup.com/pnasnexus/article/4/1/pgae522/7906554.

Yes, that means you'll have to have someone on your team (maybe even you) par-ticipating actively and regularly in forums, and you may even have to budget to attend online or in-person conferences. But sharing with humans is the best way to get the most out of your relationship with your AI chatbot.

Getting ready

As with any other customer service initiative, you can't implement and run AI chatbots with guesswork. (Unless you don't think you're getting enough stress.)

In the following sections, we give clarity to your AI chatbot implementation strategy by providing a checklist of questions you and your implementation team need to answer. By starting now, you establish the trust you need in your organization and with your customers to have a great rollout of your AI chatbot to the world.

Building the foundation

You need to start by asking the following foundational questions about your processes and your finances.

» **What's your customer journey?** If you don't know the answer to that first, fundamental question, you won't know how chatbots can help smooth that journey for everyone involved. You can learn more by bookmarking this page and reading all about mapping the user journey in Chapter 5.

» **What income streams could your AI chatbot generate?** Customer input will bring you feedback that you can use to create new products and/or services that you never thought of before. You must be able to implement your new offerings and prices to attract more customers.

» **Can your current technology infrastructure handle the load?** You need to be able to store and manage more data coming from the chatbot and integrations with your existing apps (like customer relationship management) now and as your chatbot grows.

» **Are you budgeting for the long haul?** As your chatbot capabilities grow from what's included in your current platform plan, budget for higher platform fees and potentially more specialized staff in your customer service department.

» **What happens if your chatbot platform is no longer a fit?** Reserve some money to move to a new platform if the one you have doesn't deliver on its promises and/or doesn't serve your needs at some point.

» **Are your employees ready?** Identify team members who need training in managing your AI chatbot, analyzing the data, and perhaps designing customer experience. If you can't find anyone, you need to convince the powers that be to budget for a new hire.

» **Is your culture ready?** Moving to an AI-first customer support model is a big cultural shift, and you need to train all your employees on what your AI chatbot will do, what it won't, and how the company will manage this new support system.

» **How will you tell your customers about your new chatbot?** Tell customers how to use your chatbot, but acknowledge that some people prefer the human touch. Let customers know they can still contact your human customer support team, and remind them how to do so.

REMEMBER

Always be transparent with how your AI chatbot works, how it compares with human interactions, and how it handles data privacy. As with all other business endeavors, being upfront with customers about how to work with your business and how you protect them makes them want to join you and want to stay.

Preparing for emergencies

You know that like every other human contraption ever made, anything involving computers will break down, and that includes your AI chatbot. In an emergency, you need two fallback positions at the ready.

>> **Be able to roll back to a previous version of the AI chatbot if a new version breaks.**

>> **Be able to tell website or app users they need to contact human customer support and how to do that.** If you're using SMS to connect with users, send out an alert telling them the AI chatbot is down on your website and/or app and give them a way to reach your support people.

WARNING

You should always make human customer support readily available to users no matter what. This approach helps mitigate AI chatbot downtime and ensure you don't gift customers who prefer human support to your competitors.

Remembering the R in R&D

Every new piece of tech brings its own responsibilities with it, and AI chatbots require you to keep researching as you develop your chatbot to be the best for your customers now and for years to come.

Though your chatbot platform is researching its industry, it may not share all its data with you — and that data may not pertain to your company and industry anyway. So here are some subjects that should be on your radar:

>> **Laws and regulations in the AI space, especially when regarding data privacy.**

>> **Acquisitions of small platforms by bigger ones and how they may affect what your AI chatbot platform offers:** That includes whether your platform is a target for acquisition.

>> **Unique ways to gather customer information from chatbots that customers can't replicate easily but don't compromise data privacy.**

- **University AI research:** Those discoveries and insights will make their way to commercial AI platforms in two or three years (if not sooner).

- **Customer behavior studies beyond all the glowing reports that chatbot platforms provide on their websites:** These studies give you unvarnished insights into how people use chatbots and what customers' pain points are.

TIP

One way to automate your research is to use Google Alerts (`www.google.com/alerts`) to have Google search for certain topics and email you a (free!) digest of websites that contain those topics.

Future proofing

Running a business is about constantly preparing for the future so you can stay in business against smaller and hungrier rivals. As part of our quest to make this book as relevant as possible no matter when you read it, here are some evergreen tips for ensuring your AI chatbot is valuable for your customers as time goes by:

- **Keep your staff learning.** Offer continuous education for everyone in your company to keep them apprised of your new AI chatbot features and the state of AI in general.

- **Keep your customers learning, too.** Have educational resources available for customers to learn how to use the chatbot to get the most out of it. Those resources can include a forum, such as a Facebook group, where you can update customers on new features and how to use them.

- **Build your portfolio.** Develop new offerings that take advantage of your chatbot's capabilities and your user feedback. If you don't, your competition will.

- **Go global.** Your AI chatbot's translation and localization can help your business enter markets around the world.

Chapter 15

Ethics, Privacy, and Platform Rules You Must Know

Whether you're using Messenger, Instagram DMs, WhatsApp, SMS, or web chat, violating terms of service or applicable laws can result in bans, blocked messages, or even permanent loss of access. That isn't a scare tactic. It's a fact. We've seen it happen repeatedly, especially to well-meaning small business owners and marketers who didn't know the rules.

We want to make sure you're not one of them, so in this chapter, we show you how to build chatbots that respect your customers' trust, comply with privacy laws, and stay within platform rules.

If you take away one thing from this chapter, let it be this: Compliance isn't a nice-to-have. It's a must-have.

REMEMBER

Building Ethical Chatbots

An ethical bot does the following:

>> Respects user privacy from the first interaction

>> Clearly discloses who or what is responding

>> Collects only the data necessary to complete its task

>> Follows user preferences for message timing and content

>> Is compliant with regulations for your specific industry

When someone interacts with your chatbot, they should feel informed, respected, and secure. Ethical chatbots don't just function correctly. They're designed with intention and integrity. This approach starts with four key principles:

>> Transparency

>> Honesty

>> Respectful design

>> Rule-abiding functionality

Examining what makes a bot ethical and rule-compliant

REMEMBER

Just because your chatbot works doesn't mean it's ethical or compliant. Always double-check your platform's settings and features before launching.

If your chatbot collects or shares sensitive data, such as information related to health care, finance, or legal issues, ensure the platforms you use are secure and legally compliant for that purpose. For example, if you're discussing protected health information, your platform must be HIPAA compliant.

Checking out opt-ins

Opt-ins are more than just a checkbox or a button click. They're the foundation of ethical chatbot marketing. Think of opt-ins as your permission slip. They tell platforms and your audience that you're following the rules and respecting boundaries.

Before you can send messages, especially promotional ones, your audience must actively agree to hear from you. Obtaining an opt-in is a legal requirement in most countries and a best practice in every situation.

But not all opt-ins are created equal. A compliant opt-in is:

>> **Intentional:** The user takes a clear action like clicking a button or typing a keyword.

>> **Specific:** The opt-in defines what kind of messages the user will receive, such as tips, offers, or reminders.

>> **Transparent:** The opt-in explains how often you'll send messages and how to unsubscribe.

Always include the "why" behind the opt-in. For example, "Click below to get weekly tips on growing your business" users more context. People are more likely to subscribe when they know what they're getting and why it matters.

Pre-checked boxes or vague language like "Sign up for updates" doesn't cut it. If your user doesn't know exactly what they're agreeing to, your opt-in isn't compliant.

Tackling transparency

Users should never have to wonder whether they're speaking with a real person or an automation. Being upfront improves user experience and builds long-term trust.

Try one of these approaches:

>> **Use a friendly, branded name like "Kelly's AI Assistant" to clearly indicate automation.**

>> **Welcome users with a branded message that sets expectations.** One example is something like "Welcome to the Stellar Media Marketing Chat Experience. How can I help you today?"

>> **Include a human handoff option.** Let users know they can type "Human" to talk with a real person.

Honoring honesty

One of the fastest ways to lose trust is to mislead users. Avoid tactics like fake urgency, surprise upsells, or vague messaging. Always tell people precisely what they're getting, and when. Let users know the following:

>> What your chatbot can do

>> What kind of messages they'll receive

>> How to unsubscribe or reach a human

And always lead with value. The saying "Money is the echo of value" is never truer than when you're communicating with your potential customers.

Understanding Major Platforms' Policies

In the earlier section "Checking out opt-ins," we introduce the idea that you need users' permission before contacting them through chatbot messaging, email marketing, and SMS messaging (texting). Sending emails, DMs, or SMS messages without proper consent puts your business at serious risk. You may face blocked messages, suspended accounts, or even legal penalties.

Whether you're working under the privacy laws in the United States (CAN-SPAM), Canada (CASL), or the European Union (GDPR), they all have one thing in common: They require explicit user consent. But you also have various platforms' guidelines to contend with, so we break those down in the following sections.

Facebook Messenger and Instagram

Fortunately, chatbots built on Meta's platforms, including Messenger and Instagram, come with built-in compliance features designed to help.

WARNING

If you're building chatbots for Facebook Messenger or Instagram DMs, Meta's rules aren't optional. These platforms come with strict guidelines — and they're enforced. Violating the rules can result in losing messaging access, having your page blocked, or even getting permanently banned. No amount of pleading with Meta support can fix it if you've been flagged too many times.

Getting familiar with the Welcome Screen

One of the most important tools on Messenger is what's called the **Welcome Screen, as shown in Figure 15-1,** and its **Get Started** button (see the following section). It includes the following:

» Your Facebook Page name

» Profile photo and cover image

» Average response time

» An optional greeting message

» The **Get Started** button (when you've turned that function on)

FIGURE 15-1:
The Welcome
Screen For
Messenger.

TIP

The greeting message is your chance to tell users what your chatbot can do and why they should engage. Think of it as your chatbot's elevator pitch. Keep it short, helpful, and friendly. You can personalize the message with the user's name and use it to set expectations about the experience they're about to have.

Employing best practices for the Get Started tool

This small but mighty button is what opens the messaging relationship between your chatbot and the user. When someone clicks the **Get Started** button, it sends a signal that they're initiating a conversation. This interaction counts as the opt-in you need to legally begin messaging. From there, you can send messages, collect additional information, and walk them through your experience.

REMEMBER

The Get Started button appears only for users who are interacting with a Facebook page for the first time. If a user has previously messaged the page or has an existing conversation, they don't see the button.

Do the following to stay compliant and make the most of this entry point:

>> **Be clear about next steps.** Let users know what to expect when they tap Get Started or start a conversation with your page.

>> **Use buttons and quick replies to guide responses.** Doing so helps structure the conversation and makes it easier for users to engage.

>> **Stay relevant and timely.** If your chatbot experience evolves, update your greeting and welcome flow accordingly.

>> **Avoid generic intros.** Make your greeting helpful and specific to the value your chatbot provides.

For technical setup details and current limitations, visit Meta's official documentation: developers.facebook.com/docs/messenger-platform/discovery/welcome-screen/.

All that said, your chatbot must still follow a few critical rules:

>> Ask permission before collecting and using personal information.

>> Clearly explain what the user is opting into.

>> Make unsubscribing easy.

Creating a simple and compliant opt-in flow

Your opt-in message doesn't need to be long or complicated. In fact, the simpler it is, the more likely someone is to follow through. Here's a proven structure:

>> **Deliver the value.**

>> Offer the lead magnet, guide, or resource that caught their attention

• Example: "I'm happy to give you access to this guidebook."

>> **Ask for the contact.**

   ● Request only the information you truly need.

   ● Example: "First, we'll need your email address."

>> **Confirm consent.**

   ● Double-check that they agree to receive messages.

   ● Example: "Please confirm you're okay with us emailing you at this address: [email]."

>> **Deliver the resource.**

   ● Send what you promised and confirm it was sent.

   ● Example: "Thanks! We've emailed the guidebook to you."

WARNING

Never assume that one opt-in covers every channel. If you're planning to send both email and SMS, you must collect permission for each one separately.

Managing permissions the right way

After a user gives you permission, you need to treat that data with care:

>> Store timestamps showing when and how they opted in.

>> Respect regional laws like CAN-SPAM (USA), CASL (Canada), or GDPR (EU).

>> Avoid over-messaging, which can lead to opt-outs and complaints.

>> Make unsubscribing easy and instant.

REMEMBER

Most chatbot-building platforms keep records of these things for you to make things easier.

Understanding the 24-hour messaging window

Meta follows a 24-hour rule that keeps chatbot messaging respectful and relevant. As soon as a user interacts with your chatbot (clicks a button, types something, comments on a post, and so on), you have 24 hours to send *any kind* of message, including promotional content.

This window resets with every interaction. But after 24 hours pass, you can't keep messaging users unless you've used an approved method like a Messenger List (we cover those in Chapter 11 and the following section) or a Sponsored Message.

Clicking a button that opens an external website doesn't trigger the 24-hour window. Only actions that keep the user inside Messenger or Instagram DMs can do that.

Messaging beyond 24 hours (the right way): Messenger Lists

We explain in Chapter 11 that Messenger Lists are part of Meta's Recurring Notification system and allow you to send messages to users who have explicitly opted in to receive ongoing updates. These communications are perfect for things like weekly tips, new product alerts, or content series. Messenger Lists are your safest route for staying on Meta's good side with these kinds of updates.

Here's how it works:

>> The user must click a special "Get Updates" button during a conversation.

>> Each list is topic-specific (for instance, "Weekly Marketing Tips" or "New Product Alerts").

>> You can send only one message per list, per user, per day.

>> Messages must stay relevant to the topic the user opted into.

>> Users can unsubscribe at any time.

You can't use one list to send updates on multiple topics. If someone subscribed to "Weekly Tips," don't sneak in a sale announcement. Meta sees that as a bait-and-switch and will restrict your account.

Sticking to Meta's other terms of service

Meta's developer messaging policies (see the preceding sections) are only one part of the compliance puzzle. If you're building bots on Messenger or Instagram, you also need to follow Meta's terms of service:

>> Commerce policies

>> Community standards

>> Advertising policies

>> Platform policies

Failing to follow these rules can result in message delivery failure, feature restrictions, or permanent bans.

You do need to be aware of some key content restrictions. You can't share, promote, or sell the following:

>> Weapons, ammunition, or explosives

>> Tobacco or vaping products

>> Alcohol to minors or without appropriate *age gating* (asking the user to confirm there are older than the law requires)

>> Prescription or recreational drugs

>> Adult content or services

>> Gambling or betting products

>> Cryptocurrency or forex trading without Meta's written approval

>> Multilevel marketing (MLM) schemes

>> "Get-rich-quick" offers

>> Health claims not approved by regulatory bodies (like "cures cancer")

>> Fake documents or services that facilitate deception (for example, fake IDs)

>> Misinformation, especially related to elections, health, or safety

>> Digital products that are sold directly inside Messenger or Instagram DMs

TIP

Here are some important bits of advice to keep in mind regarding content restrictions and terms of service:

>> **Selling digital products inside a Meta-hosted chatbot is strictly prohibited.** You can mention them, describe them, and even promote them, but the purchase must happen outside Messenger or Instagram through an external checkout page.

If you don't believe us, consider the well-known business coach who tried selling an e-book directly through her Messenger bot in violation of Meta's rules. As a result, her business page was blocked from using Messenger for weeks. She was fortunate to have internal contacts at Meta and eventually regained access, but most people aren't that lucky.

>> **Even if you're not running ads, your chatbot content must still follow Meta's advertising standards.** The system treats any commercial interaction with the same scrutiny.

>> **Always keep a current copy of Meta's platform and ad policies bookmarked.** They do change, and ignorance isn't a valid excuse if your page gets shut down. Neither is the defense that someone else is doing it and getting away with it.

Using comment-to-message automation

One of the most popular chatbot tools is the *comment trigger.* A user comments on a post, and your chatbot sends them a private message to follow up. Sounds simple, right? It is, but there's a catch.

To be compliant, your first message must always include an opt-in prompt. That's Meta's way of making sure the user wants to engage in a private conversation. Until the user taps a button (that stays within the chat) or replies, you can't send them additional messages or deliver the full content you promised.

WARNING

If you skip the opt-in message, you risk violating Meta's rules, even if the person has interacted with you before. The opt-in message is required every time someone enters through a comment trigger. Meta treats each entry point as a separate experience.

Influencers often use comment-to-message automations and send links without properly opening the 24-hour messaging window. Then they send follow-up messages and unintentionally violate the rules. The result? Their accounts get hit with 7-day, 30-day, or even longer restrictions. Sometimes they lose messaging access entirely.

To stay on the safe side, follow these guidelines:

>> Use clear opt-in prompts like "Tap below to continue" or "Click to receive the freebie."

>> Don't deliver promotional content or digital products until the user engages with that first message.

>> Make sure your automations stop if the user doesn't interact.

Automating story replies and keyword triggers

Instagram automation allows you to set up replies when someone reacts to your story or sends a keyword through a DM. This setup is a great way to increase engagement and offer lead magnets, promo codes, or content links.

But even though the trigger may feel casual, the same 24-hour messaging rules we address in the earlier section "Understanding the 24-hour messaging window" still apply. Here's how to keep it compliant:

>> **Your automation must start only after the user takes an action, either by sending a message or reacting to your story.**

>> **Your reply must follow Meta's platform policies and not include any restricted content.** Flip to "Sticking to Meta's other terms of service" earlier in the chapter for more on those.

>> **You must send promotional messages within the 24-hour window or through approved methods like Messenger Lists only.**

TIP

When automating keyword triggers from Instagram Stories, keep the experience short and useful. A quick thank-you, a link to the offer, and a lead capture are usually all you need.

Avoiding interaction baiting

Meta's policy team is on the lookout for chatbots that try to trick the system. That includes tactics like sending vague or low-value questions to get a user to respond so the business can reopen the 24-hour window. This practice is considered *interaction baiting* and can get your chatbot flagged or disabled.

If your goal is to sneak in a sales pitch after a meaningless prompt, you're crossing the line. Instead, focus on genuine, user-driven conversations. Every message you send should be helpful, expected, and aligned with the user's intent.

TIP

Before sending a message, ask yourself the following: Would this still make sense and offer value if the user never responded? If not, it probably shouldn't go out.

WhatsApp

If you've already been building chatbots on Messenger or Instagram, you'll be glad to know that many of the same rules from the preceding sections apply on WhatsApp. You still need to be transparent, get proper opt-ins, and follow content and privacy policies. But WhatsApp adds a few extra layers, especially around how you initiate and deliver messages.

In this section, we look at what's the same, what's different, and what to watch for.

Knowing what you can and can't do on WhatsApp

WhatsApp messaging is more tightly controlled than other platforms. You can't start conversations whenever you want. Every message outside the initial 24-hour user-initiated window must use a preapproved message template.

That means the following:

>> You must get opt-in before sending proactive messages.

>> You can send outbound messages using WhatsApp's templated format only.

>> Those templates must be reviewed and approved by Meta before you can use them.

REMEMBER

WhatsApp templates can't be sneaky. Meta reviews every template for clarity and compliance. If your message looks spammy, misleading, or promotional without user consent, it won't get approved.

Getting the opt-in right

Just like on Messenger or Instagram, users must give clear permission to be contacted. But on WhatsApp, that consent usually happens off-platform, whether that's on your website, at checkout, or through a checkbox during another interaction.

Doing the following can help keep you compliant:

>> The opt-in must clearly explain what the user will receive (say, shipping updates, appointment reminders, or special offers).

>> The user must actively take action (like checking a box or clicking a button) to subscribe.

>> You need to store a record of their consent in case it's ever requested.

TIP

If you're collecting opt-ins on your website, include a line like "Yes, I'd like to receive updates via WhatsApp," with a short description of the message type and frequency.

Understanding the 24-hour rule on WhatsApp

WhatsApp uses the same 24-hour rule as Messenger (which we outline in the earlier section "Understanding the 24-hour messaging window"). If a user sends you a message, you have 24 hours to reply with a free-form message. After that, you can't message them again unless

>> You use a pre-approved template

>> The user re-engages and opens a new 24-hour window

This protocol is WhatsApp's way of keeping the user experience clean and respectful. No one wants to get spammed because they made one comment on your ad.

WARNING

Don't try to bypass the 24-hour window by sending "just checking in" or "is this still a good number?" messages. If it's not a user-initiated message or a pre-approved template, it's not allowed.

Deciding on WhatsApp message templates

WhatsApp *templates* are structured messages that Meta must review and approve before you can send them. Templates keep things consistent and prevent spammy outreach.

Templates come in three main categories:

>> **Transactional:** These service-based messages are things like order confirmations, shipping updates, booking reminders, and appointment changes. They're the most common and the easiest to get approved.

>> **Utility:** These follow-up messages are tied to a specific user action. Think of things like password resets or payment confirmations. They must provide timely and expected information.

>> **Marketing:** This category is the trickiest. Marketing templates can include promotions, offers, and re-engagement messages, but only if the user has opted in *specifically* for this type of messaging. These templates go through stricter approval and can be denied if they're vague or overly salesy.

TIP

Here are some key hints about using templates:

>> **If your template is rejected, don't try to slip it in under a different category.** Meta has strict filters in place and may flag your account if you repeatedly submit questionable content.

>> **Keep your templates short, clear, and focused.** Avoid using overly casual language or unnecessary hype, especially in marketing templates.

>> **Even if your template is approved, you still need the right opt-in.** Approval doesn't override compliance.

SMS

SMS is one of the most personal communication channels out there. It lands directly in someone's messages app on their phone, right next to texts from their family and friends. That's why it's heavily regulated, and why compliance matters even more when you're using a chatbot to automate the experience.

Complying with the laws that apply to SMS chatbots

Whether you're sending promotions, reminders, or confirmations through text, you need to understand the legal landscape. Ignorance won't protect you if someone files a complaint. Depending on where your business or your customers are located, several different laws may apply. The main ones include these:

>> The Telephone Consumer Protection Act (TCPA) in the United States

>> CAN-SPAM Act in the United States (applies more broadly to digital communication, including some SMS marketing)

>> CTIA guidelines (industry guidelines followed by U.S. mobile carriers)

>> Canada's Anti-Spam Law (CASL) in Canada

>> General Data Protection Regulation (GDPR) in the European Union

Each of these laws has slightly different rules, but they all agree on one thing: You need clear, written consent before you text someone.

REMEMBER

For SMS chatbots, *consent* means the user has actively agreed to receive messages, and they know what kind of messages they're agreeing to. In other words,

>> No pre-checked boxes

>> No sneaky language in your terms and conditions

>> No bundling SMS with unrelated opt-ins

To stay compliant, your opt-in should clearly state the following:

>> That users are agreeing to receive SMS messages

>> What kind of messages they'll get (such as reminders, promotions, updates)

>> How often you'll text them

>> That they can reply STOP at any time to unsubscribe

TIP

Use your chatbot to collect SMS opt-ins with a simple message like "Would you like to receive text reminders and special offers? Message frequency is 2 to 4 texts per month. Reply YES to opt in." Then follow that with a clear confirmation after they reply.

WARNING

Don't text users just because they gave you their phone number for another reason, such as placing an order. Unless they specifically agreed to receive marketing messages, it's a violation.

Respecting opt-outs and frequency limits

Compliance doesn't stop at the opt-in. You also need to respect how and when you follow up.

>> **Every SMS message must include a way to unsubscribe.** Most platforms do this automatically with a line like "Reply STOP to unsubscribe."

>> **You must process opt-outs immediately.** No delays. No extra messages. This part of your chatbot's job is just as important as sending messages is.

>> **Limit how often you message people.** Blasting users daily, even if they opted in, can lead to high complaint rates and blocked numbers.

TIP

Test your chatbot's unsubscribe flow regularly. If someone replies STOP, the conversation should end immediately, and they should be removed from all future campaigns.

Phone

Remember the days when calling a business meant getting stuck in a never-ending loop of "Press 1 for this; press 2 for that," followed by elevator music and a little frustration? Those old-school phone systems are getting a major upgrade. Thanks to AI and some serious tech advancements, phone chatbots — also called *voice chatbots* or *conversational interactive voice response* (IVR) — are sounding more human than ever. Sometimes it's hard to tell whether you're talking to a person or a machine.

With natural-sounding AI voices and smarter logic behind the conversation, today's phone chatbots can answer questions, book appointments, route calls, and even hold full conversations without ever involving a human. They can be powerful tools, especially for customer service, appointment-based businesses, and high-volume support centers. But although the tech has evolved, the rules still apply. You can't just dial up anyone and start chatting. You have compliance boxes to check and expectations to meet.

In this section, we take a look at what's allowed, what's not, and how to keep your phone chatbot both helpful and legal.

WHAT'S AN IVR?

Interactive voice response, or IVR, is the technology that lets people interact with a phone system by using their voice or by pressing numbers on their keypad.

You've definitely used IVR before. Think of when you call your doctor's office and hear "Press 1 to schedule an appointment. Press 2 to speak to billing." That's a traditional IVR.

Older IVR systems are rules-based and limited. But today's AI-powered voice chatbots work more like smart IVRs. They let users speak naturally, they understand intent, and they respond in real time, often without the user's needing to press a single button. (Head to Chapter 1 for more on the difference between rules-based and AI systems.)

Understanding the legal requirements for voice and phone chatbots

Like SMS and other platforms, phone chatbots are subject to both legal regulations and user experience best practices. And yes, you can still get in trouble if you don't play by the rules.

In the United States, most voice chatbot compliance issues fall under these laws:

>> TCPA

>> State-level privacy laws, like the California Consumer Privacy Act (CCPA) and others

>> FTC Telemarketing Sales Rule (TSR), especially if your chatbot uses outbound calling or prerecorded messages

Here's what those laws generally require:

>> You must have express written consent before calling or texting someone with a prerecorded or automated message.

>> You must identify yourself and your business clearly at the beginning of the call.

>> You must offer an easy opt-out, such as saying "Press 9 to stop receiving calls."

>> You can't contact people who are on the National Do Not Call Registry unless they've given permission or are an existing customer.

Sending prerecorded or AI-generated calls without prior consent is a quick way to get fined or reported. The TCPA doesn't mess around. Violations can cost up to $1,500 per call.

Building a legally compliant voice chatbot

Even if you're legally allowed to call someone, how you build your phone chatbot still matters. Here's how to do it right:

>> **Start with a clear introduction.** Say the name of your business and explain that the call is automated or AI-powered.

>> **Give people a way to reach a human at any time.** Voice chatbots should never trap users in endless loops.

>> **Respect silence or frustration.** If a user says, "Stop calling," or hangs up quickly, that's a signal to opt them out or route to a human next time.

>> **Avoid any tricks, like using real, human-sounding names or pretending to be live.** Not only are those practices unethical, but they may also violate consumer protection laws.

Transparency is key. A phone chatbot should never pretend to be something it's not.

Use AI voice chatbots to handle repetitive, high-volume questions or bookings. Leave the sales pitches and sensitive topics to a trained human.

Web chat

Of all the platforms you can build a chatbot on, web chat is hands down the most flexible. Unlike Messenger, Instagram, WhatsApp, or SMS, no third-party platform is setting strict boundaries around what you can or can't do. That freedom is one of the biggest reasons web chat is gaining popularity, especially for businesses that want full control over the experience.

But with that flexibility comes responsibility. You may not be tied to platform policies, but you're still accountable to data privacy laws and your users' trust.

In this section, we talk about what you can do, what you still need to watch out for, and how to keep things clean and compliant when your chatbot lives on your website.

Dealing with fewer rules

When you use web chat, you're not working within a platform's policies or tele-com rules. That means you have:

>> No 24-hour messaging window

>> No template approvals

>> No restrictions on promotional content

>> The ability to collect leads, follow up however you want, and build complex flows

However, because web chat typically runs on your website or is embedded in your app, you're responsible for the entire user experience and how user data is handled.

Being responsible despite the lack of rules

Just because web chat doesn't have strict platform rules doesn't mean you can ignore compliance. Privacy laws like GDPR, CCPA, and others still apply. Here's what you need to do to stay compliant with web chat:

>> Get clear consent before collecting personal information (such as email, phone number, or anything sensitive).

>> Disclose how you'll use data, and provide a link to your privacy policy.

>> Use cookies responsibly if your chatbot tracks sessions, behaviors, or returning users.

>> Provide a way to opt out of follow-up communication (like emails or SMS) that's triggered through your chatbot.

WARNING

Web chat platforms that store data in noncompliant ways (like unsecured data-bases or servers outside the required region) can put your business at risk. Always check your builder's data policy.

Staying Compliant and Avoiding Banishment

In the other sections of this chapter, we try to give you grasp on what keeping your chatbot compliant across multiple platforms takes. Knowing the rules isn't enough, however. You have to build your chatbot with compliance baked into every flow, every trigger, and every message. That's why in this section, we explain how to keep your chatbot (and your business) in the clear.

Violating terms of service, skipping proper opt-ins, or sending the wrong kind of message to the wrong person on the wrong platform can result in more than an error message. It can mean a warning from Meta, a blocked SMS number, lost access to your business tools, or getting banned entirely from a platform. And when that happens, recovery is rarely quick (and sometimes impossible).

Knowing the rules for each platform

Don't assume what works on one platform will work on another. As we detail throughout the chapter, each channel has its own playbook, so treat them accordingly.

Create a cheat sheet for yourself or your team that outlines the key compliance rules for Messenger, Instagram, WhatsApp, SMS, phone, and web chat. It'll save you headaches later.

Collecting proper opt-ins

We say it earlier in the chapter, but we'll say it here, too: Always get permission before you message someone. Regardless of the platform, consent should be crystal clear — and distinct for all channels you intend to use to message users. Let people know what they're signing up for and how often they'll hear from you.

Keeping user trust at the center

Transparency is a trust-builder in addition to a legal requirement. Be upfront about who is messaging, how data is being used, and how someone can opt out. People are far more likely to stick around when they feel respected; if you make it hard for people to leave, they'll report you instead.

Monitoring changes in policy

Platform rules, privacy laws, and messaging limitations are always evolving. What's allowed today may be restricted tomorrow. Subscribe to platform update emails, bookmark Meta's policy center, and check in with your chatbot platform regularly.

At the end of the day, staying current on compliance isn't about fear. It's about respect. When you take the time to know and follow the rules, you create a better experience for your users and a safer, longer-lasting system for your business.

Chapter **16**

Creating a Long-Term Chatbot Strategy

A truth that a lot of people don't talk about: Many companies that saw early success with chatbots didn't always stick with them. If you go back and look at some of the businesses featured in those feel-good chatbot case studies, you'll find that many have simplified their chatbots or are no longer using chat automation at all.

What happened? In many cases, it comes down to one thing: They never created a long-term chatbot strategy.

Instead, they launched a few one-off campaigns, got some quick wins, and called it a day. No one owned the system or was responsible for maintaining it. And as teams changed and priorities shifted over time, those once-powerful chatbots sat untouched, became outdated, and were eventually forgotten.

REMEMBER

A chatbot isn't a set-it-and-forget-it tool. If no one is owning it, updating it, or measuring its value, it'll get sidelined in no time.

This chapter is all about avoiding that outcome. We show you how to build a chatbot strategy that supports your business long after the bot's launch. We also talk about how to align your chatbot with your evolving goals, what scaling your systems looks like, and how to keep your automations running smoothly as your team and tools grow. Whether you're managing everything yourself, working with a team, or planning to hire a contractor, this chapter can help you create a plan for long-term success and not just a temporary boost.

Aligning Your Chatbot with Business Goals

Your chatbot isn't just a customer service tool or a way to grab emails. It's a business asset. And like any other tool in your marketing or sales toolbox, it needs to support your overall strategy. That means tying your chatbot back to your business goals. Not once, but regularly.

Knowing your current goals

Businesses evolve, and their chatbots should evolve with them. Are you focused on lead generation right now? Driving traffic to a new offer? Reducing customer service requests? Your chatbot should reflect that priority.

Ask yourself the following:

>> What are our top three goals for the next quarter?

>> Is the chatbot helping us move toward any of those goals?

>> Where's it falling short or not being used at all?

If the answer is "I'm not sure," go back and review your flows, messages, and entry points to make sure everything still lines up with where you're headed.

TIP

Add a quarterly chatbot check-in to your calendar. Review goals, flows, and performance like you would with email or social content. We offer a more detailed punch list for that review in the later section "Your quarterly or biannual chatbot strategy review checklist."

Prioritizing high-impact use cases

REMEMBER

Your chatbot doesn't need to do everything. It needs to do the right things. Not every chatbot function carries equal weight.

You may have built out flows for everything from booking appointments to sharing blog posts, but that doesn't mean they're all driving results. Look at your analytics and your customer journey. Which chatbot flows are moving the needle? Start there.

Some examples of high-impact use cases include these:

>> Converting social media traffic into leads or subscribers

>> Automating appointment scheduling or product recommendations

>> Reducing the number of repetitive support questions in your inbox

>> Delivering content or offers that nurture leads toward a sale

If you can connect a flow to real results like conversions, clicks, or saved time, it's worth maintaining and optimizing. If it's not doing anything useful, you may want to archive or improve it.

Assigning an owner

One of the biggest reasons chatbots go stale is that no one is in charge of them. If it's everyone's job, it's no one's job.

Assign clear responsibility to someone — whether that's you, someone on your team, or an outside contractor — for reviewing, updating, and measuring chatbot performance. That person should:

>> Know how to use your chatbot platform

>> Have access to key business goals and campaigns

>> Be able to edit or request edits to flows and automations

>> Regularly report back on performance or issues

Even if it's a small role right now, assigning ownership ensures your chatbot stays aligned and doesn't get buried under everything else on your to-do list.

TIP

If you're a solopreneur, block off 30 minutes per month to review your chatbot flows and stats. You don't need a whole team; all you need is a calendar reminder and a plan.

Scaling: When to Upgrade, Hire, or Outsource

After your chatbot is up and running, you'll eventually hit a point where you need to level up. That may mean adding more features, reaching more people, or simply trying to keep up with everything your chatbot is doing behind the scenes.

But here's the deal: Scaling doesn't always mean spending more money. It means being strategic about what you upgrade, what you delegate, and how you make sure your chatbot continues to grow with your business.

Deciding when to upgrade your platform

If your chatbot platform no longer meets your needs, you may want to consider something more advanced. Maybe you've hit your subscriber limit, need better AI capabilities, or want features like built-in email or SMS integration. Whatever the reason, the platform you start with isn't always be the one you stick with.

That said, switching platforms is neither fun nor easy. Especially on Meta platforms, moving subscribers from one chatbot builder to another can be messy, time-consuming, and result in losing a chunk of your audience.

TIP

You're not limited to only one chatbot platform. If your business has multiple needs, using more than one is perfectly fine. For example, Manychat is an excellent choice for TikTok, Instagram, Facebook, and WhatsApp, but it doesn't offer web chat. If you love Manychat but need web chat options, you can continue using it for social and pair it with another platform that specializes in web chat. You just need to decide whether you prefer an all-in-one solution or a combination of platforms that each do one thing well.

REMEMBER

Choosing the right platform from the start is one of the smartest moves you can make. That's why it's so important to think long-term before you even choose a chatbot platform. Ask yourself these questions:

>> Will this platform grow with my business?

>> Does it support all the channels I use or plan to use (like web chat, Instagram, or SMS)?

>> What does it offer in terms of AI, segmentation, or compliance tools?

For more on choosing a chatbot platform, head to Chapter 4.

Outsourcing your chatbot build (or management)

Not everyone wants to build a chatbot from scratch, and that's okay. In fact, many businesses outsource their chatbot builds to specialists who know how to handle the tech, strategy, and compliance sides of things.

As someone who's built a lot of chatbots for businesses, I (Kelly) can tell you first-hand that outsourcing the build is a common — and smart — move. Chatbots aren't your average marketing tool. They have platform rules to follow, AI integrations to manage, and real strategy involved. Working with someone who knows what they're doing can save you time and prevent mistakes.

If you decide to hire or outsource, here's what to look for:

>> Experience with your preferred platform (or a strong case for the one they recommend)

>> Examples of past chatbot builds or references from happy clients

>> Knowledge of compliance rules, especially on platforms like Meta

>> Experience with the specific type of chatbot you need, such as phone, SMS, or AI-powered flows

>> An ability to keep things simple

WARNING

If someone tries to impress you with their coding knowledge for a simple chatbot project, that's a red flag. You don't need a developer. You need someone who understands strategy, platforms, and what works for your business. Most chatbots today are built 100 percent without coding. You want strategy and smart building, not unnecessary tech headaches.

REMEMBER

You can absolutely manage and scale your chatbot yourself, especially if you're a solopreneur or a scrappy small team. But what you can't do is ignore it. Ensure someone (whether they're inside or outside your organization) consistently reviews the chatbot, examines performance metrics, and determines what to improve next. The fastest way to kill a successful chatbot is to leave it unmanaged. Assign someone to own it or risk losing momentum.

Future-Proofing Your Automation Systems

Building a great chatbot is one thing. Making sure it still works six months or a year from now is another. Businesses, tools, and platforms all change. If you want your chatbot to continue delivering value over time, you need a plan to keep it updated, functional, and aligned with your business goals.

This section is all about setting up those systems and habits now so your chatbot doesn't fall apart later.

Creating an operating procedure for long-term success

One of the most important steps you can take to future-proof your chatbot is to create a standard operating procedure (SOP). This system doesn't have to be fancy, but it does need to be easy to follow.

Your chatbot SOP should include the following:

>> A list of the tools your chatbot connects to, such as customer relationship management (CRM) systems, calendars, email systems, and so on

>> Step-by-step instructions for editing or updating chatbot flows

>> What to update when something changes in your business (like services, pricing, contact info, or documentation)

>> Who's responsible for the updates

>> How to test and review chatbot changes before pushing them live

TIP

Treat your chatbot like a living part of your business. If your offers or messaging change, your chatbot should reflect that shift right away.

Building in regular check-ins

Don't wait until your chatbot breaks or becomes outdated. A stale chatbot can create confusion, broken experiences, and even lost sales. Instead, create a schedule for regular reviews based on how often your business changes.

Here's what we recommend:

>> **Weekly quick checks:** The chatbot manager should dedicate time each week to reviewing the logs, verifying that recent flows are functioning correctly, and identifying any broken links or errors.

>> **Quarterly or biannual reviews:** Set aside time to thoroughly review the chatbot. Are the flows still relevant? Have your goals changed? Are new features available that you could be using?

These regular check-ins can help you catch minor issues before they become big problems.

Your weekly chatbot review checklist

Set aside 30 to 60 minutes each week to quickly check your chatbot's health. Use this checklist to make sure everything is working as expected:

>> Check your error logs for failed messages or broken flows. Read more about these lists in the later section "Monitoring error logs and platform status."

>> Make sure all scheduled messages or campaigns are sending properly.

>> Refresh platform permissions if anything looks disconnected. "Refreshing permissions regularly" later in the chapter has more info on this task.

>> Review any new comments, DMs, or customer feedback that may indicate user confusion.

>> Update your knowledge base or FAQ content if anything has changed in your business.

Your quarterly or biannual chatbot strategy review checklist

This deeper review helps make sure your chatbot is aligned with your current goals and still functioning across all connected systems. Schedule time each quarter, or at least twice a year, to run through this checklist:

>> Check for changes to services, pricing, business hours, or documentation.

>> Audit all active chatbot flows for accuracy, tone, and performance.

>> Test all major conversation paths from start to finish.

>> Review chatbot analytics to find drop-off points or underperforming flows.

>> Confirm all connected tools like CRMs, email marketing platforms, or calendars are working properly.

>> Refresh platform permissions across Meta and third-party apps (see the later section "Refreshing permissions regularly").

>> Review any compliance updates from platforms like Meta or your SMS provider.

>> Meet with customer service, operations, and other teams to identify any updates.

Monitoring error logs and platform status

REMEMBER

Just because your chatbot looks okay from the outside doesn't mean it's working correctly. If messages aren't being delivered or actions aren't firing, you can often find the problem in your error logs.

Every quality chatbot platform should give you access to *error logs*. These logs show issues like message failures, broken integrations, and permission problems that can silently break parts of your chatbot. Make sure to locate where your error logs live and check them regularly. If you're not sure where to find them, look through the platform's automation or settings area.

For example, in Chatrace, error logs are available under the Flows section of the dashboard, as shown in Figure 16-1. Here, you can see which flows failed, what the issue was, and when it happened.

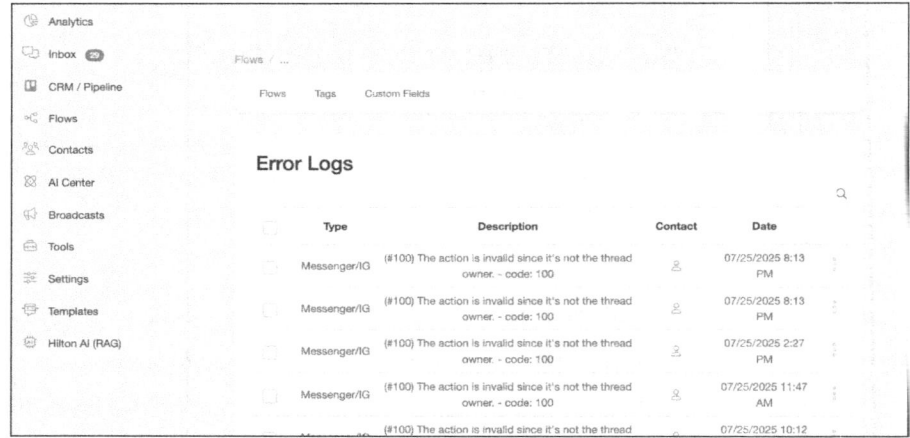

FIGURE 16-1:
Error logs in Chatrace's Flow section.

In Manychat, you can find error logs under Settings → Logs, as shown in Figure 16-2. This area shows failed messages, application programming interface (API) errors, and permission issues. It also highlights problems related to Facebook page permissions, which are a common source of unexpected issues (see Figure 16-3).

Refreshing permissions regularly

If you're using a platform like Facebook, Instagram, or external tools through Zapier or Make (see Chapter 7), permissions can expire over time. You may not get an alert when that happens, but you'll start to notice that certain parts of your chatbot stop working.

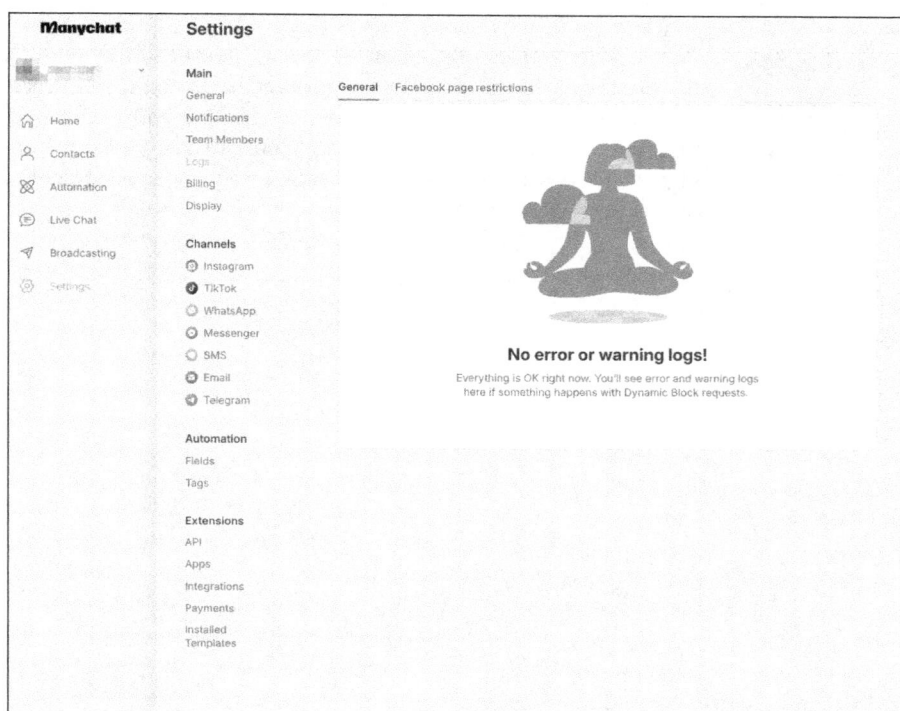

FIGURE 16-2:
Error Logs and
Page Status
in Manychat.

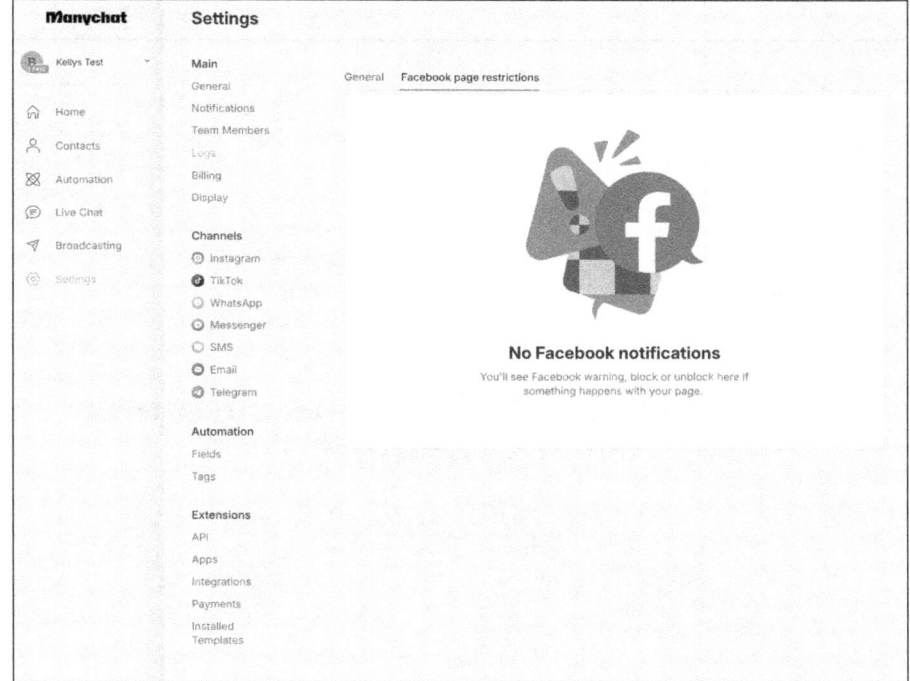

FIGURE 16-3:
Manychat status
for Facebook
page restrictions.

TIP

That's why refreshing your platform permissions as part of your regular maintenance routine like we suggest earlier in the chapter is a good habit. Doing so helps prevent many of the hidden issues that show up in your error logs — and that's more issues than you think. You can see a Manychat-based example in Figure 16-4. After refreshing, always test your most essential flows to confirm that things are working correctly.

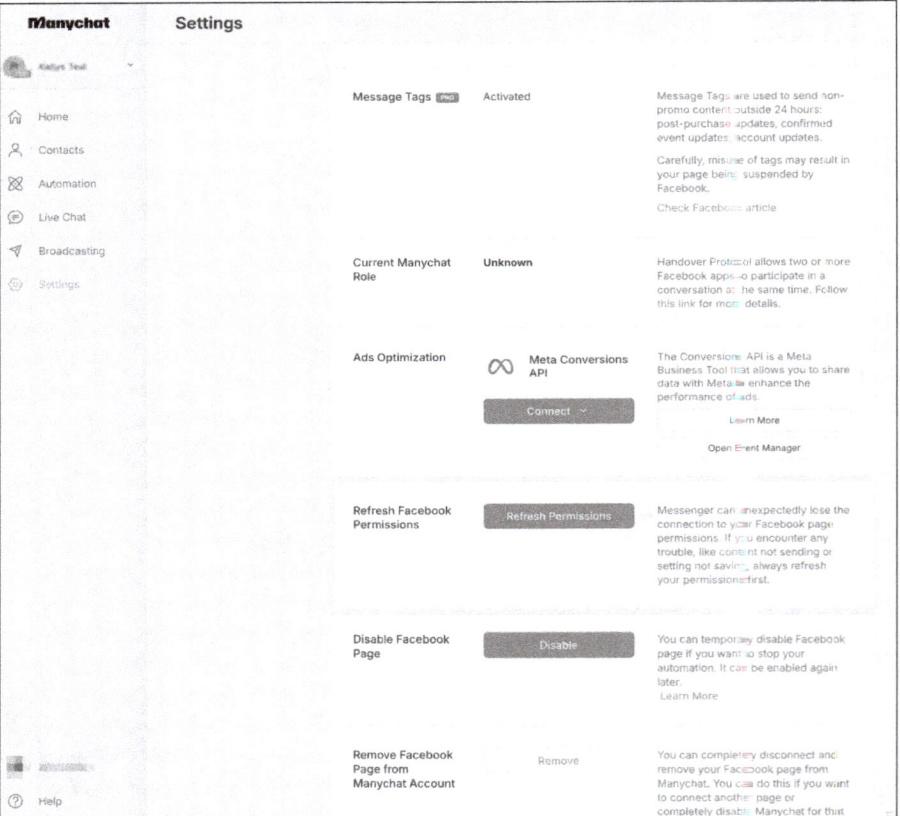

FIGURE 16-4:
You can find the Manychat refresh button in that platform's settings.

Keeping a platform's customer service top of mind

One of the smartest things you can do when selecting a chatbot platform is to test its customer support *before* you commit. At some point, you're going to run into a bug, an integration hiccup, or a compliance question. If you can't get timely help, your entire system may get delayed or, worse, break down at a critical time.

Before committing to a platform, send a test inquiry or explore its help center and community forums. See how quickly the company responds and how helpful its support team is.

Testing early is important because not all chatbot companies offer equal support. For example, Manychat and Chatfuel (platforms we discuss in Chapter 4) consistently provide fast, reliable customer service. But Chatrace, a platform I (Kelly) love for its solid features and flexibility, has customer service that isn't the most responsive. So if a platform checks all the boxes for you in terms of capabilities but you know you'll want more hands-on support than it gives, you may want to consider using one of its white label providers. A *white label provider* licenses another company's platform and rebrands it as its own, often adding more personalized support, training, or extra features to improve your overall experience.

White label platforms can be hard to identify because they don't always advertise their connection to a platform. But if you compare interfaces and features, you can usually spot the overlap. One white label I personally use is Chatibots (chatibots. com). The customer service there is decent, and though I don't usually need much support because I know the platform well, having it available when needed is reassuring.

Your chatbot is only as strong as the support system behind it. A great platform with terrible support ultimately costs you more in stress, time, and missed opportunities.

5
The Part of Tens

IN THIS PART . . .

Avoid ten common chatbot mistakes.

Explore ten tools that optimize your chatbot strategy.

Chapter **17**

Ten Common Chatbot Mistakes (and How to Avoid Them)

M aking mistakes with AI chatbots when you're first starting out is easy. We don't want that for you, and we figure you don't want that because you're reading this chapter.

In the following sections, we review the ten common chatbot mistakes. You may have heard of the old adage "a stitch in time saves nine," so after each mistake we also tell you how to stitch up your AI chatbot at the start so you don't have to go back and make time-consuming fixes later.

Making It Too Complex

When you first start training your chatbot, you may be tempted to add just one more thing to account for everything you think the user will want to ask. That's a good way to invite scope creep and never finish your chatbot's training, not to mention to confuse and frustrate your user.

So use the tried-and-true KISS method. *KISS* stands for "keep it simple, stupid," and applying it to chatbot training means you need to focus on the essential questions users want answered, keep the paths to a solution clear, and keep the interactions straightforward.

TIP

Many chatbot platforms have tutorials on their websites for training your chatbot. For example, ChatBot offers chatbot best practices on its website shown in Figure 17-1.

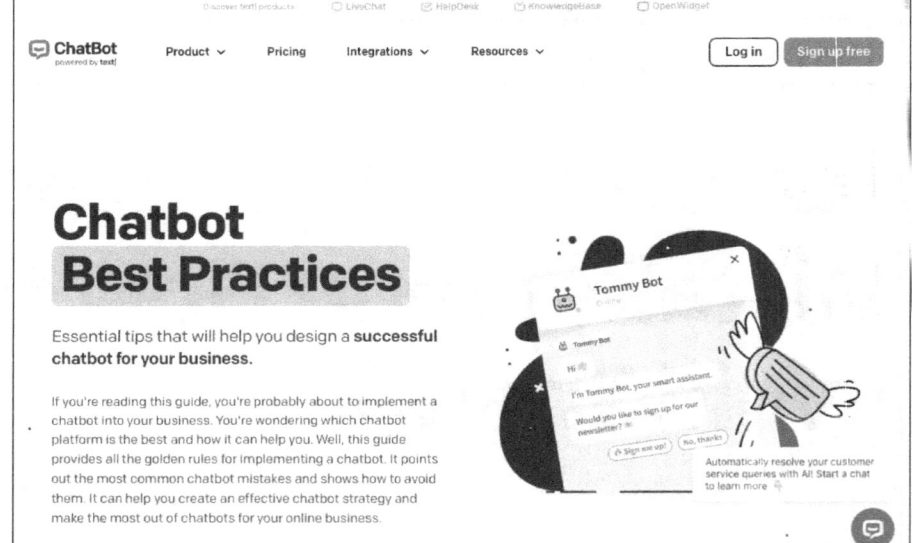

FIGURE 17-1:
The ChatBot best practices page guides you from planning to building to monitoring your chatbot.

Forgetting Human Handoff

If your chatbot doesn't make connecting with a human easy for users when the chatbot can't solve their problem, then the chatbot isn't ready for prime time. Even worse, you may lose a potential or current customer to a competitor and not even know about it. (Gasp!)

Serve your customers the right way and ensure a seamless handoff to a live human. An even better idea is to keep customer support contact information on your website and/or app, such as a phone number on every page of your site. That reassures customers that you still have human agents ready to help them if a chatbot doesn't float their boat.

Not Testing Flows

Like with any new technology, not rigorously testing your chatbot before you roll it out to customers will lead to some bad juju. (That's a technical term.)

Avoid as many errors and bugs as possible by testing your chatbot internally — and ideally with a few willing customers. (Don't forget the incentives.) Incorporate their feedback into subsequent versions so you can test it again.

REMEMBER

Don't let perfect be the enemy of the good. Have an end goal in mind before you start testing so you know when the chatbot is good enough to release to the world. If you keep saying, "one more thing," we bet you two dollars to a donut (donuts are pricier these days) that your company leaders will wonder why you're wasting their money.

Ignoring Analytics

We note throughout the book that launching a chatbot isn't a situation where you can set it and forget it. You need to use the analytics tools in your platform, and perhaps additional analytics tools like Google Analytics, to find out how the chatbot is performing.

That includes user behavior, engagement rates, and, perhaps most importantly, conversion metrics. All these data don't mean anything unless you act upon them to improve your chatbot so you can relieve users' pain points, answer their questions, and get them to buy from you.

Being Too Robotic

Even with the natural language processing powers of AI, you can still make your chatbot sound like a robot with stilted grammar or, worse, give responses with only a few words. (If your chatbot could talk, it may sound like the computer from the original series of *Star Trek*. Look it up online.)

One of the key chatbot features you need to test is how personable, relatable, and engaging the chatbot is. If your tester feedback says your chatbot isn't all that friendly, fix the problem before you introduce your chatbot to the world. Unfriendly, robotic chatbots can lead to lost customers and lost sales.

Breaking Platform Rules

Chatbot platform companies are like any other tech companies in that they have terms and conditions for their use, including content, messaging frequency, and especially data handling.

Whether you're shopping for an AI chatbot platform or you're already using one, reviewing the platform's terms and conditions — and also discussing them with your platform's sales and support teams when you have questions — is a good idea.

TIP

You can find terms and conditions on the company's website; the link is usually at the bottom of the home page with all the other links. For example, when you click Terms of Service at the bottom of the Manychat home page, the Terms of Service page appears (see Figure 17-2).

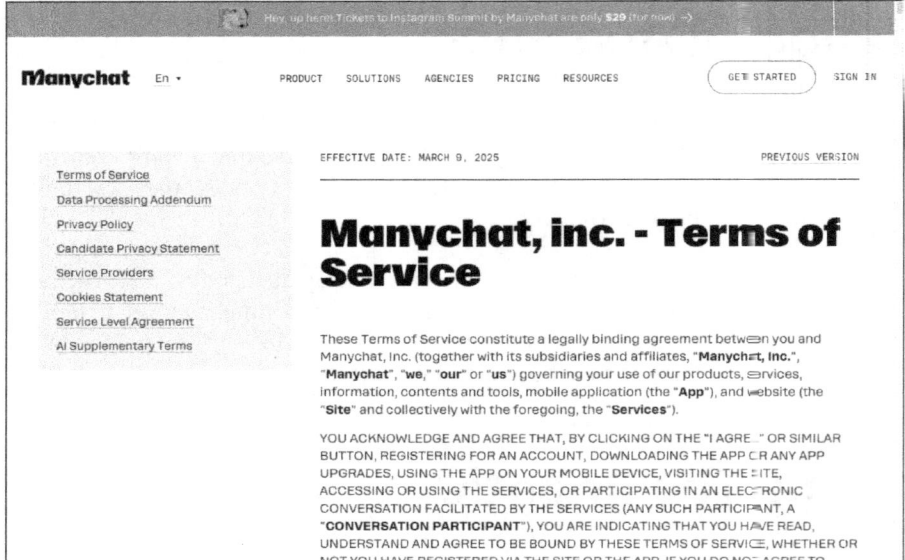

FIGURE 17-2:
The Manychat terms of service is divided into eight sections.

REMEMBER

Chatbot platforms update their terms of service regularly, so visit that page often to see whether terms have been updated and what those updates entail.

Failing to Segment Audiences

If you're naïve or lazy, you may think a one-size-fits-all approach is the way to go. But if you don't have different messages for different audience segments, you'll be left to wonder why you have fewer people using the chatbot — and buying from you.

After all, using Gen Z slang with boomers is only going to confuse and annoy the latter group, and people who are first-time buyers need a different approach than returning customers. So use your chatbot platform's abilities to segment your audiences and give them different messages that are more likely to make your customers happier. Happier customers are more likely to recommend your business to their family and friends.

Using Confusing Copy

Humans often get too close to their topics of interest and think that they need to use a lot of jargon to sound like an authority in their field. But jargon can simply confuse customers, and confused customers drop out of your chatbot (and maybe your company altogether).

If you fill your website and other marketing copy with jargon, you're going to do that with your chatbot. So the KISS method we talk about in the earlier section "Making It Too Complex" applies. Write clear, concise, user-friendly copy that keeps the geek-speak to a dull roar.

TIP

Come to think of it, de-jargoning your chatbot is a great opportunity for you to look at the rest of your marketing assets and see where you can make your message clearer.

Not Setting Expectations

If you don't set expectations about your chatbot from the outset, users will set their own. And we don't think it's a stretch of any kind to say that most of your users will be disappointed by what they find.

You may receive grumbles about the chatbot. Your human support team may not see any drop-offs in calls because calling in is easier for customers than dealing with a chatbot that doesn't do what they want. Then your powers that be may come to you asking why the chatbot isn't giving the company the cost savings you promised.

When you aren't upfront about what the chatbot can do, what it can't, and when the user should contact a human, then all people see is bad technology. And if they see bad technology on your website and/or app, they'll think your company doesn't know what it's doing. You don't want that . . . but your competitors do.

Trying to Do Too Much at Once

Part of unnecessary complexity (see the earlier section "Making It Too Complex") is trying to do too much all at once. If you add too many functions and features, your users may become confused or overwhelmed, throw up their hands, and call your human support people.

WARNING

If your leadership has decided to replace your human support with your chatbot, the lack of human support is the dictionary definition of bad foreshadowing, complete with ominous music. (Perhaps *leadership* should be in quotes.)

Save your customers (not to mention yourself) a lot of stress by planning ahead. Focus on the chatbot functions that align with your primary goals and then analyze the results. How your users respond to and use the chatbot can help you decide what features to add next.

REMEMBER

Don't forget to request feedback from your users at the (hopefully successful) end of a conversation. Specifically, ask what they think of your chatbot and what else they want the chatbot to do to help them.

Chapter **18**

Ten Tools to Supercharge Your Chatbot Strategy

S trategy is just one side of the coin of successful chatbots. The other side? The tools you use to bring that strategy to life. If you've ever felt like you're constantly juggling spreadsheets, copy drafts, calendars, or analytics dashboards while building out your automations, you're not alone.

This chapter is a roundup of tools and platforms that can help you build smarter, faster, and with more impact while saving you time. These aren't chatbot platforms themselves (we cover those in Chapter 4). They're the power-ups that work alongside your chatbot to help you capture leads, collect data, personalize conversations, and streamline delivery. Regardless of where you are in your chatbot journey, the tools in this chapter can help you level up.

REMEMBER

A strong chatbot strategy doesn't rely on just one tool. It's about finding the right combination that works for you and your business. That said, you don't need to use all ten options in this chapter. Think of it like your chatbot toolbox. Pick the tools that make the most sense for your goals, audience, and workflow, and ignore the ones that don't.

Zapier or Make for Automation

In Chapter 7, we introduce Zapier and Make (formerly Integromat), two automation platforms that let your chatbot talk to thousands of other apps, even the ones your chatbot builder doesn't natively support. Whether you're trying to move lead data into a customer relationship management (CRM) system, send an email when someone fills out a quiz, or enroll a user in an online course, Zapier or Make can help it happen behind the scenes.

Although these tools serve the same general purpose, each one shines in different ways. Depending on your comfort level, budget, and the complexity of what you're trying to build, one may be a better fit for you than the other.

Zapier

TIP

Zapier is one of the easiest automation tools to use, especially for beginners. It works off of a trigger-and-action system, meaning you can create simple workflows like "When a lead comes in and completes specific steps, send their contact info via SMS to my phone." No coding required, and the interface is super user-friendly.

Figure 18-1 shows the start of a zap between Manychat and Zapier, where an SMS message with lead information is sent.

Zapier is perfect when you need a quick connection between your chatbot and your CRM, email platform, Google Sheet, or any other tool in your tech stack. It also has tons of pre-built integrations, which makes setup even faster.

WARNING

Zapier can get pricey depending on how many tasks your automation runs. Check your monthly task count often so you don't get surprised by an unexpected bill.

Make

Make is the tool I (Kelly) reach for when a project requires more advanced logic, multiple steps, or data filtering. Make gives you a visual map of your automation so you can see how each action flows into the next and even add branching paths based on user input, tags, or conditions.

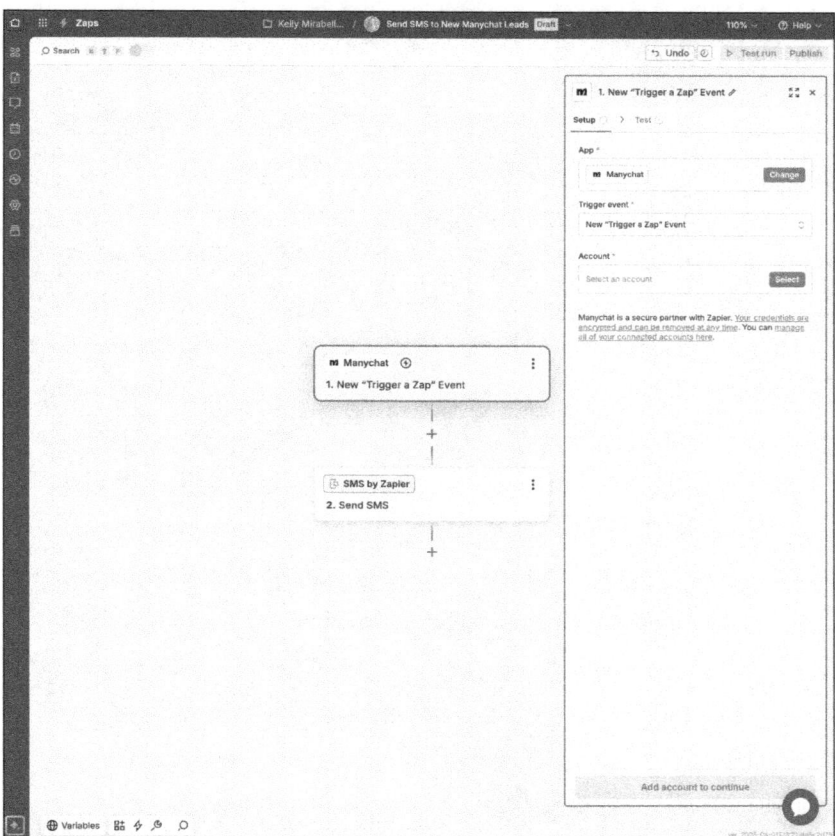

FIGURE 18-1:
Triggering a
zap event.

TIP

This functionality is especially helpful if you need your chatbot to interact with more than one platform at a time or perform checks before continuing. It's a little more technical than Zapier (see the preceding section), but after you get used to it, the flexibility is hard to beat.

In Figure 18-2, you can see one of the many templates that Make offers that can help your connect one or more external tools or actions.

REMEMBER

Make is powerful, but it does have a learning curve. Be patient with yourself during setup, and don't be afraid to lean on Make's templates and community forum when you're stuck.

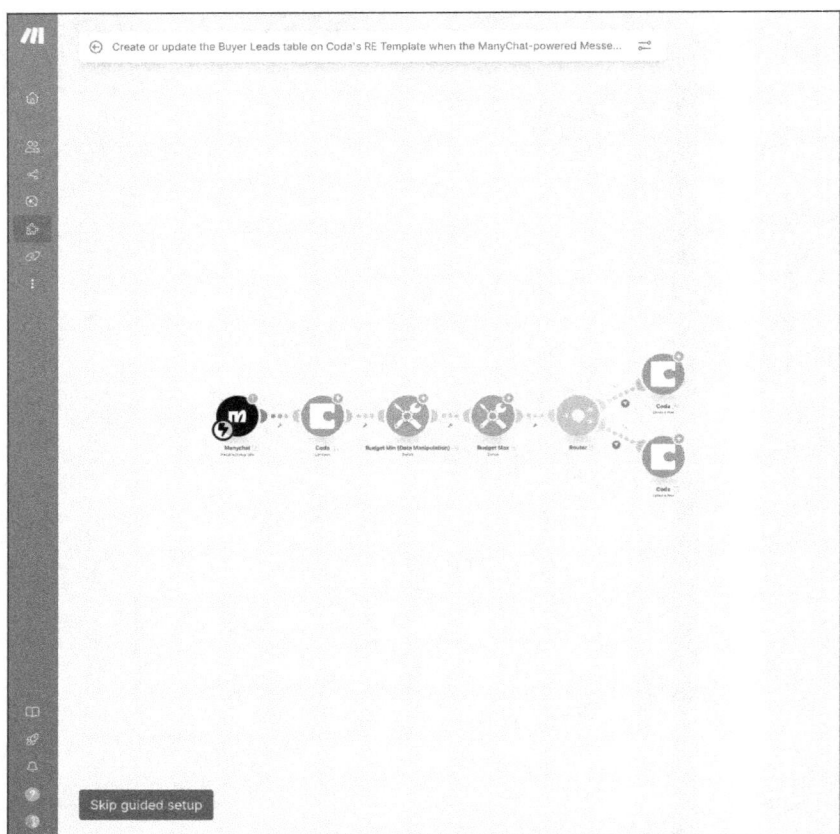

FIGURE 18-2:
Make
automations
flow.

Google Sheets for Data Collection

For many small businesses and solo marketers, Google Sheets is one of the easiest and most effective ways to organize chatbot data without needing a CRM. From lead collection to quiz answers to tracking signups, Google Sheets gives you a simple, visual way to keep tabs on what's happening inside your chatbot flows. It's a great stepping stone for data collection.

As we note in Chapter 7, most chatbot platforms integrate directly with Google Sheets or can connect through a third-party automation tool. That means you can automatically send chatbot data — like a user's name, email, or even their answers to a quiz — into a neatly organized spreadsheet. No copying and pasting, no chasing down inboxes, and no wondering where that lead went. It's also a handy way to review chatbot performance over time because you can filter, sort, and even chart the data right inside the sheet. It's fast, familiar, and flexible enough for most nontechnical teams.

WARNING

Google Sheets isn't HIPAA compliant or built for handling sensitive information. If you're in a regulated industry, like health care or finance, avoid storing anything confidential here.

Large Language Models for Copy and Logic Writing

When you're writing chatbot copy or mapping out your logic, large language models (LLMs) like ChatGPT, Gemini, and Claude can make your work a whole lot easier. These tools can help you brainstorm welcome messages, fine-tune your flows, draft quiz responses, and even troubleshoot logic paths when things get messy. Whether you're building something from scratch or optimizing an existing flow, an LLM can save you time and spark better ideas.

TIP

LLMs are great for speeding up the creative side of chatbot building, but avoid simply cutting and pasting LLM copy into your chatbot. Start your chatbot copywriting process in an LLM to get a rough draft going. Then polish and personalize it based on your brand voice and user needs.

These tools are also helpful for writing logical expressions. If you're stuck figuring out how to structure a quiz, scoring system, or conditional path, you can ask your favorite LLM to help you outline the steps. They don't replace your understanding of how your chatbot platform works, but they can help you map out a better plan before you start dragging blocks around.

REMEMBER

Not every chatbot platform supports every LLM, so always check your chatbot platform's LLM compatibility before you commit. If you're planning to connect ChatGPT, Claude, or Gemini through an application programming interface (API — see Chapter 6), your platform needs to support that connection.

The following list can help you choose among ChatGPT, Gemini, and Claude:

» **ChatGPT (OpenAI):** This option is best for general chatbot writing, conversational tone, and quick idea generation. ChatGPT is beneficial if you want to write in a warm, friendly voice or need a fast second brain to brainstorm flows, messages, or quizzes. It's also the most widely supported by chatbot platforms, making it an easy plug-in choice.

» **Gemini (Google):** Gemini is best for integration with Google's ecosystem. It shines when you're working on content that touches Google Docs, Sheets, Calendar, or

Gmail. It can speed up the copy process when you're juggling multiple Google tools or planning content that lives both inside and outside the chatbot.

>> **Claude (Anthropic):** This choice is best for long-form and complex logic planning. Claude handles longer context better than the others, which makes it ideal for working on quizzes with lots of conditional logic; product recommenders; or even chatbot flows that simulate deeper conversations. Its tone also feels more cautious and balanced, which can be a plus in regulated industries.

TIP

You don't have to pick just one. Use each tool where it shines and adapt your workflow around what works best for the task at hand. I (Kelly) personally use a tool called Magai to access all the major LLMs in one place. It gives me the flexibility to use the following options — plus many more LLMs on the market — without having to pay for each one separately. Although Magai doesn't support API connections for chatbot integration, it's perfect for content creation, brainstorming, and logic planning. If you want to try it out, I have a special affiliate link that gets you 30 percent off your first month: `Magai.co/kelly`.

Canva for Visuals Inside Bots

A picture is worth a thousand words, and the right image can make all the difference in chatbot engagement. When you're designing banners, thumbnails, product images, or playful graphics, Canva makes creating professional-looking assets that fit right into your flow simple.

You don't need to be a designer to get great results. Canva offers pre-sized templates and drag-and-drop elements, allowing you to quickly build visuals for Messenger, Instagram DMs, and web chat. Use it to make lead magnet previews, cover images for guides, and quiz results graphics.

TIP

Use Canva to create visual "confirmation" cards that show up right after someone books a call, signs up for a freebie, or completes a quiz. It reinforces their action and adds a polished, branded — but also human — touch.

Just remember that most chatbot platforms have file size limits, especially Meta platforms like Messenger and Instagram; they typically max out at 100 MB, depending on the content type. Keep your images optimized for web and mobile. PNGs usually look best for graphics, but JPEGs tend to load faster.

WARNING

Using large images or sending too many files at once can slow down delivery and cause frustration. Always test your visuals on mobile before publishing your chatbot.

Calendly or Google Calendar for Bookings

If your chatbot's goal is to drive calls, consultations, or appointments, then integrating a scheduling tool is a must. Tools like Calendly or Google Calendar let your chatbot hand off the booking process without any back-and-forth emails or missed messages. The user picks a time that works for them, the system handles the reminders, and your calendar stays up to date.

Calendly is especially chatbot-friendly, as we explain in Chapter 7. You can build a flow that asks for the user's name, email, and reason for the call and then send them to a custom Calendly link to complete the booking. If you want to take it a step farther, you can use automation tools like Zapier or Make (which we discuss earlier in the chapter) to push that booking data into your CRM or notify your team in real time.

TIP

Collect basic info in the chatbot before sending someone to your calendar. That way, your form is pre-filled and your booking page stays clean and focused. The fewer steps between your user and the confirmation screen, the better. Make your booking flow feel like a natural part of the conversation.

If you're using Google Calendar directly, note that some chatbot platforms don't have a native integration for it, but you can still make it work. Use a connected form or automation to generate an event, or link to a Google Form that feeds into a calendar automation using Zapier. It's not as seamless as Calendly, but it's a free and flexible option if you're just getting started.

Stripe or PayPal for Payments

Integrating payment options like Stripe and PayPal is the way to go if you want your chatbot to close sales or take payments. These tools enable secure transaction processing without redirecting users to a separate checkout process.

Most chatbot platforms offer native support for Stripe, which makes setup painless. It's also a good option if you're planning to scale or expand internationally. It supports multiple currencies and payment methods, and its dashboard makes keeping track of everything in one place easy.

PayPal is still one of the most recognized and trusted names in online payments, though not all chatbot platforms support it natively. Be sure to check compatibility before you commit. Offering PayPal as an option can boost conversions, especially with customers who already have a PayPal balance or choose not to enter card details. If you're selling on a website chatbot or want to keep things simple, PayPal is a great addition to your payment flow.

TIP

If your chatbot is hosted on a website, you often have more flexibility. Web chat allows you to offer both Stripe and PayPal as payment options or even embed your own checkout pages.

You can read more about the nitty-gritty of setting up payment tools — and staying compliant with special sets of rules, like those for Meta platforms — in Chapter 7.

Twilio or AudioCodes for SMS and Voice Calling

If you're looking to expand beyond Messenger, Instagram, or web chat, SMS and voice calls are excellent additions to your chatbot strategy. Tools like Twilio and AudioCodes allow you to send text messages, place automated voice calls, or even trigger call forwarding directly from your chatbot. These functions are especially helpful when you need to reach users quickly or communicate outside the 24-hour Meta messaging window (see Chapter 11).

When used correctly, adding SMS or voice functionality to your chatbot can boost engagement and make your automations feel more human. But make sure your messages are timely, relevant, and respectful of your audience's preferences.

WARNING

Before sending any SMS messages, you must collect proper opt-in and follow all local laws around text marketing. That includes providing an easy way to opt out.

Twilio is the more commonly used of the two tools, especially for SMS. AudioCodes is a more specialized option typically used in enterprise environments or by developers working on voice-first systems. We break them down further in the following sections.

REMEMBER

As with any tool, not all chatbot builders have native integrations with Twilio or AudioCodes. In some cases, you may need to connect using an external tool like Make or a webhook (we discuss those in Chapter 7). That extra step may take a little longer to set up, but it gives you more control over how and when your chatbot sends texts or places calls.

Twilio

Twilio offers voice capabilities if you need to set up automated calls or simple call routing. But it really shines when used for text-based messaging. It integrates with many chatbot platforms and can handle a wide range of tasks like appointment reminders, real-time alerts, event follow-ups, and promotional messages.

What makes Twilio especially valuable is its reliability and scalability. You can start small and grow over time without changing systems. It also supports two-way messaging if your platform allows it, which means users can reply and your chatbot can respond accordingly.

AudioCodes

If your chatbot strategy involves voice assistants, call routing, or complex telephony logic, AudioCodes offers the power and flexibility to build it out.

AudioCodes isn't usually necessary for smaller chatbot projects focused on marketing or lead gen. Its integration options may require more technical know-how, and the platform is geared toward teams with IT resources or a dedicated developer. Still, if you're working in customer service, health care, or support-driven industries where voice calls are a key part of the experience, AudioCodes is worth exploring. For the correct use case, it can handle advanced call flows, voice bot integrations, and even voice-to-text capabilities.

Meta Business Suite for Channel Management

If you're using Messenger or Instagram DMs for your chatbot, Meta Business Suite is the central hub for managing your connected Facebook and Instagram pages. It gives you access to your inbox, page settings, ad tools, and basic analytics. Technically, it's where Meta expects you to manage your chatbot communications.

In practice? Meta Business Suite can be frustrating at best. It's a bit clunky. Features change without notice, the interface isn't always intuitive, and sometimes it feels like you're just clicking around hoping things will work.

Here's the good news: For most chatbot tasks, you don't need to spend much time in Meta Business Suite. Your chatbot builder platform likely gives you all the tools you need to create, manage, and track your automations without dealing with Meta's dashboard.

That said, you still want to check in with Business Suite from time to time. It's where you manage your page access, confirm your Messenger setup, and handle any permission issues or page connection problems. You may also need it if you're running ads that trigger your chatbot, especially if you're using Click to Messenger or Sponsored Messages.

Notion or Trello for Chatbot Project Planning

When you're juggling chatbot builds, automations, content, and client feedback, having a solid project management tool is a lifesaver. Tools like Notion and Trello help you organize your chatbot strategy, map out flows, track progress, and collaborate with your team or clients. They keep your head clear and your projects moving forward.

Trello is great if you love a visual layout. You can create a board for each chatbot project and use cards to represent different stages, such as research, copywriting, build, testing, and launch. It's simple, clean, and easy to update, even if you're working solo.

Notion is more flexible and works well if you're managing a lot of moving parts. You can combine notes, task lists, flowcharts, content calendars, and links all in one place. I (Kelly) like using Notion for planning out chatbot logic, documenting API steps, or storing prompt ideas when I'm integrating AI features.

REMEMBER

No matter which tool you choose, the goal is the same: Keep your chatbot projects organized, repeatable, and less stressful. A little structure goes a long way when you're building bots that actually get results.

TECHNICAL STUFF

If you're looking for something with a bit more horsepower, ClickUp is another excellent option. It combines features from tools like Notion, Trello, and Asana into one workspace. You can manage tasks, store documents, automate reminders, and assign roles or due dates to team members. ClickUp is ideal if you're managing multiple chatbots or running a larger team with lots of moving parts.

Using Leading Analytics Tools

One of the most significant benefits of using chatbots in your business is how trackable everything becomes. You're no longer guessing whether something is working; you can measure it. But if you're not actually looking at those numbers, you're flying blind.

In Chapter 13, we explain that the chatbot-building platform you're using most likely includes the most detailed analytics for chatbot-specific performance, such as open rates, click-through rates, and so on. You can see how users move through your flows, which messages get the most clicks, and where users drop off. These stats give you a clear look at how well your chatbot is functioning inside the platform so you can improve your strategy over time.

But that's only part of the story. You also want to track what happens after the chatbot. Are users converting? Are they purchasing, signing up, and/or engaging with your brand elsewhere? To get the whole picture, you need to pull in external analytics tools such as those in the following sections.

WARNING

Don't rely on chatbot stats alone. If someone clicks a link in your chatbot but doesn't convert, you won't know why unless you're tracking behavior on the destination page.

Google Analytics

Google Analytics is a must-have if your chatbot sends people to your website or landing pages. It helps you track what users do after they leave the chatbot, such as how long they stay on your site, which pages they visit, and whether they complete a form or make a purchase.

TIP

The easiest way to tie your chatbot to Google Analytics is by using *urchin tracking module* (UTM) parameters on any link the chatbot sends out. It's a fancy name for adding little tags to the end of your URLs so you can track where your traffic is coming from. That way, you know exactly which conversations or flows are generating traffic and results.

Understanding how to use UTMs with Google Analytics

When you use UTMs in your chatbot links, you're telling Google Analytics, "Hey, this user came from my chatbot flow." That way, when someone clicks a link in your chatbot and lands on your website, you can see exactly which message, campaign, or channel drove that traffic.

Here's a simple example:

>> **Without UTMs:** `https://mywebsite.com/free-guide`

>> **With UTMs:** `https://mywebsite.com/free-guide?utm_source=chatbot&utm_medium=messenger&utm_campaign=lead-magnet`

That second version gives Google Analytics context. You can see that someone clicked from a Messenger chatbot during your lead magnet campaign.

Setting up UTMs the easy way

You don't have to write those long links by hand. You can simply use Google's free **Campaign URL Builder** tool to create UTM-tagged links in just a few steps.

Here's how:

1. Go to `ga-dev-tools.web.app/campaign-url-builder/`

2. In the Website URL field, enter the link you want your chatbot to send people to.

3. Fill in the necessary fields.

   You want to complete the following areas:

   Campaign Source: This is where the traffic is coming from. (For example, "chatbot.")

   Campaign Medium: This is the type of traffic. (For example, "messenger," "instagram_dm," or "web chat.")

   Campaign Name: This is the name of your campaign. (For example, "spring_promo" or "quiz_flow.")

4. Copy the full URL that's generated at the bottom.

5. Paste that link into your chatbot's button or flow.

Now when someone clicks that link, Google Analytics can tell you exactly how they got there.

TIP

Use consistent naming in your UTMs so your analytics stay clean. For example, always use "chatbot" as the source and avoid mixing in things like "bot" or "dm-bot" unless you really need separate tracking.

Meta Ads Manager

If you're running ads that send people into your chatbot, Meta Ads Manager is your tracking headquarters. You can see which ads generate the most clicks, which audiences convert better, and how those users interact with your chatbot. This data is beneficial when you're testing new offers or targeting strategies.

Use Meta's built-in tools to track lead events, message replies, and conversions. You can even use custom conversions and pixel tracking to go deeper.

Dashboards for combining chatbot and other analytics

If you want to see chatbot data alongside your website, email, ad, and sales data, tools like Databox, Looker Studio (formerly Google Data Studio), or Dashthis can help you bring it all together. These dashboards let you pull in data from multiple sources and visualize your entire customer journey from chatbot to sale.

These tools are especially useful for agencies or teams that need to show results to clients or stakeholders. Instead of flipping between platforms, you get a clear, centralized view of what's working across all channels.

Index

Alexa, 36, 54

Amazon Influencer Program, 32

analytic features, 24, 33, 64, 173, 216

Anthropic's Claude, 89

API key *see* OpenAI API key

Apple, 225

application programming interface (API), 21, 35, 51, 279

appointments booking, 12

appointment setters *see* Get Matt Deals

AudioCodes, 37, 282, 283

augmented reality (AR), 225

automation

  collaborate with live agents, 145–147

  customer service, 264–265

  customer service capabilities, chatbot, 136

  FAQs, 136–138

  monitoring error logs, 262

  operating procedure for long-term success, 260

  permissions, 262, 264

  quarterly/biannual review checklist, 261

  real-life examples, 147–149

  real-time routing, 140–145

  regular check-ins, 260

  ticket deflection, 138–140

  weekly review checklist, 261

B

Basic Builder, 92–94

behavior, 172, 173

  tracking, 200, 203

  triggers, 173

benefits, in business, 13–14

blog posts, 186, 187

Bonvoy chatbot, 202

Botpress, 180

  automation examples, 149

  customer support, 57

  Google Analytics integration, 201

  key features and prices, 51–52

  marketing agencies, 56

  strengths and weaknesses, 54–55

brand voice, 81, 100

break-even analysis, 14

budget, 60–61

business

  AI chatbot integration, 15

  description/mission, 100

  development, 12–13

  hours and availability, 101

  profile, 100–101

business goals

  current goals, 256

  high-impact use cases, 256–257

  owner assigning, 257

About the Authors

Kelly Noble Mirabella is the owner of Stellar Media Marketing and founder of Baby Got Bot, where she helps businesses and marketers harness the power of chat automation and digital technology responsibly. For more than 15 years, she has trained thousands of professionals through her courses, YouTube channel, and speaking engagements worldwide. She is also the co-author of *Digital Etiquette For Dummies* and is known for making complex technology approachable and practical for small business owners and solopreneurs. When she's not teaching or creating content, Kelly enjoys time with her husband and two daughters, coaching youth softball, and volunteering in her community.

Eric Butow is the owner of Butow Communications Group (BCG) in Jackson, California. BCG offers writing, online marketing, and web development services for businesses. Eric has written 54 computing and user experience books. His most recent books include *Funding a New Business For Dummies*, *Ultimate Guide to Influencer Marketing* (Entrepreneur Press), and *Instagram For Business For Dummies*, 3rd Edition. When he's not working or writing books, you can find Eric enjoying time with his friends, walking around the historic Gold Rush town of Jackson, and helping his mother manage her infant and toddler daycare business.

Dedication

To my grandmother, Deloris Wilson (1932–2025), a strong-willed, sharp-tongued, and hilarious woman. Truly the monarch of our family and a queen among women.

—Kelly Noble Mirabella

To Tony Barcellos (1951–2024), a good friend, enthusiastic bibliophile, and intrepid technology guy.

—Eric Butow

Authors' Acknowledgments

I'd like to thank my co-author, Eric Butow, for being such a wonderful collaborator and for his steady guidance throughout this project. My thanks also go to Matt Wagner, our agent, for helping make this book a reality, and to the incredible team at Wiley, including Steve Hayes, Kristie Pyles, and our editor Tim Gallan, whose patience and expertise made the process a joy.

To my husband, Jeff, thank you for being my constant support, my sounding board, and my biggest cheerleader. And to my two amazing kids, thank you for inspiring me every single day and reminding me why I do what I do. Finally, thank you to every reader who picked up this book. I'm so glad you're here learning with us.

—Kelly Noble Mirabella

I'd like to thank my co-author Kelly Noble Mirabella for being a wonderful person to work with and teaching me a lot about chatbots. My thanks as always to Matt Wagner, who served as the agent on this book. I also want to thank all the pros at Wiley who made this book possible, especially Steve Hayes, Kristie Pyles, and our editor Tim Gallan, who was a pleasure to work with. And *thank you* for buying this book!

—Eric Butow

Publisher's Acknowledgments

Executive Editor: Steve Hayes
Senior Editorial Assistant: Hanna Sytsma
Development Editor: Tim Gallan
Copy Editor: Megan Knoll

Senior Managing Editor: Kristie Pyles
Managing Editor: Murari Mukundan
Production Editor: Magesh Elangovan
Cover Image: © TippaPatt/Shutterstock